# Beyond Perestroika

## The Future of Gorbachev's USSR

———◆———

### ERNEST MANDEL

*Translated by Gus Fagan*

**VERSO**

London · New York

Published by Verso 1989
© 1989 Ernest Mandel
All rights reserved

**Verso**
UK: 6 Meard Street, London W1V 3HR
USA: 29 West 35th Street, New York, NY 10001-2291

Verso is the imprint of New Left Books

**British Library Cataloguing in Publication Data**

Mandel, Ernest
    Beyond perestroika : the future of
    Gorbachev's USSR.
    1. Soviet
    I. Title
    947.085′4

    ISBN 0-86091-223-X
    ISBN 0-86091-935-8 Pbk

**US Library of Congress Cataloging in Publication Data**

Mandel, Ernest.
    Beyond Perestroika : the future of Gorbachev's USSR/Ernest
    Mandel.
        p. cm
    Includes bibliographical references.
    ISBN 0-86091-223-X : $42.50. – ISBN 0-86091-935-8(pbk.) : $14.95
    1. Soviet Union–Politics and government–1982– 2. Soviet Union–
Economic conditions–1978– 3. Gorbachev, Mikhail Sergaevich, 1931–
    I. Title.
DK288.M35 1988
947.085′4–dc19

Typeset by Leaper & Gard Ltd, Bristol
Printed in Great Britain by Bookcraft (Bath) Ltd

*To the memory of*
*Pierre Frank*
*and*
*Emile Van Ceulen*

# Contents

# Preface

The changes currently taking place in the Soviet Union are the most important international development since May 1968, if not since the victory of the Chinese revolution in 1949. They are having a profound effect on the whole world situation and those effects will make themselves felt for years if not decades to come. They will stamp their mark on the social and political dynamic in key sectors of the world. The fact that the people of the main capitalist countries will no longer be repelled by the political system of the Soviet Union, although socially and economically it will remain unattractive, is in itself a major change in what has been a constant factor in the world since the end of the Second World War. The essential change in the situation is not so much the democratic reforms that have been introduced or that will be introduced in the near future. Nor is it the personal role of Gorbachev and his undoubted success in the field of public relations, although we shouldn't underestimate the importance of these phenomena. The most important change has been the reemergence of the independent mass political activity of the Soviet working class, as evidenced in at least sixty major strikes in two years, many lesser disputes, often involving democratic rights, and massive mobilizations in Estonia and Armenia.

For more than forty years the working classes of the Soviet Union and of the United States of America, the two largest and most highly qualified working classes in the world, constituting more than one quarter of the whole world working class, have been absent from the political scene, as actors with a minimum of class independence. This has been an essential factor in the relation between the classes on an international level and has been one of the principal factors acting as a brake on the world struggle for socialism. The fact that the Soviet workers have begun to act on the political plane constitutes a major change in the world situation. It is comparable, in its significance, to a resurgence of independent class activity on the part of the American workers, a resurgence which, at a single stroke, would radically transform the whole world situation. The events in the Soviet Union today will facilitate this development which is not only possible but, all appearances to the contrary, is actually inevitable. Two facts already underline the progressive dynamic of this evolution. The first is the Soviet withdrawal from Afghanistan, a withdrawal caused in part by the growing opposition within the Soviet Union itself and the second is the impossibility today of a Soviet military intervention in Eastern Europe as happened in East Germany in 1953, in Hungary in 1956 and in Czechoslovakia in 1968. Such intervention is ruled out today because it would not be tolerated by public opinion within the Soviet Union. These are two very significant changes in the world situation which have already been brought about by the changes within the Soviet Union.

There are certain features of the analysis offered in this book to which we would like to draw attention. We do not seek to explain the current transformations in the Soviet Union in terms of the personal role of Gorbachev, nor do we see them as the result of his particular initiatives or projects. For us, Gorbachev and Gorbachevism are more the *product* of all the contradictions that have characterized Soviet society since the death of Stalin. We also reject any interpretation of those transformations which sees them as exemplifying an alleged constant feature of Russian history, namely, that change can only come from the top. Such a vision of Russian history and politics seriously underestimates the scope of peasant rebellions throughout Russian history and ignores the scale and the spontaneity of the mass involvement in the three great revolutions of this century: in 1905, February 1917 and October 1917. It also ignores the colossal transformation of that country which has taken place since the thirties and forties. The Soviet Union today is not only modernized and urbanized, with an urban majority which is already second generation: it is a society which, in terms of scientific and cultural qualifications, is one of the most developed in the world. A quarter of all the world's scientists are Soviet and 40 per cent of its working class has some form of diploma in higher education. Soviet workers have an interest in science and in literary and artistic culture to an extent that bears no comparison with the workers of any other country. The scale of the production of literary and scientific journals, of novels and collections of poetry, is indicative of this. Under those circumstances, the continued existence of a mediocre living standard, of an oppressive and brutal political regime, of structures of domination and control which are both ineffective and universally rejected, has become intolerable for the mass of the Soviet people and not just for the intelligentsia.

Gorbachev and Gorbachevism are the product of this contradiction between all the dynamic forces of Soviet society and all its conservative structures. It is a specific crisis of this system which has been developing for decades, most clearly expressed in the constant decline in economic growth and in the social misery of millions of its citizens. Over the past ten years there has been a growing awareness of this crisis within a number of important milieus. Public opinion has been irreversibly awakened. Herein lies the cause of the transformations that are now taking place. Gorbachev represents the response of the modernist wing of the bureaucracy to the threat to the stability of its rule represented by this crisis and by the rise of public awareness. To channel these changes and to try to keep them under the bureaucracy's control — this is the historical project of the Gorbachev wing of the Soviet bureaucracy. Hence the panic which we can observe among the more lucid of Gorbachev's supporters. 'If these radical reforms do not succeed in reversing the crisis, then the Soviet Union, within very few years, will be technologically a second-rate power, a fact which would have unavoidable consequences from the point of view of national defence.' This is the conviction which animates and motivates the Gorbachev wing. It is a conviction firmly based in reality.

Gorbachev has set in motion a dialectic, which should not be underestimated, between reforms from above and increasing pressure from below accompanied by independent mass action pushing in the direction of greater reforms. Although the root cause of this transformation is to be found in the depths of Soviet society, there is no denying the detonating effects of Gorbachev's initiatives. From the point of view of the political role which he plays in this process of transformation, Gorbachev is indeed a remarkable political leader. The parallel which springs to mind, although one should be aware of the limits of every historical analogy, is that of Franklin D. Roosevelt. Like Roosevelt, Gorbachev leads one of the key countries of the world. He exercises power through the medium of persuasion and manipulation without recourse to the apparatus of repression or terror; he confronts a specific society which, after an unprecedented development, is faced with a profound crisis which threatens to undermine the fundamental values on which this development was based; and he is convinced that a rapid and thorough reform is necessary to avoid an explosion, even a revolution. Like the big bourgeoisie in the USA at the time of Roosevelt, the top levels of the Soviet bureaucracy, in their majority, fail to comprehend the scale of the crisis and the need for radical reform. There are also other similarities: the appeal to the popular masses while at the same time trying to keep the popular mobilization under control and compatible with the survival of the system; the widespread popular support and the ability to use the media to strengthen this.

There are, of course, important differences. It was much easier for Roosevelt to convince American big capital of the need for reform of American capitalism through the New Deal than it is for Gorbachev to convince or win over the *nomenklatura*. The bourgeoisie is a ruling class, confident in its role, deeply anchored in the system through its ownership of property and wealth. The *nomenklatura* is not a ruling class but a fraction of a class which has usurped the power of the working class and can continue to rule, in the final analysis, only as a result of the passivity of that class. It has less confidence in itself, is very vulnerable and is much less able to channel a vast popular movement. The essential difference, however, is the fact that the USA was the richest country in the world, where the bourgeoisie disposed of enormous resources, enabling it to make real concessions to the masses. The Soviet Union today has an economy in desperate plight, whose large resources cannot be mobilized for the benefit of the mass of the people until there has been a radical change in the system of economic management and political power. It is this which makes the realization of Gorbachev's project much less certain. This analogy, however, highlights the historic dimension of Gorbachev and of the battles that have begun in the Soviet Union.

The ensemble of changes that have begun in the Soviet Union are often summarized under the two headings: perestroika and glasnost. Perestroika (which we examine in detail in chapter 5) refers to the totality of reforms which Gorbachev is attempting to introduce into the economic system. Glasnost is the collection of political reforms which, in general, take the form of a democratization of the system. (This aspect of the reform is looked at in chapter 6.) In an earlier phase, Gorbachev attempted what was in essence a bureaucratic reform of the system of bureaucratic rule. He attempted to eliminate some of the worst aspects of the system (corruption, alcoholism) exclusively by means of initiatives from the top, by administrative measures, even by the use of repression pure and simple. The limits and the almost total ineffectiveness of these measures were soon apparent. Then began a second phase in which Gorbachev combined economic reforms with increasing appeals for the democratization of political life, for initiatives from below. Increasingly, glasnost is being presented as an essential precondition for the success of perestroika. This turn in Gorbachev's policy resulted also from an analysis of the reasons for the failure of the Khrushchev reforms. Gorbachev and his close allies affirmed that the cause of the failure of the Khrushchev reforms lay in the fact that these reforms were not supported by independent initiatives on the part of the masses. The apparatus was therefore able to integrate the Khrushchev reforms and eventually to stop them and partly reverse them. With the nineteenth Party Conference, held in June 1988, a third phase in Gorbachev's policy began in which the political institutions themselves have begun to be transformed. We will examine this aspect in chapters 12 and 13 and attempt to draw a balance sheet of the discussions and decisions of this conference.

In agriculture and services perestroika amounts to a partial reprivatization. The black market in goods and labour has been legalized. This represents, in effect, a mini-NEP, the goal of which is clear. Perestroika has an altogether different significance, however, in the field of heavy industry and in the planning system. Although the proposals are somewhat vague here, they fit into the general framework of a choice between market socialism and the utilization of market mechanisms by the 'socialist' plan. The balance sheet up to now in this area has been one of failure. The economy has not grown; there is still an inadequate supply of consumer goods; the standard of living of the workers has actually deteriorated further. This is the source of the real fear among the supporters of Gorbachev, that popular discontent might be used by conservatives in the apparatus to obstruct the reforms. This explains also their very real fear that perestroika may actually fail. From the point of view of the working class, perestroika has a number of very negative features which partly explain the scepticism of the workers. From the point of view of its immediate effect on living standards, perestroika is a form of austerity. Social inequality will increase, which is offensive to the people's sense of elementary justice and is not likely to encourage a greater productive effort. The organization of labour will be changed in ways that undermine the elementary cohesion and class solidarity which has been established in the big factories. What is even more important, full employment seems to be threatened and there is no question that large-scale lay-offs will provoke profound hostility on the part of the workers, if not open resistance.

Under such conditions perestroika and glasnost, far from reinforcing each other, will come increasingly into conflict. The logic of the conflict of social interests will lead the workers to seize the opportunities offered by glasnost to articulate their aspirations, their demands and their discontent. With increasing freedom of expression and demonstration, the workers' actions will begin to breach the fortresses of the bureaucratic dictatorship. The number of strikes will grow, as will the demand for the legal recognition of the right to strike. Organs of self-management will begin to appear, as they already have in Yerevan. In other words, the workers will use the democratic space opened up by glasnost to fight for their own class interests in the field of perestroika. The contradiction between perestroika and glasnost will eventually lead to the opening up of a contradiction within the dynamic of glasnost itself. Up to now this has been limited by the maintenance of the single-party system, a system identified with the existence of censorship, the absence of real trade union freedom and with the presence of the KGB. It will become increasingly clear that the soviets do not exercise real power, that a genuine workers' power does not exist. Real power in the soviets would presuppose that the workers have the right to select their own candidates. It would also presuppose that candidates have the right to organize themselves around alternative political platforms distinct from the platform of the Communist Party leadership. The absence of the legalization of all soviet parties – parties that accept in reality the soviet constitution regardless of their ideology – is in fact a powerful restriction of democracy inside the Communist Party itself. It leads to the prohibition of tendencies, the absence of any right for minorities within the party to organize themselves around an alternative platform, since any minority within the party is seen as a potential second party. In the months and years ahead, all of those contradictions will be exposed and will become the object of political action, including action by the masses themselves. In fact, this has already begun.

The foreign policy of Gorbachev is no less contradictory than his internal and economic policies. Its underlying motive is the need to increase the material resources available for economic growth and improvement in living standards by reducing spending on arms and by obtaining credits from the West to finance the import of new technologies. The initiatives in the field of disarmament, the withdrawal from Afghanistan, the moves to resolve 'regional conflicts' and the attempts to 'deepen' peaceful co-existence and co-operation with imperialism all are in keeping with this orientation. It is an orientation which it is impossible either to approve or reject en bloc. The disarmament measures, the withdrawal from Afghanistan, similar measures in Kampuchea and Ethiopia and even in Eastern Europe are all very welcome. They will lead to an important clarification of the world situation in the eyes of the labouring masses throughout the world, for it will become clear that it is imperialism and capitalism which, by their very nature, are aggressive and militaristic. The claim that the Soviet Union, because it is 'socialist' is even more aggressive and menacing than imperialism will lose much of its credibility. This will increase the space for anti-imperialist and anti-capitalist political initiatives especially in the imperialist countries themselves. But these positive openings are accompanied by a new phase of theoretical 'revisionism' which attempts to rationalize the turn towards greater peaceful co-existence in terms which characterize imperialism as 'peaceful' and which envisages an end not only to conflicts between states but between classes. Of course, the international Social Democracy and the liberal bourgeoisie welcome this. After all, for over seventy years they have claimed that world revolution was a myth and that the foundation of the Third International was a catastrophic mistake. They have proclaimed the gradualist and not the revolutionary road to social change. Now Moscow and Beijing seem to agree. 'Marxism is now well and truly dead', proclaim the Social Democrats.

Revolutions, however, in spite of the wishes of Gorbachev and the Social Democrats, are the product of exacerbated social and political contradictions and are not created by hidden conspirators. There will still be revolutions, even if they are not supported from Moscow. Marxism explains why these revolutions occur. It also explains the contradictions in Soviet society which gave rise to Gorbachev. It offers a coherent account of the whole crisis of our epoch and is capable of inspiring workers and youth. This does not, however, minimize the negative effects of the 'new doctrine' coming from Moscow because the latter can only reinforce ideological confusion and encourage scepticism with respect to anti-capitalist action. This revisionism from Moscow, combined with real political pressure, could force revolutionary movements to moderate their course and could help to bring about capitulations and defeats in many important sectors of the international class struggle.

Where is the Soviet Union headed under Gorbachev? What are the possible outcomes of the process that has begun in that country? If pressure from the masses (limited and channelled) is adequate to neutralize the obstruction and sabotage of the more conservative layers of the bureaucracy; if the apparatus is progressively modernized and rejuvenated; if capitalist credits are made available; if Gorbachev's reforms are allowed to continue and the impetus is not lost or reversed: then perestroika will begin to deliver fruits after a period of time and the living standards of the people will improve. In such a case the Gorbachev experience will succeed. Of the four possible scenarios that we outline here, we consider this one the least likely. It underestimates the resistance to reform and the social and political contradictions which are an obstacle to any 'reformist' solution.

Another possibility is that Gorbachev will be outflanked by the radicalization of a section of leading cadres in the party which combines with a mass anti-bureaucratic mobilization. This will lead to a 'Moscow spring'. In this case, the conservative wing of the bureaucracy would prefer Gorbachev as a lesser evil rather than risk a real revolution from below. Whether or not this happens depends on the scale of the mobilization in the next two or three years and on the degree of radicalization that takes place inside the party. We think that this is not a likely outcome.

The third scenario is a more pessimistic one: the failure of the Gorbachev reform. If a mass mobilization does not develop, largely as a result of deteriorating conditions of life and work; if perestroika is an economic failure; if the conservative fraction of the *nomenklatura* decide that glasnost is too risky: then the democratization process could be brought to a halt. This wouldn't automatically mean the elimination of Gorbachev, but this eventuality could not be excluded. The reform course would be halted or neutralized, purges would follow in the party and in the media and opposition groups would be dealt with as before. But it would be difficult, if not impossible, to return to the status quo. Too much has already happened: social forces have been awakened; freedom of criticism has gone too far. There could not be a 'normalization' of the kind we saw in Czechoslovakia.

The fourth variant remains. Delays in the improvement of living and working conditions will transform working-class scepticism into virulent discontent and eventually mass action. The masses will seize the opportunities offered by glasnost to begin a vast movement of self-organization which becomes more and more centralized. The slogan 'All Power to the Soviets' will be revived in its classic form and meaning, and in socio-economic conditions much more favourable than existed in 1917, 1923 or 1927. A new political leadership will emerge from the working class and from the socialist intelligentsia which will help the masses in the achievement of their fundamental objectives. The political revolution, in the classical Marxist sense of the term, will triumph.

Some combination of this third and fourth scenario is also possible. In any case, these two latter scenarios seem more likely to us than the first two. They are both based on a more realistic assessment of the profundity of the social contradictions at work in Soviet society. The conclusion which follows is that Soviet society has begun to move and no one can bring this movement to a halt. Stalinism and Brezhnevism are definitively at an end. The Soviet people, the international proletariat, the whole of humanity can breathe a great sigh of relief. The world is no longer as it used to be.

15 July 1988

# 1

# The Objective Contradictions of Soviet Society

There are two mistaken views of Soviet reality prevalent in the West. The first presents the Soviet Union as a frozen and totalitarian society. The control of the bureaucracy over all areas of social life creates almost total immobility and stability. The bureaucracy has succeeded in integrating everything into its system, including the black market, corruption, crime, economic dysfunctions, the attraction of the Western model of consumption. The apoliticism of the population is the ultimate proof of its success. Because of this, the system is capable of going on reproducing itself indefinitely. A good number of right-wing 'dissidents' would go even further in this assessment, in particular Alexander Zinoviev.[1] It is a view which is shared by most bourgeois 'Sovietologists'.

The second version presents Soviet society as essentially in movement. Economic progress, the rise in the standard of living, and the increasing skills of the workers explain both the lack of popular political opposition and the constant pressure for progressive reforms, which the bureaucracy cannot avoid for ever. Since Stalin's death in 1953 successive waves of reforms have been on the agenda. These are bringing the Soviet Union closer and closer to the model of Socialist society envisaged by Marx and Lenin. The Gorbachev reforms are viewed as only the last in a long series; demonstrating the vitality and basic health of the system. The course of radical reforms and democratization is irreversible. This second view is not only prevalent within the pro-Soviet Communist parties. It is also increasingly present among Eurocommunists and within a growing wing of European Social Democracy, particularly the Social Democratic Party of the Federal Republic of Germany and the British Labour Party.[2]

An objective analysis of Soviet reality and its evolution over the last

*1*

thirty years leads to the conclusion that both these views are mistaken. They do not take into account the nature and the contradictory development of Soviet society, which is precisely a product of the combination of dynamism and immobility. The dynamism results from the economic and social growth (product of what remains of the conquests of the October revolution), which is impressive over the long term, even if this is slowing down year by year. This growth has profoundly changed the country from what it was in 1940, 1950, or even 1960. The immobility results from the bureaucratic stranglehold on the state and society as a whole. This is an obstacle to further growth. It deprives the country, particularly the working masses, youth, the creative intelligentsia, women, the national minorities, and the 'new poor', of a good share of the fruits of past growth.[3]

This is the contradiction which is today dominant in the Soviet Union.[4] This is what determines its immediate future, what explains the concern, the worry, indeed the anguish of the Gorbachev team. This is at the root of both its populist demagogy in favour of 'radical reforms' and its failure to implement them on a sufficient scale to give a new spurt to economic growth and progress towards Socialism.

Since the Brezhnev era the Soviet Union has gone through a real crisis of the regime. The most superficial observers have been struck above all by the superstructural phenomena which reflect the crisis: the ageing and unchanging leading figures at every level; a growing immobility when faced with political choices; the increasing rigidity and ineffectiveness of the dominant ideology. The more serious critics relate this to the crisis of socio-economic structures which is hitting Soviet society.

The most striking manifestation of this crisis of the regime is the slowdown in economic growth. The fall in the growth rate has been regular from one five-year plan to the next over the last twenty years, as we can see from tables 1, 2, and 3.

As Jacques Sapir has pointed out, these figures exaggerate the real growth of the Soviet economy. The concept of 'gross social product' or 'net material product by use' designates the amount of turnover. If from one year to another there is an inflated consumption of intermediary products (through waste or declining efficiency), with final production remaining the same, there is still an increase in net material product (NMP) and gross social product (GSP). Furthermore, the hypothesis of a stable or declining price index is unrealistic when one considers the ability of managers to raise prices for so-called new products, which make up on average 25–30 per cent of current production. Sapir concludes that it is necessary to reduce the official figures. He proposes the set of figures shown in table 4. Mark Frankland gave similar figures,

**Table 1**   *Average growth in Soviet national income:*
*(annual percentage by five-year plan)*

| | |
|---|---|
| 1951–55 | 11.2 |
| 1956–60 | 9.2 |
| 1961–65 | 6.6 |
| 1966–70 | 7.75 |
| 1971–75 | 5.75 |
| 1976–80 | 4.75 |
| 1981–85 | 3.5 |

**Table 2**   *Percentage of increase per five-year plan*

| | *1966–70* | *1971–75* | *1976–80* | *1981–85* |
|---|---|---|---|---|
| Total social production | 43 | 36 | 23 | 20 |
| Net material production by use | 41 | 28 | 21 | 17–18 |
| Net material production per person | 33 | 24 | 18 | 15 |
| Gross industrial production | 50 | 43 | 24 | 20 |

drawing his deflated growth rates from CIA estimates submitted to Congress (see table 5). Abel Aganbegyan, chief economic advisor to Gorbachev, goes even further than this in his latest book, *Perestroika* (Paris 1987). He states quite bluntly that during the course of the eleventh five-year plan (1981–85) the rate of growth of the Soviet economy was zero, taking into account price rises connected with quality changes and the substitution of more expensive goods for cheaper ones without thereby improving the quality for the consumer. This is demonstrated in figure 1 which appeared on page ten in his book.

We find a confirmation of this tendency towards stagnation in the fact that, in absolute figures, there has been a decline in the production of coal in 1979, 1980, and 1981; of steel in 1979, 1980, and 1982; of machine tools in 1979, 1980, and 1981; of cars in 1981 and 1982; and once again in 1985 we find a fall in the production of oil, coal, steel, paper, cement, and even radios. Aganbegyan adds that, except for 1979 and 1982, the physical volume of industrial production declined by 40 per cent.

The continuing decline in the rate of growth confronts the bureau-cractic leaders of the Soviet Union with an agonizing choice. When the rate of growth is at or above 4–4.5 per cent they are able to increase simultaneously investments (industrialization and modernization), military spending (in the pursuit and maintenance of 'military parity' with imperialism), and the standard of living of the masses, although at a

**Table 3**  *Percentage of annual increase*

| | 1966–70 | | 1971–75 | | 1976–80 | | 1981–85 | | 1986–90 |
| --- | --- | --- | --- | --- | --- | --- | --- | --- | --- |
| | plan | real | plan | real | plan | real | plan | real | plan |
| Net material product by use | 6.9 | 7.1 | 6.7 | 5.1 | 4.7 | 3.8 | 3.4 | 3.2 | 3.5–4 |
| Gross industrial production | 8.5 | 8.4 | 8.0 | 7.4 | 6.3 | 4.4 | 4.7 | 3.7 | 3.9–4.4 |
| Construction | | 7.4 | 7.5 | 6.2 | | 2.1 | | | |
| Agricultural production (gross) | 4.5 | 3.9 | 3.7 | 0.5 | 3.0 | 1.0 | 2.5 | 1.1 | 2.7–3 |
| Real income per person | 5.4 | 5.9 | 5.5 | 4.4 | 3.9 | 3.4 | 3.1 | 2.2 | 2.5–3 |
| Investment | 8.2 | 7.5 | 6.7 | 7.0 | 3.2 | 3.4 | 1.5 | 3.5 | 3.5–4 |
| Productivity of industrial labour | 6.0 | 5.7 | 6.8 | 6.0 | 5.5 | 3.2 | 4.2 | 3.2 | 4.2–4.8 |

**Table 4**    *Annual rate of growth (average percentage)*

|                         | 1975–79 | 1980–84 |
|-------------------------|---------|---------|
| Gross social product    | 2.64    | 1.74    |
| Industrial production   | 2.24    | 0.63    |
| Industrial productivity | 0.47    | −0.07   |

*Source*: Jacques Sapir, 'Crises et mutations de l'économie sóvietique', *La Nouvelle Alternative*, no. 4, 1986

modest rate. If this rate drops to 3 per cent or below, the simultaneous pursuit of these three objectives, the goal of the bureaucracy since the death of Stalin, becomes impossible. The slowdown in economic growth is accompanied by an even clearer slowdown in consumer spending (see table 6).

It is true that the situation is somewhat better as far as consumer durables is concerned (see table 7). The low rate of growth in these products is a reflection of the fact that need has shifted from basic provision to repair and maintenance. The poor quality of so many of these products, and the difficulty in finding spare parts, has created serious problems and a great deal of dissatisfaction among consumers.

The housing crisis is still acute, although the situation is slowly improving, as can be seen from table 8. Fourteen per cent now have private cars, but annual production has stagnated at around 1.3 million new cars and delivery time is on average seven years.[5]

The masses are strongly aware of this stagnation in living standards. According to a study carried out by the Sociological Institute at the Academy of Sciences and reported in the English-language *Moscow News* (but not in the Russian press), 45 per cent think that medical services are worse than they were ten years ago; 52 per cent think that shops are less well stocked and 54 per cent think that public transport has deteriorated.

The most dramatic expression of this slower rate of growth is the quasi-stagnation in cereal production, particularly animal feed, which for years has made the USSR dependent on massive imports of agricultural products from capitalist countries (Argentina, Canada, USA, France and Australia).

For the same reason, the effects of the long depression of the international economy on the Soviet economy have increased. The export products of the USSR (essentially gold and oil) have been subject to violent price fluctuations. The necessary resources for importing high-technology goods are not automatically ensured. The depression is stimulating imperialist rearmament, which is in turn increasing pressure

**Table 5** *Rate of growth (average percentage)*

|  | 1951–56 | 1956–60 | 1961–65 | 1966–70 | 1971–75 | 1976–79 | 1981–85 |
|---|---|---|---|---|---|---|---|
| *National Income* |  |  |  |  |  |  |  |
| Official sources | 11.4 | 9.1 | 6.5 | 7.7 | 5.7 | 4.2 | 4.0 |
| CIA estimates | 6.0 | 5.8 | 5.0 | 5.5 | 3.7 | 3.0 | 1.5–2.5 |
| *Industrial output* |  |  |  |  |  |  |  |
| Official sources | 13.1 | 10.4 | 8.6 | 8.5 | 7.4 | 4.7 |  |
| CIA estimates | 11.3 | 8.7 | 7.0 | 6.8 | 6.0 | 3.5 |  |

*Source:* Mark Frankland, *Observer*, 7 December 1980.

**Figure 1**   *Growth of national revenue*

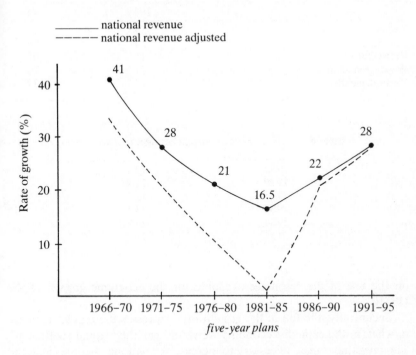

_____ national revenue
−−−−− national revenue adjusted

**Table 6**   *Rate of annual growth of consumer spending per head of population in the Soviet Union (percentages)*

|  | *1966–70* | *1971–75* | *1976–80* | *1981* |
|---|---|---|---|---|
| Global consumption | 5.1 | 2.9 | 2.2 | 1.8 |
| Goods | 5.4 | 2.8 | 2.1 | 1.8 |
| including: foodstuffs | 4.3 | 1.6 | 1.0 | 1.4 |
| non-durables | 7.1 | 3.0 | 3.1 | 2.1 |
| durables | 9.1 | 10.05 | 5.4 | 1.7 |
| Services | 4.3 | 3.0 | 2.5 | 1.9 |
| including: foodstuffs | 5.8 | 4.6 | 3.4 | 2.1 |
| education | 2.9 | 1.5 | 1.6 | 1.3 |
| health | 3.2 | 1.4 | 1.4 | −0.2 |

*Source*: G. Schroeder, 'Soviet Living Standards', in *Soviet Economy in the 80s*, part 2.

**Table 7**   *Units of household equipment per 100 families*

|  | 1965 | 1975 | 1984 |
|---|---|---|---|
| Radios | 59 | 79 | 96 |
| Televisions | 24 | 74 | 96 |
| Refrigerators | 11 | 61 | 91 |
| Washing machines | 21 | 65 | 70 |
| Vacuum cleaners | 7 | 18 | 37 |

**Table 8**   *Living space per urban resident (square metres)*

| | |
|---|---|
| 1965 | 10.2 |
| 1970 | 11.2 |
| 1975 | 12.2 |
| 1980 | 13.1 |
| 1984 | 13.9 |

on the use of the resources available for the economic growth of the USSR.

Technically, the fall in the growth rate expresses the regular increase in what, in the capitalist economy we would call the 'capital coefficient'. The investment mass necessary to increase the national income (material production) by 1 per cent increases from one five-year plan to the next. This is caused in the last analysis by the growing non-utilization of material resources, resulting from the general malfunctioning of the economy, as well as by the low productivity of human labour (see table 9).

The concentrated result of this malfunctioning is summed up in Andropov's succinct phrase, repeated by Gorbachev: *a third of the paid work hours in the USSR are wasted.* Contrary to what is claimed by technocrats East and West, this is not due mainly to workers' 'laziness' or 'lack of drive' (Stalin put it more crudely: sabotage), but to the generalized waste engendered by bureaucratic mismanagement.

This is characterized by an irregular flow of raw materials as well as by a lack of balance between production and the transport and distribution system. This is partly caused by decades of insufficient investment in these last two areas; a lack of spare parts and many related problems; a gradual ageing of the machinery; chaos in prices and bonuses discouraging technical progress; and so on. Just to cite one example of this chaos (others are reported in successive chapters): the USSR has become the world's primary producer of mineral fertilizers,

**Table 9**   *Annual rate of increase in labour productivity (percentages)*

|  | 1966–70 | 1971–75 | 1976–80 | 1981–85 |
|---|---|---|---|---|
| Industry | 5.7 | 6.0 | 3.2 | 3.2 |
| Agriculture | 6.6 | 1.3 | 2.9 | 2.6 |
| Construction | 3.9 | 5.0 | 1.9 | 1.6 |

**Table 10**

|  | Energy | Steel Products |
|---|---|---|
| USSR | 1,490 | 135 |
| GDR | 1,356 | 88 |
| Czechoslovakia | 1,290 | 132 |
| Hungary | 1,058 | 88 |
| Britain | 820 | 38 |
| West Germany | 585 | 52 |
| France | 502* | 42* |
| Switzerland | 371* | 26* |

*These figures are not really comparable: the manufacturing industry plays a smaller role in the formation of GNP in these countries than in the other countries mentioned
Source: The Economist, 6 July 1985.

but according to the daily newspaper *Trud*, a quarter of the 30 million tonnes produced annually is lost. Stored 'in sacks that fall apart during transport' the fertilizer is carried on open-backed lorries. Whatever survives transport is stored in the rain and exposed to the wind (reported in the French daily, *Libération*, 2 October 1985).

The main problems of the Soviet economy, criticized by Gorbachev himself in his report to the plenum of the Central Committee on 11 June 1985 were: technological backwardness; the low quality of many industrial products; the low return on generally excessive and unfinished (frozen) investment; unbalanced planning, and chronic wastage of energy and raw materials.

A report drawn up by the Polish Academy of Sciences (quoted by the British weekly, *The Economist*, 6 July 1985) calculated average spending on energy (in coal kilogram equivalents) and on steel products (in steel kilogram equivalents) for every thousand dollars of the gross national product (at the official exchange rate) for the year 1979–80 (see table 10).

## The Computer Test Case

Soviet backwardness in the use and distribution of computers in some ways sums up the scientific, technical, economic, social, and political problems facing the Soviet Union at the present stage of its development. The Soviet Union does not lag behind the United States, Europe, or Japan in the field of pure scientific research. Soviet mathematicians are among the best in the world. Vladimir Gurevich stated on 20 January 1985 on Radio Moscow that the Soviet Union was producing the most advanced super-computers in the world at Severodenetsk. We do not know if this was a boast but in itself it is not impossible.[6]

However, there is a huge gap between the project, building prototypes, the first tests, and regular production or generalized use. In this field the backwardness of the Soviet Union is striking. The only type of computer to which the enterprises, administration, and schools have access in practice – and even here we should not overstate the case – is what is known as 'third generation'. The production of 'fourth generation' – general in the West – has hardly begun. Only 32 per cent of the big enterprises (employing more than five hundred people) have a computer, while the comparable figure in the USA and Japan is almost 100 per cent. Although the five-year plan for 1981–85 planned an annual production of software (computer programmes) of 2.5 to 3 thousand million roubles, real production in 1983–84 reached hardly 1 per cent of this figure. On average these computers are only used twelve hours per day, against a scheduled use of eighteen to twenty hours per day.

The mass introduction of computers into schools is a burning necessity in order to prepare the young Soviet generation for the generalized use of the new work and research tool. Given the insufficient production in the Soviet Union itself, and the limited export capacity of the GDR, the Soviet authorities have approached British and American firms with a view to importing 'personal' computers of the Apple Macintosh or IBM PC–AT type. But the Soviet Union is estimated to be ten to fifteen years behind the United States and five to ten years behind the British and Japanese in the quantity and quality of computers widely distributed.

There is an even greater delay as far as their use is concerned. At the beginning of the 1970s there was a widely held idea in the Soviet Union and the GDR that the planned economy was much more suited than the capitalist economy to the use of computers for planning and managing production, investment, or economic life as a whole. Projects for a central unified system of information on the whole of the national economy of the Soviet Union were drawn up. Today, Soviet philosophers, economic managers, and *apparatchiks* must be very disappointed. The generalized and rational use of the computers in managing the enterprises and the national economy has come up against numerous and, it seems, growing difficulties.

Certain of these difficulties are of a technical nature, but are difficult to eliminate in the short or medium term: insufficient infrastructure (particularly the telephone and telecommunications system); lack of electronic technicans and, particularly, software specialists; difficulties in justifying the advantages of using computers in financial or productivity terms (the introduction of computers does not lead to the elimination of mechanized or even manual accounting or clerical departments).

But the main difficulties are socio-economic and socio-political. The generalized use of computers presupposes clarity and unimpeded dissemination of information, which is guaranteed within capitalist enterprises by private property. It remains true, of course, that their extension to the whole of the national economy does not flow automatically from the functioning of the market economy.[7]

Within the Soviet economy, given the bureaucracy's material interests in getting the maximum possible resources for the minimum possible goals for the plan, not only is open information between the enterprises and the higher bodies not assured, it is practically excluded. It is even limited within one enterprise. The bureaucratic management system works largely on the basis of wrong information, as is recognized by all those concerned. That is what the former Hungarian Communist prime minister, Andras Hegedus, called 'generalized irresponsibility'.[8] How can a unified computer system be used 'rationally' in these conditions? The bureaucratic management system itself seems to be an obstacle.

Alongside the socio-economic difficulties there are also the socio-political ones. The personal computer normally has a printer attached – that is, a printing machine that can play the role of a small offset or duplicator. Millions of personal computers in the schools and universities and enterprises would be so many samizdats, so many publications avoiding censorship. What a nightmare for the KGB, what a godsend for what the authorities call 'anti-Soviet agitation', which is only the perfectly normal and natural exercise of the workers' rights to express their own opinion on real life in a workers' state, as Marx and Lenin expected and defended.[9]

The crisis of the system is as obvious in the social field – in social relations as a whole – as in the strictly economic field. A whole series of the relations that Stalin and Khrushchev had tried to freeze have gradually relaxed or even decomposed under the combined effect of the frustrations provoked by the lack of self-determination, of self-management, and of liberty; and of the attempt to substitute individual solutions for collective solutions.

Thirty years of almost uninterrupted growth in the standard of living of workers and collective farm workers, although at a very slow rate, have been accompanied by a scandalous backwardness in social allocations. The result is the appearance of a widespread layer of 'new poor' in the country. Tens of millions of people, including invalids, the disabled, widows, single mothers (they are still called 'deserted wives' in the Soviet Union), alcoholic down-and-outs, and youth on the fringes of society, are living well below the breadline. A not negligible section of the poorer paid workers also live below the breadline. According to Professor Léonid Gordon (interviewed in *Moscow News*, 3 January 1988), these people earn around 100 roubles a month. The average salary in the services is 117.3 roubles a month. Households of three or four that have to live on such salaries fall immediately below the breadline.[10] The authorities as well as the general public are indifferent to the plight of these new poor. At the beginning of 1987 *Izvestia* published an article on the condition of handicapped children, based on evidence from the region of Kemerovo, near Novosibirsk:

> For years we have closed our eyes, pretending that among us there are no blind, no deaf, no invalids, no mentally handicapped people.... In this region the percentage of women employed in industries that endanger health is very high. In factories that produce nitrogen the number of premature births is three times above the average.

The least that should be done, according to the author, would be to prohibit this type of work for women 'as happened in the mines' (*Le Monde*, 8 January 1987):

> It is essential to take all necessary measures to ensure normal births.... When handicapped children reach school age then another headache begins. In the region of Kemerovo there are no longer any special schools for children who have had polio or who are paralysed. The few institutions that do exist for handicapped children are filled up and in a deplorable state.

Writing about price rises in Poland in 1985 the Polish journal *Politika* reported that the rich were becoming richer and the poor were finding it more and more difficult to make ends meet. This is true of the Soviet Union as well, although to a lesser degree. This 'marginalization', on all the evidence, brings about demoralization, a sharp rise in alcoholism, in the crime rate, and, to a lesser extent, in drug use. Realistic estimates put the number of poor in the Soviet Union at fifty million; including the children in such households this is 20 per cent of the Soviet population.

Their income barely reaches 50 roubles per month per household. The salary of a qualified worker is 300 roubles, and the average salary is around 200 roubles per month.

Alcoholics and criminals do not emerge only from among the poor and the marginals. They are also products of the widespread feelings of frustration and dissatisfaction. Criminality also feeds off the almost universal corruption which, under Brezhnev, had begun to show even at the summit of the bureaucratic pyramid.[11] It is further stimulated by the malfunctioning of the bureaucratic management of the economy, the 'privileged relations', the middlemen (*tolkach*), and the system of 'pull' (*blat*), which attempt to overcome the vacuum left by the non-functioning of the plan. (Even during the worst period of the terror there was a very common saying in the Soviet Union: *blat* is stronger than Stalin.)

The low quality of consumer goods, the slowness of the official distribution and allocation system, and the insufficient supplies are in part corrected by the black market, semi-legal trade, and moonlighting, which also obviously help to increase incomes. The whole set-up wallows in a climate saturated with the search for individual advantages, money, and private enrichment. The official ideology which talks about 'material interest' is obviously not unconnected.

In Moscow there are 5 murders, 60 burglaries, and 750 cases of arson in a week. In New York the respective figures are 30, 2,319, and 1,806. But in the capital cities of northern Europe, where an advanced form of social welfare exists, crime is not as big a problem as in the Soviet capital.

Marx expressed himself with great clarity on this subject in an article in the *New York Daily Tribune* (18 February 1853):

> Legal punishment is nothing but society's defence against violations of its own conditions of existence. But what kind of society is it that has no better defence than a penal judge? If there are a large number of crimes, of a nature and frequency as if they were a phenomenon of nature ... isn't it necessary, instead of glorifying the judge, who eliminates one group of criminals simply to make room for another group, to reflect seriously on the need to change the system which produces such crimes in the first place?

Those words remain true today. And they apply as much to the Soviet Union, where there is a prison population of some millions, as they do to the capitalist countries.

The French journalist Liliane Sichler reported in *L'Evénement* (5 November 1987) that in the small town of Sovietsky, thirty kilometres from Moscow, a man was sentenced to seven years for having stolen a handbag in a crèche. According to a recent report in the Polish press, a judge sentenced two young people to ten years in prison for having stolen a pair of sheets from a youth hostel. It seems that similar sheets were not available in the shops and these 'honest gentlemen' were outraged over such a crime. Seven years in camp, ten years in prison for crimes of petty theft – these facts say more about the Soviet Union than 100 volumes of 'Marxism–Leninism' adapted to the needs and interests of the bureaucracy.[12]

The figures for life expectancy and infant mortality are further confirmation of this process of social decomposition in the years 1965–85. According to official Soviet statistics, life expectancy, having risen from 67 to 70 between 1955 and 1959, and stabilized at that level until 1971, fell to 68 in 1978, to rise again to 69 in 1984–85. Life expectancy for men, having fallen from 66 to 62 between the 1960s and 1978–79, has risen again to its level of 1971, that is, to 64. Aganbegyan states quite frankly in his book that in the twenty years between 1966 and 1986 life expectancy did not rise in the Soviet Union.[13] In the United States life expectancy for men is 70.9, for women, 78.4; in Britain it is 71.3 and 77.3 and in France 70.9 and 79.1 respectively. Even more disturbing is the rate of infant mortality in the Soviet Union. In 1971 it was 22.9 per 1,000, whereas in 1985 it was 26 per 1,000. This was the highest level in Eastern Europe where in 1985, the rate of infant mortality in Czechoslovakia was 11 per 1,000, in Hungary, Bulgaria, and Poland 18 per 1,000, and in Romania 22 per 1,000. [14] The comparable figure for the United States was 11.5, for Britain 10.8, and for France 9.7. According to Dr V.A. Tabolin, member of the Academy of Sciences of the USSR, one of the reasons for this rise in infant mortality is to be found in the 'excessive self-confidence' of doctors (*Sovietskaia Rossiia*, 31 October 1986). He argues that medical developments in the 1970s made it possible for women in poor health to give birth. 'These sick women gave birth to sick children and we had neither the equipment nor the qualified staff needed to care for these children.' But what kind of society is it in which advances in medical technology lead to increased infant mortality? The explanation is obviously inadequate. In fact, medical spending has declined from 5.3 to 4.6 per cent of the total budget for the USSR. In 1987 it declined further to 4.4 per cent. Agenbegyan modifies these official figures: 'Less than 4 per cent [of national revenue] is devoted to health, although in other countries the rate varies from 8 to 12 per cent.'[15] (This is indeed true: in Britain the figure is 6 per cent, in France 9 per cent, in the United States 10.5 per cent, and in the Scandinavian countries 12 per cent, although these figures include both public and private health care.)

One of the causes of the high rate of infant mortality which Dr Tabolin does not mention is the disastrous hygienic conditions in the maternity wards of Soviet hospitals. On 11 October 1985 *Pravda* revealed that following an infectious epidemic affecting more than 60 infants in a maternity hospital in Rostov-on-the-Don (of whom a number died), an inquiry discovered numerous violations of elementary rules of sanitation: swaddling clothes were not sterilized, milk was unpasteurized, wards were overcrowded. This was a very dangerous situation, but on 31 August 1986 *Pravda* affirmed that there were many similar cases.[16]

Soviet propaganda chiefs point proudly to the fact that the Soviet Union has more doctors per head of population than the United States. But what they do not say is that unfortunately these doctors spend a great part of their time filling out forms. The bureaucratization of medicine has reached incredible proportions. The *Izvestia* of 7 January 1987 published a letter from Dr Tomachevsky of Lviv who claimed that administrative tasks absorbed more time than caring for patients. A doctor in a polyclinic is supposed to see eight patients in an hour, in other words, he or she is expected to spend on average seven-and-a-half minutes with each patient. On average, five of these are spent filling in forms. Dr Tomachevsky adds: 'The work of doctors has to follow certain statistical norms.... Our method of working is determined by figures.' This claim by Tomachevsky prompted a flow of letters to *Izvestia* from doctors, many asking that their names be withheld.

One of the results of this deterioration of the public health system is the expansion of a private healthcare system, comparable to the black market in consumer goods. According to *Izvestia* (21 January 1986), there are twenty private polyclinics in Moscow. The current five-year plan predicts an increase of 60 per cent. By the year 2000 their number will have increased fivefold (*Pravda*, 15 August 1987). A director of one of those private polyclinics, Dr Shutornenko, explains the reasons for this increase: 'People turn to us in the first place because here they can get qualified and highly specialized treatment without paying a bribe' (*Izvestia*, 21 January 1986).

It is beyond doubt that this extension of the private and black market into the area of health care further accentuates social inequality. The opening of the first entirely private hospital in Moscow in September 1987 was accompanied by the announcement of a daily charge of 5.70 roubles for public hospital care, with an extra 2.50 roubles for food. A week in hospital would thus cost the equivalent of an average two weeks' salary. According to Dominique Legrand:

Is a two-tier system being created, whereby the state will provide a basic minimum but the patient will have to pay for anything extra? This is still a long way off. But the statements of the new minister for health, appointed seven months ago, clearly point in that direction. Citizens, according to him, have to demonstrate a greater individual responsibility: 'Free health care encourages people to lose interest in their health' (*Nedelia*, no. 34, 1987).[17]

A remark such as that made by the health minister is worthy of Mrs Thatcher or President Reagan.

# 2

# The Rebirth of Public Opinion

Alongside the deepening objective contradictions, what is most characteristic of the evolution of the Soviet Union over the last few years is the
gradual reappearance of a consciousness of the crisis in different
sections of society. A real public opinion has taken shape in this country.
This has been, of course, an opinion fragmented into different social
mini-milieus. There is no overall vision of social ills. Such a vision could
only be political and the Soviet Union continues to be marked by a real
depoliticization, a product of more than sixty years of bureaucratic
dictatorship.

Nevertheless, the reappearance of a public opinion independent from
the Kremlin higher-ups marks a major change in the situation. It was in
part a product of the crisis in the system itself. It also corresponded to
the long-term consequences of the disappearance of the terror, the
wearing away of fear,[1] the slow easing-up of repression of the mass of
the population, except for political opponents against whom political
repression has increased since 1968. This has resulted in intermediary
groups and subsectors exercising a certain pressure within the higher
layers of the bureaucracy itself.

We can very schematically distinguish the following social mini-
milieus which have given a more or less open expression to the phenomena of social unease and discontent during the Brezhnev era.

## The Non-conformist Intellectuals

Their number has grown considerably during the 1970s and 1980s. This
distancing from the 'party line' has been manifested among social

17

science researchers (philosophers, sociologists, historians, economists), writers, theatre and cinema people,[2] and painters and sculptors. Despite the heavy, stupid, and ignorant censorship, these dissonances and demonstrations of non-conformism have appeared in a growing number of articles in reviews and books, even outside the samizdat and the 'wild' exhibitions of non-figurative art.

Themes once considered taboo have been cautiously evoked, including the transition to Communism, the nature of economic equality, the 'contradictions within Socialism', the existence within the Soviet Union of classes and social groups with different interests, the influence of these different interests on daily social behaviour and even on political decisions, the existence of poverty in the Soviet Union, the history of the first months of the Soviet regime seen through the archives of the period, that is to say without flagrant historical falsification.

In general only accessible to specialists and distributed in small numbers – as is also the case for the non-conformist novels and short stories such as those of Trikhonov – these products of artistic and literary creation or scientific research independent of the *nomenklatura* have begun little by little to change the intellectual climate of the country. Stalinist monolithism was dead long before the sensational 'opening up' of the Gorbachev period. Boris Kagarlitsky has written an important work on the role of intellectuals in the Soviet Union since the October revolution (*The Thinking Reed*, London 1988). Chapter 6 in this book is devoted to the intellectual revival of the seventies.

The decomposition of this monolithism does not in any way imply an automatic return to the golden age of Soviet art and science of the 1920s. The thorough discrediting of Communism, Socialism, and Marxism by its transformation into a state doctrine (or even a state religion), the overall balance sheet of the Stalin and Brezhnev eras, and the gap between reality and the official ideology continue to have a profound effect. In these conditions the diversification of thinking feeds as many backward, mystical–religious, Slavophile, pan-Slavist, chauvinist, racist, anti-Semitic, or, on the fringes, outright fascist currents as it does liberal or left- or right-wing Social Democratic, anarchist, or authentic Communist (oppositional) currents. The Russian nationalist and Slavophile tendencies have at their disposal reviews and publishing houses, notably *Nash Sovremennik* and *Oktyabr.*

It would be worthwhile to take a particular look at the development of anti-Semitism as a viewpoint not only tolerated but defended by certain sectors of the bureaucracy. What is striking is the number of works published during this period, which, under pretext of attacking religion or Zionism contain the kind of 'arguments' and hysterical vocabulary not all that different from the anti-semitism of the Tzarist epoch. What can one say of the following titles: *The Octopus of Zionist Espionage*; *The Sinister Secrets of Zionism; the Poisonous Virus of Zionism*? One of the themes developed by these modern-day 'Black Hundreds' and nazis is that of the 'world conspiracy' of Zionists who control the world's armaments industry (L. Korneev in the review *Ogonyok*). V. Begun, in *The Fragmented Counter-Revolution*, defends the idea that the pogroms in Tzarist Russia were examples of the class struggle of the Russian people against the 'Zionist exploiters'. In his novel *The Promised Land* Y. Kuchevnikov proposed that Eichmann was a Zionist agent and that the extermination camps were the work of Zionism. There is no shortage of official writers who state quite clearly that 'imperialism and international Zionism are the chief enemies of the working class'.

The objective social roots of this rebirth of anti-Semitism in a section of the Soviet intelligentsia are linked to the phenomenon of 'cadre stability' of the Brezhnev era. This stability represented a slowing down of vertical social mobility. Victor Zaslavsky points out that the average age of film directors in the 1930s was thirty or less, but in 1974 it was sixty.[3] The criterion of national origin had gradually replaced the criterion of class origin in the selection of cadres. Between 1976 and 1981 the category 'social origin' was removed from internal passports. Under such circumstances competition for posts in education, in administration, in the so-called 'liberal' professions, created a fertile climate for anti-semitism among certain sections of the intelligentsia. For instance, the vice-director of the Institute of Philosophy of the Academy of Sciences of the USSR in the 1970s openly stated the number of Jews (then, at least, they were still called Jews and not Zionists) among university professors and among the 'prestigious professions'. He stated quite bluntly that their 'massive presence' was shameful and irrational from the point of view of the other Soviet nationalities. He demanded that there be a limitation placed on the number of Jews who could enter such professions in the USSR.[4]

In fact, the number of Jews who entered Soviet universities between 1969 and 1977 was reduced by 40 per cent from 112,000 to 67,000. The number of Jewish students doing doctoral research dropped from 5,000 in 1970 to 3,000 in 1975.[5] Those anti-semitic measures explain in large part the increase in the demand for emigration among Soviet Jewish intellectuals.

In addition to this development of reactionary ideologies, there was also a development of non-conformist ideologies of the left, although on a much smaller scale. There was the samizdat review, *Twentieth Century*, which appeared in 1975 in Moscow edited by Roy Medvedev and Raisa Lert. The material published was generally of a left-wing kind, and among those who worked with the editors were Lev Kopelev, P. Egorov, S. Elagin, and A. Krassikov.[5] There was also the Social Democrat, Yuri Orlov, living today in emigration, and the Communist oppositionists who published the *Appeal to Soviet Citizens* in 1968. The review *Poiski*, which began to appear in 1978, contained articles of various ideological orientations, but among them were writings of left-wingers such as Raisa Lert, Piotr Egides, and Vladimir Gershuni. The most important development was the group known as *Left Turn* (they were later known as *Socialism and the Future* after the name of their journal). The leaders of this group were all arrested in 1982. They were in contact with the Italian Communist Party and other Eurocommunist groups. One of those arrested and sentenced at this time was Boris Kagarlitsky, who later played an important role in establishing the Federation of Socialist Clubs in 1987.

It would, however, be premature to conclude from this that, in the case of the eruption of the broad masses on to the political scene, all these currents would share more or less equally the favours of the wage-earners who today constitute the big majority of the population of the Soviet Union. Ideas are going to pass through the sieve of social interests, above all material interests, whether consciously or instinctively grasped. It is not very probable in these conditions that Solzhenitsyn's apologies for tzarism – to take just one example – will find much of an echo in the working class or among the mass of the intelligentsia.

Sometimes this original thought even percolates into the official ideology. Thus, under the anodyne title of 'Methodological Problems in Marxist–Leninist Sociology' (*Voprosi Filosofii*, no. 8, 1986), the director of the Sociology Institute of the Soviet Academy of Sciences, V.N. Ivanov, emphasizes the different interests of different social classes and groups in the Soviet Union, who retain their specificity – and thus their opposition – even if they come together 'overall'. This discontent of a section of intellectuals, indeed their sometimes daring initiatives,[7] have undoubtedly come into play since the end of the Brezhnev era.

## Scientists who have Rebelled against the Abuse of Science

The most well-known case in this field was the battle of Zhores Medvedev and others to expose the Lyssenko scandal which did so much damage to Soviet genetics. This battle led, in the end, to the rehabilitation of the great biologist, Vavilov, and the condemnation of the repressive practices by means of which Lyssenko and his clique, protected by Stalin, defended their unproven theories.[8] One of the consequences of this episode is not widely known in the West. During the Brezhnev era, when the 'spirit of the times' was moving in the direction of partly rehabilitating Stalin and Stalinism, the geneticist N.P. Dubinin was rewarded with rapid advancement in his career when in 1973 he published his book *Perpetual Motion*, in which he claimed that Stalin had nothing to do with the arrest and death of Vavilov and that political considerations played no role in the destruction of Soviet geneticists and of Soviet genetics in this period.

Special honour must go to the many courageous Soviet psychiatrists who have denounced the abuse of psychiatry for political purposes. Among the victims of this abuse were the left-wing dissidents Pyotr Grigorenko and Leonid Plyushch, as well as many others. Among those who fought against this abuse, special mention must go to Dr Anatoly Koryagin who bravely defended the miner, Aleksey Nikitin, who had made a perfectly legal attempt to obtain overtime payment for a group of twenty-two Donetsk miners and was punished with imprisonment in a psychiatric hospital.[9] The writer Mark Popovsky, has written about a whole series of courageous scholars who opposed the dictats of the state in their discipline. Professor Makhailov, a remarkable medical specialist, refused to accelerate the production of a polyvalent vaccine for the ministry of defence because experiments had not yet proved the vaccine safe for humans. He suffered a heart attack when he learned that, in spite of his explicit prohibition, the dangerous vaccine was about to be tested on humans.[10]

## The Young Technocrats and their Ideological Transmission Belts

The malfunctioning of the economy has become so striking that at least a section of young cadres in the enterprises cannot avoid thinking critically and making proposals for reform. The plan/market relation or, what comes down to the same thing, the bureaucratic despotism/law of value relations, the fundamental contradiction of the economy, has been present in official thinking, not to mention potentially oppositional thought, since the start of the Stalinist era. We see from time to time attempts to express this contradiction.

The purpose of the discussion has been more or less the same for a quarter of a century: the need to pass from extensive industrialization (economic growth) to intensive industrialization, given the exhaustion of existing reserves. O. Lacis did not hesitate to recall that the terms of the discussion and the proposals put forward have hardly changed from those advanced by Nemchino, Kantorovich, and Novochilov in around 1964 (*Kommunist*, no. 13, 1968, pp. 32–41). He could also have added

Kosygin's proposals ten years later.

The difficulty is not the lack of a diagnosis, but applying the remedies in a systematic manner on a broad scale, in the economic system as a whole, without too much incoherence or too many contradictions. Partial reforms are not enough for this. It is the whole of the 'economic mechanism' which has to be turned upside down. This thorough shake-up is impossible without a parallel shake-up of the political system. The economist Tatiana Zaslavskaia and her 'Novosibirsk report' – under the auspices of academician Aganbegyan, who was one of the principal advisers at the time of the Kosygin reforms and became one of the main advisers of Gorbachev – played a key role among the ideologues of the young technocrats oriented towards a radical reform of the Soviet economy.[11] But the failure of the Liberman reforms in the 1960s and the Kosygin reforms of the 1970s led them to be very prudent – and very vague – about practical proposals, which stands in contrast to the clarity of the diagnosis.

## The Non-Russian Nationalities

Through the effects of a very uneven demographic dynamic the Soviet Union is becoming a federal state in which the Russian people will soon be only a minority of the citizens.[12] The bureaucratic top level under Brezhnev reacted with a dual approach, on the one hand developing internal colonization, which increases national oppression, and on the other developing the 'national' bureaucratic apparatus in each of the territories inhabited by the non-Russian nationalities, in order to integrate them into the defence of the status quo.

There is no doubt, in the light of the evidence, that national oppression and discrimination exist in the Soviet Union. According to official statistics, the print-run of daily newspapers in Russian is 3.5 times greater than those of the daily newspapers in all the other languages spoken in the Soviet Union, even although the latter concern 50 per cent of the population. Of the books published in the Soviet Union, only 18 per cent of their print-run is in non-Russian languages, again for 50 per cent of the population. In Urkaine 70 per cent of the books and pamphlets published are in Russian while only 20 per cent of the population in this republic have Russian as their native language. In Tadzhikstan, Turkmenia, and Uzbekistan the number of doctors per ten thousand persons is 24.2, 28.6, and 29.7 respectively, while in Russia the figure is 41.4, in Estonia 42.4, and in Lithuania 44.9. The national income per head of household in these three Asian republics is 51 per cent, 71 per cent, and 58 per cent of the average income in the USSR, whereas in the Russian republic and in Lithuania it is 113 per cent and in Estonia 133 per cent.

## The Rebellious Youth

Although less developed than in Western Europe, the United States, and China, the expression of cultural rebellion among young people began to be seen in the Soviet Union towards the end of the 1970s. They were particularly concerned with popular music, jazz, and pop songs. Some of these demonstrations had (and retain) a quasi-political character, insofar as they involved a constant clash with the censorship if not its open rejection.

Contemporary technology played an important role in this rebelliousness – particularly the habit of making cassettes with the aid of tape recorders often imported from abroad. In Estonia the reproduction of Finnish radio and television programmes has taken on the scope of a real 'domestic industry'.

The most typical case of this youth cultural rebelliousness was the poet–singer Vladimir Vysotsky, who died in 1980 at the age of 42. He had become the idol of Russian youth. His songs played a similar role to that of the protest songs of the Beatles, Joan Baez, and Bob Dylan in the USA and Britain in the 1960s. They were increasingly repressed and banned by the authorities – to be reproduced illegally by young people. Nicole Zand speaks of 'millions of pirate cassettes' (*Le Monde*, 16 October 1987). Vysotsky was very popular among the workers. He became a veritable spokesperson for all the underprivileged of Soviet society, dedicating one of his songs to the prisoners in the camps. On the day of his funeral tens of thousands of people gathered near the Taganka theatre where Vysotsky had also been an actor. This was the biggest spontaneous demonstration which the Soviet capital had seen since 1927.[13]

The 'Independent Song Club', with its musical, literary, and poetic programmes played an important role in its articulation of youth rebelliousness. In 1975 the club was closed down by the authorities but some of its members continued their activities elsewhere. During this same period the Student Club in Moscow put on a pantomime which poked fun at the classic sophisms with which the majority of the people (both East and West) justify their refusal to get involved in politics:

> a single actor came on the stage. He walked around repeating to himself: 'Alone, I can do nothing.' A second actor then walks behind the first, repeating his words and gestures. Then a third, and a fourth ... finally a tenth

person has joined the stage and they are all walking around in unison, repeating the same words and gestures: 'Alone, I can do nothing.'

The show was banned.[14]

Alongside these 'libertarian' rebels there are also young conservative thugs, similar to British skinheads, including the 'Lyuberists' in Moscow. They are said to be manipulated by conservative groups inside the KGB. We will return to this phenomenon in chapter 12.

## Ecology Activists

The ecological approach has gradually spread among certain layers of the intellectuals, timidly supported by a small number of local state and party cadres, and some groups of citizens. The writer Zalygin is the most prominent representative. He already made himself noticed by his campaign against the industrial chemical pollution of Lake Baikal (this is the biggest fresh water reserve in the Euro-Asian land mass). He has again taken the lead in the fight against the project of diverting the Siberian rivers Ob and Irtich towards the south. The goal of this project was to increase cereal, rice, and cattle-feed production in Kazakstan and Uzbekistan by at least thirty-five million tons a year. Up to the 27th Congress of the CPSU this project was maintained despite the protests of ecologists. At the end of the Congress it was mysteriously abandoned, without a vote being taken or any discussion at the Congress itself.

Zalygin took up the question again during the sixth Writers' Congress of the Russian republic. His speech was reproduced in *Literaturnaia Gazeta* of 18 December 1985. He won a significant success, taken further by the Gorbachev team which made a sharp attack on the minister who had made the proposal.[15]

Mark Popovsky, in *Science*, describes the timid protests (too timid!) when emissions from the atomic centre for the desalination of water, situated in Shevchenko, polluted the Caspian sea, poisoning the fish and killing the flora for many miles. There was also the case of the destruction of the thin layer of polar soil at Magadan which resulted from the intensified search for and mining of gold.[16] There are other less well-known examples of ecological protest in the Soviet Union. In the Moscow suburb of Kuskovo there were protests from 1979 on about dangerous waste from a chemical factory, but the factory wasn't closed until 1987.

But it is obviously the Chernobyl catastrophe and its regional – that is, national/Ukrainian – implications which made the biggest contribution to provoking widespread public opposition on ecological issues.

The Ukrainian press at the time mentioned the fact that the authorities had wished to speed up the construction and operation of the plant at the cost of safety measures.[17] We will deal with this question in greater detail in chapter 12.

Until very recently ecological activists were subject to persecution. Two members of the *Trust Group* in Moscow, an independent peace group, lost their jobs at the Academy of Sciences because of their position on the Chernobyl disaster.

## Feminist Activity

The difficult situation of the vast majority of women in Soviet society is above all the result of the difficulties in buying food and the lack of child-care centres. But it is also a reflection of obvious sexual discrimination. For example, although women were 27 per cent of the delegates at the 27th Congress of the CPSU, only 7 women were able to speak there – only 8 per cent of the speakers list. Fifteen women were elected to the Central Committee composed of 307 members, less than 5 per cent. Not one single woman was elected to the Politburo of 12 full members and 7 candidate members. One woman was elected to the Secretariat, without being a member of the Politburo. Adding it all up that makes 1 woman (less than 4 per cent) among the 26 people at the top of the bureaucratic pyramid.

The structure of the medical profession is another reflection of this sexist discrimination (see table 11).

A feminist sensibility is gradually becoming visible in the Soviet Union. Its first appearance was through the samizdat by women of Leningrad entitled *Women in Russia* at the end of 1979.[18] This publication had a broader popular success than had been foreseen, in any case broader than that of other samizdat publications. The collection contained significant information on the work, wages, and living conditions (including in prison) for women, as well as poetry. Among the

**Table 11**   *Women in the medical profession (percentages)*

| | |
|---|---|
| General Practice | 90 |
| Administration of personnel | 50 |
| Surgery | 30 |
| University professors | 20 |
| Members of Academy of Medical Science | 10 |

*Source*: V. Navarro, *Social Security and Medicine in the USSR*, 1977.

authors were Socialists like Tatiana Mamonova who, without considering herself a Leninist, does not reject the Leninist tradition, as well as
deeply religious and anti-Marxist women. The group suffered severe
repression in 1980.

The revelations of *Women in Russia* were sensational. There are
precise figures on the'second (domestic) work day for women'; on the
fact that there are only 1.5 million crèche places for a population of 270
million; on job discrimination in the machine-building industry (70 per
cent of the women employed in this industry are in non-skilled jobs,
only 1.3 per cent of the women employed there have a post which
carries some sort of responsibility); on the dreadful conditions for
abortion in one hospital in Archangel, etc.

There was a spectacular expression of this rise in consciousness at the
congress of the Union of Soviet Women on 30 January 1987, notably in
the speech by Valentina Tereshkova, summarized by the French daily
*Libération* (3 February 1987). According to this report, most Soviet
women still do tedious and unskilled manual jobs. They waste hours
every day queueing for low-quality products and doing housework
which in itself constitutes a second working day. The report criticizes the
lack of crèche and nursery places, the lack of health safeguards,
responsible for the rise in contagious diseases among children, and the
rise in infant mortality which is twice the rate of the advanced capitalist
countries.

## Protests against Social Evils

The new poverty, crime, the severe repression of 'anti-social' elements,
and, in particular, the scourge of alcoholism have been the subject of
courageous protests by writers, academics, and journalists as well as by
the left, in spite of the frenetic efforts on the part of the authorities to
deny the very existence of such phenomena, under the pretext that such
'slanders' against the Soviet state are only grist to the mill of enemy
propaganda.

One such example of this kind of protest was the article by A.
Krassikov, 'The Number One Commodity', which appeared in the
samizdat journal, *Twentieth Century*, and which claimed that Soviet
consumer spending on alcoholic drinks in 1972 represented 27–8 per
cent of all Soviet consumer spending on food in state and co-operative
outlets and 15 per cent of all consumer spending (i.e. 27 thousand
million roubles on alcohol!). Of those 27 thousand million, 19.2
thousand million or 74 per cent was state revenue, equivalent to more
than 10 per cent of total state revenue, a percentage which has been

more or less stable since 1927 when Stalin estalished a 'provisional' state monopoly on the sale of vodka. Between 1960 and 1973 the sale of alcohol passed the 100 index to 267, while the sale of clothing and linen reached 251, meat 224, and the index for the total of commodities reached 238.[19]

## Workers' Resistance

There has been no wave of workers' strikes and demonstrations comparable to the rebellious activities of the social milieus we have just detailed. But it would be wrong to conclude the the working class was satisfied with the Brezhnev regime or that it held back from reacting to the accumulation of problem resulting from the growing crisis of the system. The reality is more complex.

There were a number of strikes: at the hydro-electric plant in Vyshhorod near Kiev; in the armaments factory in Gorky; in the rubber plant in Sverdlovsk in 1969; in Vladimir in 1970; in the Kirov factory in Kopishche in the early 1970s; in a number of factories in Dnipropetrovs'ke in September 1972; the biggest factory in Vitebsk in 1973; bus drivers in Togliattigrad in August 1979; in a motorcycle factory in Kiev in 1981.[20]

The behaviour of the working class was above all a result of the shift in the relationship of forces in the workplaces in the workers' favour. This resulted from a long period of full employment:[21] combined with slow but constant improvement in the standard of living. The result was a growing pressure within the enterprise against stepping up work speeds, overtime (particularly unpaid overtime), the lack of security and hygiene, the high number of work accidents, manipulation of bonuses, etc.[22] Very widespread workers' resistance was often quite successful.

The improvement in the standard of living slowed down considerably after 1975, or more or less disappeared as far as good-quality food was concerned (food still accounts for two-thirds of consumer spending by the Soviet worker). This is clear from the figures in Table 12, drawn from official Soviet annual statistics.

The workers' reaction has been a growing use of 'do-it-yourself': moonlighting and the black market. From Soviet sources we estimate that seventeen to twenty million people are involved in the provision of services outside work hours. *Izvestia* (19 August 1985) estimates the value of these services as 5–6 thousand million roubles per year, while the turnover of the state enterprises in the service sector was 9.8 thousand million roubles in 1984. According to the review *EKO*, 60 per cent of spending on maintaining or repairing private cars goes through the black market.[23]

**Table 12**    *Food consumption per head in kilograms per year*

|  | 1964 | 1975 | 1980 | 1984 |
|---|---|---|---|---|
| Meat/fat | 41 | 56.7 | 57.6 | 60.4 |
| Milk and milk products | 251 | 366 | 314 | 317 |
| Eggs (in units) | 124 | 216 | 239 | 256 |
| Fish/derivatives | 12.6 | 16.8 | 17.6 | 17.5 |
| Fruit | 28 | 39 | 38 | 45 |

This area of consumer-spending is characterized more and more by inequality. Few workers can afford to buy a car. Few are able to avail of the services of a private garage. The same applies to goods for sale on the black market, where prices are well above what the average worker can afford. Inadequate provisions of textile and leather goods, their poor quality and high prices, are a constant source of workers' discontent. The figures in table 13 speak for themselves.[24]

Of course these figures need to be slightly adjusted to take into account a certain division of labour within COMECON. However, the different levels of provision are still so striking that the conclusion remains. The situation is aggravated by the fact that to obtain these insufficient and low-quality goods the Soviet worker has to pay a very high percentage of his or her salary for essential clothing and footwear: in Moscow 15.9 per cent, compared with 10.3 per cent in the GDR, 8.8 per cent in Hungary, and an average of 7.4 per cent in the countries of Western Europe.[25]

Workers' resistance and their discontent as both producers and consumers is therefore increasing. They aspire to a standard of living comparable to that of the proletariat of the imperialist countries, from which they are still far removed.[26] The fact that this discontent does not yet take very collective or active forms does not mean that it will not be expressed. The rapid increase in the number of critical letters in the daily newspapers is an indication of this. The number of these letters officially noted by the three dailies, *Pravda, Izvestia,* and *Trud,* rose from 300,000 in 1955 to 720,000 in 1960, 1.4 million in 1965, 1.26 million in 1970, 1.47 million in 1975, and more than 1.5 million at the beginning of the 1980s.[27]

These letters sometimes touch on political and institutional criticism. Zhores Medvedev has pointed out that the Politburo, the Central Committee, and other organs of power were inundated by thousands of letters denouncing corruption after Andropov's first public allusion to this social evil. In the same way, 'the Politburo began to receive thousands of protest letters about illegal interventions by the police, and as the Politburo had committed itself in December (1982) to reply to

**Table 13**   *Production of textiles and leather goods per person*

|  | Bulgaria | Hungary | Poland | GDR | Romania | CSSR | USSR |
|---|---|---|---|---|---|---|---|
| Cotton (sq.m) | | | | | | | |
| 1975 | 39.1 | 33.4 | 28.0 | 28.1 | 27.3 | 37.3 | 26.1 |
| 1980 | 38.3 | 31.0 | 27.0 | 29.0 | 33.0 | 35.8 | 26.6 |
| 1985 | 39.2 | 29.1 | 23.8 | 28.2 | 30.0 | 37.4 | 27.7 |
| Wool (sq.m) | | | | | | | |
| 1975 | 6.3 | 3.4 | 5.3 | 6.3 | 3.7 | 5.7 | 2.9 |
| 1980 | 6.7 | 3.7 | 5.1 | 6.4 | 4.3 | 5.9 | 2.9 |
| 1985 | 6.9 | 3.1 | 4.2 | 5.5 | 4.0 | 6.2 | 2.4 |
| Leather shoes (pairs) | | | | | | | |
| 1975 | 2.7 | 4.1 | 4.0 | 4.7 | 3.3 | 7.7 | 2.7 |
| 1980 | 2.8 | 4.0 | 4.0 | 4.7 | | 7.8 | 2.8 |
| 1985 | 3.3 | 4.2 | 4.0 | 5.0 | | 8.1 | 2.8 |

*Source: Annual Statistics of the CMEA Countries 1986.*

workers' letters, it was forced to reconsider its own tactics.'[28]

This systematic recourse to individual protest has to be understood in the context of the difficulty for workers to organize. The bureaucracy systematically places obstacles in the way of informal organization – different income levels, informers, and so on.[29]

## General Political Opposition

All those manifestations of protest are temporary and fragmented. There are a number of indications, however, of a more generalized political opposition, although not so well articulated. One of those is electoral behaviour, studied in detail by a samizdat of the *Group 68–80* and based on the results of three elections: to the Supreme Soviet of the USSR in 1979; to the Supreme Soviet of the Russian republic in 1980; to the local soviets in 1982. According to the results of this study, 10–12 per cent had their names voluntarily removed from the electoral register so they wouldn't have to vote. A considerable number of electors did not vote but had their family or neighbour do it for them – as much as 30 per cent of the electorate in certain districts. Finally 8–10 per cent of the electors simply refused to vote.[30]

Although it isn't possible to say that all three groups of voters were opposed to the official candidates, they do reflect to different degrees a rejection of the electoral comedy that takes place in this one-party system.

# 3

# The Deepening Crisis of the Soviet System

From a Marxist point of view, it is obvious that the serious problems described in the first chapter of this book, and fully acknowledged today by the Soviet leaders themselves, could not be the result simply of 'mistakes' in the political orientation or political ideology of individuals or groups.[1] The fundamental cause of these phenomena has to be examined. For a materialist, these causes are not to be found in behavioural patterns such as 'bureaucratism', conformism, conservatism, or what Andras Hegedus, the ex-prime minister of Hungary, calls 'generalized irresponsibility'. Of course these forms of behaviour as well as the mentality, the way of thinking and acting which inspires them, are an important aspect of Soviet reality. But the task of social science is to explain the root, the ultimate sources of the problems. And this is to be found in *material interests and conflicts of interest among social groups* – social classes and major sections of social classes.

This approach, sometimes referred to as 'the materialist interpretion of history', represents the principal contribution of Marxism to social science. Nothing in the historical and sociological knowledge which has been acquired over the past 140 years provides us with any reason to doubt the well-foundedness of this central thesis of Marxism. There is no other element in the reality of Soviet or Chinese society, present or past, which provides a better key to understanding the problems confronting those societies than this key fashioned by Karl Marx.

The conflicts of material interest between different social forces are explicable, in the final analysis, in terms of the specific and different positions which they occupy in the relations of production which prevail in each given social formation. The relations of domination flow from the relations of production. These relations of domination cannot,

30

except during brief periods of dual power or revolution, be in fundamental opposition to the relations of production.

The essential law which emerges from the history of different societies is that the social group (social class or major sector of a social class) which controls the social surplus, because of its place in the production process, controls to a large extent, all the other social activities, too, including those which belong to the so-called 'superstructure': the state, political activities, ideological and artistic production, law, morality, etc. Of course, this control is never total. Other social classes or minority sections of this class may partially evade this control, fight against the established order, rebel against it. But as long as they do not succeed in reversing the fundamental structures – the power of the state and the relations of production – they will not assume control of the social surplus and their weight in superstructural activities will never be hegemonic.

There are certain groups that deny there is a crisis of the system in the Soviet Union.[2] And this is in spite of the evidence presented by Gorbachev himself and his team. These groups want to be more catholic than the pope, more 'campist' than the leader of the camp.

It is a crisis of capitalism? To defend this thesis, it is first of all essential to demonstrate that capitalism has been restored in the Soviet Union. (But when? In 1921? In 1928? In 1933? In 1956? And why was this restoration not accompanied by a fundamental change in the economic system?) It would also be necessary to demonstrate that during, let's say, the last four decades, the Soviet economy has evolved in accordance with the laws of development and the contradictions of the capitalist mode of production. It would be essential to show, finally, that the crisis in that country is the same in all its fundamental traits as the crisis which has hit the capitalist countries. (Think, for instance, of the stock market crash of October 1987!)

Such a demonstration is, of course, impossible. Without going into the kind of detailed analysis available elsewhere,[3] it will suffice to recall that the economic crisis in the West – like every other capitalist economic crisis – is characterized by *overproduction of commodities and overaccumulation of capital,* whereas the crisis in the Soviet Union is characterized by *underproduction of use-values.* There is a world of difference between shops which are stocked with a supply of commodities that exceeds the buying power of the mass of consumers, and shops with supplies that fall far short of consumers' needs and their ability to buy. Only a sophist could claim that one situation is merely a variant of the other, or that this is only a 'minor' difference.[4]

Is it a crisis of Socialism? To answer in the affirmative it would be essential, first of all, to demonstrate that Socialism has been achieved in the USSR, that it is already a society without classes and without major social antagonisms.[5] In view of what has been presented in the previous two chapters, this would be an impossible task. Such a characterization of the Soviet Union would involve a revision of everything that Marxist theory (or pre-Marxist theory) proposes as a definition of the nature of Socialism. Nothing is gained by seeking refuge behind the phrase 'really existing Socialism'.

To affirm that the difference is purely semantic is an even greater sophism. Behind the attempt to give a reductionist definition of Socialism – 'Socialism means the absence of private property in the major means of production' – lies a refusal to recognize the reality of the historical process in its entirety, a refusal to accept the analysis of the origins of the contradictions of bourgeois society and the conditions of their elimination. This brings to mind the famous dialogue between Diogenes and the sophists who defined humans as 'bipeds without feathers', a typically reductionist definition. Is a plucked chicken a human? In the empire of the Pharaohs, where the major means of production were not privately owned, do we have an example of 'Socialism'? It was not by accident that for more than a century socialism was understood by practically all thinkers as a society without classes, without major social differences, without alienated and alienating labour.

The truth of the matter is quite the reverse. The crisis of the system in the Soviet Union is the best proof there is that the construction of Socialism, as a classless society, is a long way from having been achieved, contrary to the affirmation of Stalin.[6]

The recognition of this crisis by Gorbachev himself is complete and impressive. In his book *Perestroika*, recently published in the West, he writes:

> Any delay in beginning perestroika could have led to an exacerbated internal situation in the near future, which, to put it bluntly, would have been fraught with serious social, economic and political crises ... Perestoika is a revolution.... And yet, why in the seventieth year of the October revolution do we speak of a new revolution? ... Historical experience has shown that socialist society is not insured against the emergence and accumulation of stagnant tendencies *and not even against major socio-political crises.* And it is precisely measures of a revolutionary character that are necessary for overcoming a crisis or pre-crisis situation.'[7]

If the crisis is not a crisis of capitalism, and not a crisis of Socialism, is it then a crisis of a new mode of production, of a new system of class domination? For reasons of charity we will not insist too strongly on the fact that not a single theoretician, up to now, has been able to give a coherent and substantial analysis of this so-called new mode of production, of its laws of development, of its place in history. What is most striking in this crisis, and what undermines the thesis of a new ruling class, is the fact that the dominant layer in that society seems incapable of developing the system. Historically, this is not the behaviour of a dominant class, particularly a *new* dominant class. The parasitic and non-proprietary character of this dominant layer has never been clearer than today.

The crisis of the system which prevails in the Soviet Union today is a *specific crisis of a specific society*: a society in transition between capitalism and Socialism, still incapable of self-regulation and spontaneous self-reproduction, fixed at a transitional stage of its development by the delay in the world socialist revolution on the one hand and, on the other, by the power over society and the state of a privileged and parasitic bureaucracy.[8]

Fixed obviously does not mean immobile; it would be profoundly undialectical to make such an assumption. Soviet society is a society *in movement*, like every other society. This movement, like every other movement, is the result of internal contradictions. But the limits of this movement, its parameters, are precisely determined by the specific situation of transition and bureaucratization. In other words, they cannot be radically changed without some qualitative jumps, some new revolutions – either a political revolution in the Soviet Union itself or new advances in the world Socialist revolution outside the Soviet Union.

The origins and the causes of this specific crisis of the regime in the Soviet Union could be summarized as follows:

(1) In the state sector of the economy (which produces more than 80 per cent of the national product) there is a monopoly of management in the hands of a bureaucratic layer (caste) which perpetuates its power by means of the *nomenklatura* system.[9] This system reserves the power to select personnel for all leading posts at every level of social life to organs of the CPSU. This doesn't mean, of course, that only members of the party are chosen for such posts.[10] The mass of producers, the workers and peasants, have no power over management decisions as a whole. Their interests are opposed to those of the directors/managers, even if the latter do not constitute a new ruling class.[11]

(2) This bureaucratic layer monopolizes political power just as it does economic power. This monopoly of political power constitutes the basis of its material privileges.

Those privileges are considerable. The upper layer of the bureaucracy, which one can estimate at around four hundred thousand persons, earns four to five times more than the average salary and has numerous additional advantages: special shops, special places in holiday homes, special rooms in hospitals, special rights to travel abroad, privileged access to special schools for their children, etc. Well-known academics, writers, and artists can easily earn ten times more than the average wage.[12]

> Stalin ... institutionalized a system of secret payments of large sums of money to all high officials, from the rank of *obkom* party secretary upwards, in addition to their official salaries. The banknotes were delivered in special envelopes, and these monthly payments were supposed to be confidential – the recipient was expected not to tell anybody else about it. Were they a kind of bribe? The idea behind them was to prevent individuals becoming dependent on the usual type of bribe or other illegal sources of income, since the average salary was not sufficient to support a reasonably good standard of living and it was taken for granted that people would be open to bribery. The payments were clearly against the law. On the other hand, they had been introduced by the government as an 'extraordinary measure' during the war, and retained after it. Khrushchev abolished them in 1956, but he soon introduced additional payments in kind, through a system of special shops and distributors where high officials could purchase items, or order them for delivery, at a very low cost or entirely free of charge. Khrushchev's intention was to save the very valuable time of officials which would otherwise be wasted queueing, shopping, and waiting around. Soon, however, the number of fringe benefits began to grow rapidly.[13]

Under a democratic Socialist regime, where the mass of the people had real freedoms and democratic power, these privileges would be abolished immediately and for good. The workers are very well aware of these privileges. *Pravda*, on 13 February 1986, published a letter from a worker, V. Ivanov, who wrote: 'Between the party central committee and the working class there is yet another layer which has no interest in change. All it wants from the party is its privileges.'

Unlike a real ruling class, the bureaucracy is unable to base its material privileges on the coherent functioning (i.e. the reproduction) of the economic system, on its role in the production process. Feudalism is unthinkable without the feudal nobility. Within the framework of the feudal mode of production its income from the land was assured. Capitalism is impossible without the bourgeois owners of the means of production. Capitalism is inconceivable without surplus value and profit. But a planned economy, even state planning (which is simply the most primitive form of a Socialist economy), is perfectly possible without bureaucratic privileges, even without bureaucratic management, since management, the power to dispose of the means of production, of goods and of the social surplus, is distinct from the function of so-called 'cadres' or intellectual labour which will survive without doubt until the advent of Communism.

The specific and hybrid form of the relations of production and distribution in the Soviet Union is perfectly reflected in the origins and the hybrid form of the privileges of the bureaucracy. The privileges of a bureaucrat are tied to the exact position he occupies in the hierarchy. These advantages are increased by an additional money income which allows easier access to rare commodities, and by corruption which, in its turn, adds to the standing and the power of the entire bureaucratic layer.

(3) Bureaucratic management of the economy, combined with the bureaucratic monopoly of political power, makes the *material interests of the bureaucracy* the principal if not the only motor force of plan fulfilment, of the daily functioning of the system. This robs the entire economy of any form of economic rationality. The material interests of the bureaucracy push in the direction of increasing access to goods and services for the bureaucracy itself and not in the direction of optimizing the output of enterprises – not to mention the economy as a whole – and certainly not in the direction of maximizing the rate of accumulation.[14] The contradiction between the private interests of the bureaucracy as consumers, and the interests (the possible rationality) of the economic system as a whole expresses itself in the day-to-day behaviour of the bureaucrats, which is the source of increasing waste of human and material resources: false information which makes optimal planning impossible; illegal stockpiling of reserves;[15] massive theft; parallel markets, black markets and moonlighting; generalized corruption and the non-transparency of economic life, etc.

(4) The 'natural' tendency towards hyper-centralization on the part of certain sections of the bureaucracy, their brutal incursions into the management of enterprises, is simply the reaction, ineffective in the long term, of the planners to this fundamental tendency towards the malfunctioning of the system which results from the material interests of individuals and separate groups within the bureacracy.[16] The periodic recourse to extension of the market mechanism as a way of correcting the excess of bureaucratic centralization is incapable of resolving this crisis which is endemic to the system since it does not question but, in the long run, reinforces the material interest of the bureaucracy as principal motor force of the economy.

(5) The monopoly of political power in the hands of the bureaucracy means an almost total absence of self-activity on the part of the working class in the political domain, especially in relation to society as a whole. It means an atomization and depoliticization of the working class which can achieve political class consciousness only as a result of self-activity.[17]

This atomization and depoliticization reached its peak under the Stalinist dictatorship, but it was by and large maintained by Khrushchev and Brezhnev. This is why the conquest of democratic liberties by the working class, political and ideological pluralism, the freedom of debate, free horizontal and vertical links between enterprise collectives, are indispensable conditions for the re-establishment of genuine workers' control over the economy, for the development of a genuine and planned workers' management (planned at national, regional, local and enterprise level) which is the only solution to the permanent dys-functioning of the system.

(6) The depoliticization of the working class and the decline in class consciousness have been limited, however, by the maintenance of an elementary class solidarity at the level of the enterprise. This was progressively reinforced during the Brezhnev era as a result of the long period of stable employment and gradual improvement in the living standards and qualifications of the mass of workers. Full employment (the guaranteed 'right to work') appears, in the eyes of the Soviet workers, as their most important conquest which they have not yet lost and which they vigorously defend against successive attempts on the part of the bureaucracy to put it into question by means of an increase in the 'rights of directors'.[18]

The rejuvenation of the working class and the raising of its levels of qualification have had the same effect. Already by 1970 half of the Soviet workers were under thirty years of age. During the five-year period 1971–75, 90 per cent of new industrial labourers were recruited from youth. They couldn't find jobs appropriate to their levels of qualifi-cation. This is one of the main causes of their discontent. In the mid sixties a study in Leningrad showed that 40 per cent of young workers were unhappy with the content of their jobs. A study carried out in 1976–77, published in the Soviet Union, estimates this percentage to have risen to 65 per cent. The recent education reforms only reinforce this tendency. This discontent, and this self-confidence, strengthens among young workers a critical attitude towards management and towards the bureaucratic *establishment* as a whole.

(7) In addition to all the advantages that flow from the collective ownership of the means of production – in the economic and not just in the juridical sense of the term – the full employment of human and material resources and the absence of periodic crises of overproduction have guaranteed up to now a long-term growth of the Soviet economy which is superior to that of the industrialized capitalist countries. The malfunctioning of the system and the waste of resources have been a relative and not an absolute brake on the development of the productive forces.

It has to be stressed that, in the long term, economic planning and the absence of the defects inherent in the capitalist mode of production have allowed the Soviet Union to grow at a much faster rate than the capitalist countries and to overcome in a more global manner its problems of economic, social, and cultural underdevelopment.

Professor Mel Leiman has correctly stressed the fundamental difference between an efficient allocation of resources at the micro-economic level (at the level of the enterprise) and the optimal allocation of resources at the level of the economy as a whole. The second, macro-economic allocation is not simply the sum of the first, the micro-economic allocations. The second is compatible with a non-optimal allocation of resources from the point of view of certain individual enterprises. Independently of whether or not the market assures a better allocation of resources at the micro-economic level, the plan, in any case, assures a better allocation at the macro-economic level.[13]

One must, however, guard against giving some absolute significance to this statement. Growth of production is not a goal in itself, but rather a means of satisfying social need in the most efficient manner, with a maximum of satisfaction and a minimum of effort, especially on the part of the producers. If production continues to grow while consumer satisfaction decreases, and this at the cost of a growing utilization of productive resources, then the system is manifestly functioning in an irrational manner.

Recently, Soviet sources claimed that the USSR produces 80 per cent more steel, 78 per cent more cement, 42 per cent more oil, and twice as much iron again than the USA. But these impressive figures must be seen in the light of a statement made by Aganbegyan. 'Our country produces four and a half times more tractors than the United States in order to produce a smaller quantity of vegetables.'[21] The same problem arises in the case of consumer goods, where the quality is so poor that consumers are dissatisfied and go in search of new products. It would be a mistake, however, to reduce these 'decreasing gains' of planning and nationalization to the simple question of technical–organizational efficiency. This problem has evident *social* roots.[22]

The picture becomes even bleaker when we consider the overall social costs of this growth, especially in the ecological field. In 1980 a courageous writer, Boris Komarov, published a work in which he revealed that 10 per cent of the habitable land of the Soviet Union – 1.45 million square kilometres (the equivalent of the total territory of France, Italy, Britain, West Germany, the Benelux countries, and Switzerland) – had become unusable; in 10 Soviet cities the level of toxic gas was 100 times greater than the permitted maximum; during the previous decade the number of lung cancers in the Soviet Union had doubled. Each year 5–6 per cent of children are born with genetic deformations.[23]

(8) As natural reserves of resources are used up, as the need for a

shift from an extensive to a more intensive industrialization becomes more pressing, as the rate of growth declines and as the dysfunctioning of bureaucratic management risks becoming an absolute brake on economic development, the effect is an increasing tendency of the system towards stagnation. This dysfunctioning expresses itself more as a generalized penury of resources and goods than as stockpiling and non-use, and as low quality.

(9) The 'spontaneous' tendency of society is to correct these deficiencies by a growing recourse to parallel circuits (black market, moonlighting, etc.) which, together with the private sector in agriculture, represent about 20–25 per cent of the production of goods and services in the Soviet Union.[24]

(10) The decreasing rate of economic growth, in the given national and international context, inevitably creates a tendency towards a slower rate of improvement in the quality of life. Economic stagnation engenders stagnation in the field of social progress. Flowing from the general characteristics of bureaucractic management, and the ideological–moral climate which accompanies it (corruption, growing inequality, cynicism, privatization of consumption, etc.), this tendency towards stagnation of social progress has produced the spectacular phenomena of *social regression* that we have described in previous chapters (new poverty, decrease in life expectancy, etc.).

(11) In this general context, the pressure of the world capitalist market on the Soviet economy and on Soviet society increases. It takes two forms. *Objectively*, the developed capitalist countries are trying to force the Soviet Union – the state, the government, the managers – to imitate their technology and armaments. *Subjectively*, they are trying to persuade Soviet citizens to imitate their consumption model.[25]

These pressures lead to inevitable constraints, demonstrating once again the impossibility of 'Socialism in one country'. But an already highly developed country like the Soviet Union could partly escape from these constraints on the basis of an *alternative model of development*. This could not be founded merely on ideological–moral or political indoctrination. It needs material as well as solid and permanent socio-institutional foundations, which are unachievable without workers' management, workers' power, and an institutionalized pluralistic Socialist democracy.

(12) The position of the USSR in world commerce has declined during the course of recent years, as has also its weight in the overall world economy (see table 14). This decline on the part of the USSR in world trade is a reflection of the structure of its external trade, which resembles that of an underdeveloped country rather than that of the second most industrialized country in the world. Sixty-two per cent of

**Table 14**    *Share in world gross national production (percentages)*

|  | 1960 | 1980 | 2000 (projection) |
|---|---|---|---|
| Japan | 3 | 10 | 12 |
| USA | 33 | 22 | 20 |
| Rest of OECD countries | 26 | 31 | 26 |
| USSR | 15 | 13 | 12 |
| China | 5 | 4 | 5 |
| Third World | 14 | 15 | 20 |

*Source*: Figures from Economic Planning Agency, Japan, quoted in *Neue Züricher Zeitung*, 12 May 1987.

Soviet exports are made up of natural resources such as oil, natural gas, minerals, wood, and gold. More than 35 per cent of Soviet imports are items of equipment and transport, more than 20 per cent are food products, and around 12 per cent are industrial consumer goods. As a result of the fall in the price of oil and gas in 1986, the value of Soviet exports fell by 8 per cent in that same year and again by a further 4 per cent in the first quarter of 1987.[26] This decline in exports could not be neutralized by an increase in the export of industrial goods and equipment because of the poor quality of these products.

According to Soviet sources, the decline in trade with capitalist countries has been greater than its decline in world trade in general. From 1985 to 1986 exports to non-Socialist countries declined by as much as 19.5 per cent and imports from these countries by as much as 23 per cent (in dollar terms). In the preceding period East–West trade had been financed to a large extent by bank credits from the imperialist countries. The foreign debt grew rapidly. Both governments and banks in the West have begun to adopt a more cautious attitude since 1983 which, in turn, has tended to depress East–West trade even more.

In general, the indebtedness of the Soviet Union and of the countries of Eastern Europe tended to get worse in spite of the attempts to limit this in 1983–84 (see table 15).

(13) Just as twenty years of stagnation, if not decline, in life expectancy in the Soviet Union expresses in synthetic manner the crisis of that system, so also the progress and the backwardness of Soviet science are a perfect reflection of the socio-economic crisis, its origins, and its profound contradictions.

The Soviet Union has 1.5 million scientists, a quarter of all the qualified scientists in the world and half of the world's engineers. At the same time, it suffers from a technological backwardness relative to the advanced imperialist countries which has become more pronounced

**Table 15**   *Net East European debts (thousand million dollars)*

|  | 1984 | 1985 | 1986 |
|---|---|---|---|
| Bulgaria | 0.74 | 1.55 | 3.69 |
| Czechoslovakia | 2.13 | 2.50 | 3.04 |
| German Democratic Republic | 6.80 | 7.04 | 9.15 |
| Hungary | 7.30 | 9.47 | 12.99 |
| Poland | 25.25 | 28.10 | 31.80 |
| Romania | 6.56 | 6.26 | 5.76 |
| USSR | 11.17 | 15.40 | 19.23 |
| Total | 59.95 | 70.32 | 85.66 |

Source: *Neue Züricher Zeitung*, 3 December 1987.

over the past decade. This backwardness takes two forms. The transition from technological innovation to mass production is much slower than in the imperialist countries. Entire sectors are underdeveloped and backward, which has cumulative effects for the whole system. Civilian telecommunications are an obvious example.[27]

What are the causes of this backwardness? Certain writers have claimed that it is to be found in the poor quality of numerous scientific researchers, in the 'forced' character of their rapid increase, in the corruption and in the arbitrariness with which scientific leading personnel are chosen, in the *general bureaucratization of science* – similar to the bureaucratization of medicine. Mark Popovsky, one of the principal defenders of this thesis, has painted a terrifying picture of the atmosphere in the famous Siberian 'city of scientists', Akademgorodok:

By the late sixties a general change had set in. The forests and villas were still there, squirrels still hopped across the streets, but the spirit had gone out of the place and it was rapidly losing its original atmosphere. The decline was something like that which in the past afflicted utopias such as Fourier's 'phalansteries' or the dreams of Vera Pavlovna in Chernyshevsky's novel *What is to be Done?*

The first trouble with the scientific cities was, as I have already mentioned, a shortage of foodstuffs. This in turn immediately highlighted the class divisions that prevailed. Junior scientists were allocated one type of food coupons, doctors of science another, while academicians received 'Kremlin' rations. The most serious shortage was of meat. As a junior researcher walked home with the modest piece of beef to which his rations entitled him, he would see a van drive up to an academician's villa and a pair of strong young men lift out heavy hampers covered with napkins under which were concealed choice meats and other delicacies. There was also a special academicians' club with a first-class restaurant, and it appeared that in the club reserved for ordinary scientists there was a serious discussion as to whether 'candidates' might be allowed to use it as well as doctors.

The highly stratified system that thus developed led to a sharp decrease in mutual trust. Scientists who already tended to associate with others in the same discipline now began to stick to their own 'class' as well. 'Everything is cut and dried', said sociologist A.A. on the first day of my start at Akademogorodok. 'Candidates have their place and doctors have theirs. As for academicians, they are invisible and inaccessible, like gods.' Juniors no longer get a chance to discuss scientific problems with their elders on equal terms, let alone social problems. Hence there was a wave of unbridled career-ism, with everyone doing his best to scramble up the ladder as fast as possible.

The unprincipled character of social relations spread to scientific matters as well. The atmosphere was well described by academician and physicist, Lev Andreyevich Artsimovich (1909–73): 'A peaceful quiet life in conditions of extreme specialization and complete indifference to what one's neighbour is doing – this, unfortunately, is common form in a good many of our institutes. It is about as hard to achieve important scientific discoveries in such an atmos-phere as to buy Aladdin's lamp or a magic wand in a Moscow department store.' And indeed the performance of the Akademogorodok institutes has been falling off for the last decade, even as the number of scientific 'cadres' increases year by year.

Within ten years of the foundation of Akademogorodok, the quality of its staff took a sharp turn for the worse. Researchers who had made a name for themselves and achieved higher degrees gravitated to Moscow, partly owing to the changed social atmosphere and partly because of the shortage of consumer goods, including the same old problem of beef.[28]

This account, undoubtedly accurate, was written by Popovsky after having spent many years in the Soviet Union as a journalist/reporter. He had numerous contacts with scientists and he frequently visited Akademgorodok. The account reveals the nefarious effects of bureau-cratic structures, both 'internal' and 'external', on the development of Soviet science.

A number of Soviet scientific institutes lead the world in their research. The spectacular advances made by the Soviet space industry are just one example.[29] Those examples of Soviet success suggest that the causes of technological backwardness are not to be found in the system of central planning – as Marshall Goldman suggests – nor in Communist ideology, which is the view of Mark Popovsky, but rather in the structures of bureaucratic domination which could be got rid of in the Soviet Union without calling into question collective ownership of the means of production or the planned economy.[30]

It is also true that Soviet scientists and technologists, to their credit, have made numerous discoveries and inventions which were applied first outside the Soviet Union. Aganbegyan cites a number of examples, for instance the hydraulic extraction of coal and the technology of sinking mine shafts.[31] The reasons why such advances were not applied first in the Soviet Union have to do with the material interests of the bureaucracy – in other words, with the characteristics of the bureaucratic management of enterprises – and not with collective ownership or central planning in themselves. This is what emerges from the descriptions which Aganbegyan himself provides. Aganbegyan emphasizes organizational obstacles while Goldman and Lohmann concentrate on economic obstacles.

But, as should be clear, none of this has anything to do with the 'inherent traits' of collective ownership or planning. On the contrary!

(14) Any crisis of the system produces reactions which are founded on the different interests of the various social classes and the major sectors of social classes. It also promotes a rebirth of critical thought, of ideological debate, and of political life. This rebirth is a precondition for a positive resolution of the crisis, i.e. renewed progress towards Socialism. But, in itself, it does not automatically guarantee this progress.

The ideological, political, and social conflicts, of which Gorbachevism is a reflection at this stage of development, could lead either to a positive solution or to a generalized attack on the remaining conquests of the working class. The outcome depends on the relation of forces and the political consciousness and leadership of the main forces in the conflict.

With the extension of the market mechanism, there has emerged within the bureaucracy a fraction which is clearly 'restorationist', or at least objectively tending in that direction. With the growing possibilities of discussion and relatively free activity, real possibilities have begun to emerge for the working class to overcome its relative atomization and to take up once again the road of self-organization and self-activity. The struggle between those two basic tendencies will decide the future of the Soviet Union in the years ahead.

If we speak of a specific crisis of the system in the Soviet Union – and, in a more general manner, in all the post-capitalist societies under bureaucratic rule – then we use this term in a precise sense. It is a crisis which is *fundamentally different* from that which is hitting late capitalist society, which is a classic crisis of overproduction. One cannot reject this definition as long as one accepts that the Soviet Union is not a capitalist country.[32]

But the formula 'specific crisis of the regime' does not imply in any way that what has happened in the Soviet Union in recent decades is totally unconnected to events in the international capitalist economy or to the convulsions in the crisis of capitalist society.[33] We have just mentioned the growing pressure which the world capitalist market exercises on the Soviet economy, resulting in tendencies towards stagnation which are manifest in Soviet society. This is just one aspect of the reciprocal relations between the crisis of the capitalist system and the crisis of the system of bureaucratic rule.

The long economic depression which has plagued the capitalist world, the increasing difficulties faced by the Soviet Union and the countries of Eastern Europe in their dealings with the capitalist market,[34] their major debts to the capitalist banks, the pressures which those banks exercise in favour of 'greater budgetary and financial discipline' with a view to redressing their balance of payments,[35] and the pressure from some sections of the bureaucracy in the East for their countries to join the IMF, all illustrate another aspect of this interaction.

But it is a reciprocal action of two distinct crises. The agricultural crisis in the United States had the effect that overproduction in that country was compensated for by underproduction in the Soviet Union. The problems of the Soviet economy are illustrated in Soviet reliance on imported wheat. At the same time agricultural depression in the countries of agricultural abundance has made them dependent on Soviet purchases of grain, without which thousands of farmers would be bankrupt.

At the same time, the crisis which has hit the Soviet economy, this specific crisis which is bringing about deterioration in all spheres of activity, has, throughout the seventies and the first half of the eighties, acted as a formidable argument against Socialism in the imperialist countries and in the majority of the underdeveloped countries. It has erected a powerful obstacle to an anti-capitalist solution in the struggle of the international working class against the capitalist crisis. It has been one of the principal supports of the bourgeoisie in its reactionary 'counter-reform', in its neo-conservative and pseudo-liberal offensive.

It has not been bourgeois propaganda which has hoodwinked the workers in the capitalist countries into rejecting the image of Soviet reality. The working masses perceive this reality themselves and it gives nourishment to bourgeois propaganda, just as the delays in the proletarian revolution in the West have nourished and continue to nourish the specific crisis of the regime in the Soviet Union, a crisis which has slowed down the development of the revolution in the main capitalist countries.

But the reciprocal effect is also real. Every qualitative step in the anti-bureaucratic struggle in the Soviet Union, every step towards democratization, towards improvement in the conditions of life and of work, towards self-activity and freedom of action of the masses, is a blow to the international bourgeoisie because it wipes out its principal argument against socialism and stimulates the emancipatory struggle of the working masses in the imperialist countries and in the countries of the so-called 'third world'.

A reflection of the specific nature of both crises is to be found in the differences of collective mentality which one finds in the Soviet Union and in the West. In the West the crisis brings with it a mood of scepticism and pessimism, in the working class as well. In the Soviet Union, this pessimism is combined with optimistic hopes for change in a significant section of the population.

Almost alone among 'Sovietologists' in the English-speaking world, Stephen Cohen and Moshe Lewin have rejected the Manichaean vision of the evolution of the Soviet Union. With an approach similar to that of the present author, both have recognized the contradictions at work inside Soviet society. This enabled them to foresee many aspects of 'Gorbachevism' even before the coming to power of Gorbachev. Cohen's account tends to err in the direction of 'subjectivism' while Lewin is more inclined towards an 'objectivist' explanation. The truth, undoubtedly, lies in the middle.[36]

One of the inevitable consequences of the specific crisis which has hit Soviet society are divisions within the bureaucracy between 'reformers' and 'conservatives'. Cohen has emphasized correctly that this is a structural and not a conjunctural phenomenon.[37] But the explanation which he offers for this division is essentially psychological and political. He recognizes that the reformist wing of the bureaucracy desires guarantees against the return of the terror. But are the conservatives also not motivated by the desire to ensure their 'stability of employment'? Obviously, it is essential to add the more deeply rooted group interests involved here, including material interests, in order to explain this division of which Gorbachev is a product.

# 4

# Gorbachev: his Background and what he Represents

One can comprehend the 'Gorbachev phenomenon' as the coming together of a developed social need and a personality with the requisite qualities to give striking expression to that need at a certain historical moment. *Gorbachev is the product of an already existing social ferment in Soviet society who, in turn, will accentuate that social ferment.*

This classical Marxist approach to the role of the individual in history runs the risk of underestimating the weight of social factors rather than exaggerating them.[1] It is essential to integrate into our analysis the social forces at work in the *selection* of leaders in any society, recognizing them as *social* forces, even if the mechanisms at work are not the same in every society.

It is not enough to be ambitious, clever, or a good manoeuvrer to reach the top of any hierarchy, whether bourgeois or state-bureaucratic (not to mention the feudal hierarchy or that of ancient Asiatic society). Specific channels of selection exist in all these societies and are inter-twined with the processes of socialization (family, schools, institutions) as well as with the successive tests which prove one's particular abilities, tests which enable the concentric circles of authority (local, regional, sectoral, national) to register and evaluate the qualities or defects which accelerate or put a brake on one's career.

There is one test which is generally crucial: individual behaviour in the crisis situations with which one is sooner or later confronted, a test which can be a springboard into the future or which can as easily ruin everything. The ultimate test, that of winning power, comes only after a succession of earlier tests. A biographic study of any leader, of whatever country, in this or in previous centuries, will demonstrate in every case the existence of a process analogous to progressive social selection.

It is only when the individual has climbed through the successive echelons of power that individual personal characteristics begin to have a significant influence on social development. The example of Gorbachev is particularly eloquent in this respect.

There are some unanswered questions about the earlier stages of what was an altogether modest career. As a young man he did not attract any particular attention in his job as junior official in Komsomol (the youth organization). He was selected by his provincial town to study law at Moscow University. Obviously he combined a good intelligence with an ability not to draw too much attention to himself, not to demonstrate too much zeal or innovative spirit. He appears to have been a typical conformist. In Moscow, during the height of the hysteria surrounding the Stalinist purges, he remained in the party. According to many witnesses he always took a hard line when dealing with the slightest offence by Komsomol members. Did he disapprove of the bloody purges? Probably.[2] But he was a master in the art of dissimulation. He was a conformist adapting to the sombre conditions of the Stalinist regime, marked with the stamp of the social milieu within which he developed.

Having finished his university degree and married he was sent to Stavropol to work in the Komsomol apparatus. In 1962, at the age of thirty-one, he entered the party apparatus in the department of agriculture. He strengthened his position (a sign of the times) by acquiring a second higher degree, this time in agrarian economics. At the same time he acquired a powerful protector: F.D. Kulakov, party leader in Stavropol, member of the Central Committee, soon to be in charge of agriculture, made member of the Politburo in April 1971.

In 1966 he was chosen by Kulakov to be first party secretary in the city of Stavropol and, in 1968, he was chosen as second party secretary for the Stavropol district, becoming first secretary in 1970. Kulakov was obviously preparing him for higher things. The fact that he met Suslov, Brezhnev, and Andropov at the power station in Kislovodsk, which was in his district, is an indication of this. Here again we perceive his ability to dissimulate. He didn't have high regard for Brezhnev but in the eyes of the party apparatus he was a 'Brezhnev man'. In November 1978 we find him in Moscow, taking over Kulakov's post of responsibility for agriculture in the Central Committee after the death of his patron.

If we assess this career by means of objective criteria, a career which began in a rather routine manner but then made spectacular leaps, we find that it conforms to very general rules. History offers us numerous examples of qualities and defects of 'great men' (and 'great women') which blossom only in the context of quite definite historical circumstances. Individuals excel in exceptional circumstances into which they are precipitated by history.

Of course the abilities and the talent have to be present. Emile Vandervelde, leader of the Second International, who travelled in the same train that took Trotsky to Petrograd at the beginning of May 1917, admitted later:

> Up until the time of the October revolution, I never believed it possible that a man like Trotsky could organize or direct anything. For me, he was an incarnation of the pure intellectual who spent half of his day reading and writing and half of his night discussing over a samovar or in a cafe.... He had the appearance of a bohemian pianist, with that uncontrolled nervousness which is characteristic of this type of artist. When he was celebrated later as organizer of the Red Army, I thought this was just a propaganda bluff. But, in the end, I had to admit that one cannot judge people in the course of a revolution according to what they had been in pre-revolutionary exile.[3]

The talents of Mikhail Gorbachev were put at the service of a larger social group – the Soviet Bureaucracy – because his behaviour conformed to the rules and to the objective consequences of that group's domination.

But this social group, the bureaucracy, is structured in a particular manner; its structure is not rigid, at least not as rigid as we would be led to believe by theories of 'totalitarianism'. And Mikhail Gorbachev made his appearance at certain crossroads in the molecular transformations that were taking place inside the bureaucracy, transformations that were largely independent of his will or of any personal calculation. Those transformations were a constant accompaniment to his career.

He was born into a family which Schmidt–Häuser and Martin Walker, two good observers of Soviet reality, characterize as 'new middle class' (although we would prefer to call it a 'new middle layer'), itself a product of 'Socialist' industrialization. His grandfather was a middle-ranking official, director of a kolkhoz. His father was a tractor driver who later became chairman of a combine brigade. His wife is a philosopher and sociologist, whose father was a journalist and economist. His daughter is a doctor. He himself studied law and agricultural economics. He has experienced neither class struggle, revolution, civil war, nor world war. He is the first Soviet leader who is representative of the generation of post-Stalinist Soviet 'Communists', free from the great traumas and battles of the past.[4]

It is a generation not naturally inclined to dramatize its problems, well-established, attracted by 'consumer society' – although in somewhat more modest fashion than the yuppies of Western capitalism. At the same time, it is a generation which is better trained, better educated than the previous generation and naturally inclined towards a technocratic vision of reality.

What's more, it is a generation marked by the rise of the new media, especially television. Gorbachev was one of the first of the young apparatchiks to understand the importance of television in the party's relations with the population. Soviet viewers were largely indifferent towards programmes that were mostly regarded as boring. Gorbachev's visits abroad, especially his trip to France in 1966, reinforced his conviction that this had to change. He became the first 'public relations expert', the first 'TV personality' in the history of Soviet leaders.[5]

The Stalinist era is something profoundly repugnant to the Gorbachev generation. They detest its purges, its arbitrary brutality, the enormous cost of its successes, the avoidable waste. (It seems that Raisa Gorbachev's father spent a few years in the Gulag, together with Dmitri Likhachev who is today a prominent academician.)[6] This same generation desires stability of employment. But after the decade of hope, 1953–63, recent Soviet history, characterized by increasing immobility, appears to them to be weighed down with the same problems of inefficiency as the era of Stalinist tyranny. It is a generation with a secret longing for change, even if they don't proclaim it publicly, even a gradual, prudent change, a change which avoids the excesses and mistakes of the Khrushchev era.

Alongside the spectacular successes in its competition with the West, the Soviet Union is confronting enormous handicaps of the kind we have described in earlier chapters. These handicaps limit the chances, the success, the ambitions of every member of the bureaucracy, especially the more ambitious among them. These people dream of profound changes which could lift the country out of the rut.

Objectively, what is at stake is the consolidation and extension of the power and privileges of the bureaucratic layer of which they are a part. The point is to make the system function better, not to change it fundamentally. The mechanisms of leadership selection that exist in the Soviet Union are such that the apparatus is assured in advance that no person will reach the top who has the intention of radically transforming the structure of power at the expense of the social and material interests of the bureaucracy.

The formula *Gorbachev represents the technocratic–modernizing wing of the bureaucracy* should not be interpreted in a functional sense. It is not so much a professional differentiation as one of mentality, of priorities, attitudes, and political orientations. A grouping together of academics and experts against the non-academic apparatchiks is not possible in the Soviet Union. Likewise, there is no question of a division between politicians (party and state) and technicians (economy and scientific–cultural institutions). The division that exists cuts across all seven principal components of the bureaucracy: the state (including the central economic organs); enterprises; the army; the KGB; the cultural organizations and those that deal with health, education, etc.; the mass organizations (unions, Komsomol, women's organizations); the party.

Ursula Schmiederer is certainly right in considering the party apparatus as, in the final analysis, the central one. It leads and supports the other six branches of the bureaucracy.[7] But this leading role is exercised in a context in which the degree of autonomy of each of the branches fluctuates according to the precise historical situation.

During the worst moments of the Stalinist terror, the police and security apparatus was, for all practical purposes, independent of the party apparatus. In the period 1934–41 and 1948–53, the police were controlled only by Stalin, his personal secretariat, and Beria, Yagoda, and Yezhov. The military apparatus, on the other hand, after the execution of Tukhachevsky and his comrades and at least until the big military defeats of 1941–42, had practically no independence. But after the defeats in the spring of 1942, the military apparatus, symbolized by Marshal Zhukov, regained an increasing independence which reached its peak at the time of the semi-coup of 1953, which made it possible for Khrushchev and Malenkov, within the space of a few hours, to eliminate Beria and the worst elements of the GPU/NKVD.[8]

Enterprise managers, however, acquired a large degree of autonomy with the consolidation of the Stalinist dictatorship, an autonomy which was only partly relinquished during the great purges. They have systematically sought to extend this autonomy, first at the time of the Liberman reforms in the sixties, then under Kosygin in the seventies, as well as under Andropov and Gorbachev in the eighties, although their success has been limited up to now. The cultural apparatus tried to move away from party control at the height of Khrushchev's 'destalinization'. This was the 'liberalization' of the sixties, which was followed by severe repression from the party apparatus under Suslov. Today there is a second wave of 'autonomy' in this sector which has gone beyond that achieved in the Khrushchev period.

When we say that the division between conservatives and reformers cuts across all seven sectors of the bureaucracy, this means, first of all, that in all sectors of the apparatus, including that of the party, there are partisans of change, of *aggiornamento* not altogether unlike that which happened inside the Catholic hierarchy at the time of Vatican Councils I and II.

One must not forget that in all the upper echelons of the bureaucracy nominations for key posts pass through party bodies. This is the *nomenklatura*. If first Andropov, and then Gorbachev, were elected as general secretaries of the party, it was because there was a majority of party apparatchiks, at least in the Politburo and Central Committee, who were partisans of change, who waited to end the immobility of the Brezhnev era. It was not because the 'technocrats' imposed this choice on the politicians and ideologues from the outside. The rumour still persists that the election of those two partisans of change (prudent and gradual change, of course) was promoted by none other than Suslov, considered by everyone as the incarnation of 'party orthodoxy' within the Soviet establishment.[9]

The *political* nature of the decision in favour of change also has a deeper significance. *This option corresponds to the interests of the bureaucracy as a whole* in this present period, even if it is clearly articulated and expressed by only one wing of the bureaucracy. One section of the bureaucracy, including the top leaders, had lost touch with the country as it really was, with society as a whole. Its manner of governing was becoming more and more ineffective, even dangerous from the point of view of the defence of the power and privileges of the bureaucracy as *a social layer*. In every branch of the apparatus, people were becoming aware of this.[10] They began to whisper, to worry, to demand that things be taken in hand. It is of these men and women that first Andropov, later Gorbachev, became spokesman and representative.

The need for reform was confirmed by the progressive loss of control of the party over the various social 'mini-milieus', where a rebirth of public awareness was taking place, even if fragmented. This led to a real fear that the authority of the party would be challenged by a renewal of autonomous mass activity. *Fear of a 'change from below' stimulated the bureaucracy to undertake a preventative 'change from above'.*

It is at this point in the analysis that we can deal with another contradictory aspect of the Gorbachev phenomenon. The fragmentation of Soviet society under bureaucratic dictatorship leads not only to the political atomization of the working class. It leads also to a growing inability of the apparatus to recognize, even to understand, the real situation in the country and the evolution of Soviet society as a whole.[11] Ossification and doctrinal sterility, professional super-specialization (what the Germans call *fachidiotentum*), undoubtedly all contribute to this, but its real roots are political–institutional.[12]

Under such circumstances it is once again no accident that it is the KGB, supported by an enormous network of spies and informers, which is in a better position to grasp theoretically or at least analytically the totality of Soviet society.[13] Certain key aspects which emerge from this overall picture are beginning to promote a kind of panic. The fish has already begun to go bad at the head. Corruption, to which even the KGB itself is not immune, was first exposed in the case of the Politburo's number-two man, F. Kozlov, and then it was revealed that the Brezhnev family itself had been corrupted.[14] Surgery was obviously needed.

This explains the fact that both Andropov and Gorbachev were raised to power with the support if not the direct intervention of the KGB. A number of writers correctly described Gorbachev as 'Andropov's man'.[15]

It was also significant that Gorbachev's candidature was proposed by Gromyko, one of the longest serving members of the Politburo. Gromyko's speech at the Central Committee plenum in which he officially proposed Gorbachev as new secretary general underlined his personal character and his quality as a leader. He is reported to have said of Gorbachev that 'this man has teeth of steel behind an enticing smile'. This sentence was omitted from the published version of his speech. But one important sentence of Gromyko's dealt with the concerns of the bureaucracy:

> There are some questions which it is difficult to deal with in black and white terms. There are intermediate colours, intermediate decisions. Mikhail Sergeevich always knows how to find these kinds of solutions, solutions which correspond to the line of the party.

This was an assurance for the Brezhnevites that change would be pursued gradually, that there would be no radical change. Gorbachev, in his speech, eulogized the KGB.[16] He also emphasized the 'leading role of the party', which would acquire new tasks as a result of the necessary changes.[17]

Gorbachev kept a low profile during his first year in office and during the 27th Congress of the party held in February/March 1986. He strengthened his base in the Central Committee and the Politburo.[18] He didn't want to upset the apparatus, hence the rather colourless character of the 27th Congress. This was a congress of bureaucrats, not of workers and peasants. Of the eighty-eight speeches only eight – less than 10 per cent – were made by people working in enterprises. These numbers alone are sufficient confirmation of the judgement of revolutionary Marxists that the Soviet Communist Party is a party of the bureaucracy and not a party of the working class.

> At one time, the party used to organize meetings at least once a year. Today, the majority of communists in the enterprises engage in no exchange of ideas whatever, and it has been like this for quite a few years now.

This was what one letter to *Pravda* said on 7 January 1986.

The was one new proposal in Gorbachev's speech. It was for the creation of 'councils of worker collectives' in the enterprises. These councils were to be made up of representatives of party committees, of the unions and Komsomol, of the work brigades and experts. The control by the bureaucracy is thus assured in advance. These councils are far from being democratically elected workers' councils. Although the phrase 'Socialist democracy' was mentioned in Gorbachev's speech and in a number of speeches at the Congress, its meaning was left very vague. 'One must remember,' said Gorbachev, 'that for Lenin, Soviet power is based on the self-management of workers.' But then he added: 'This self-management does not develop outside the institutions of the state, but within those institutions themselves.' In other words, there will be no new organs, just those that already exist within the bureaucratic dictatorship.

The source of the problem is clear. *Socialist democracy* is not a normative demand, nor is it an ideal to be realized little by little. *It is an immediate practical necessity for the proper functioning of the Soviet economy and Soviet society.* Without this democracy it is impossible for the planners to know the workers' preferences both as producers and as consumers. Ignorant of these preferences, it is impossible to allocate the social product and the social surplus in the correct proportions. The mobilization of the potential knowledge and initiative which still remains hiddens in the Soviet working class remains a mirage. Gorbachev's plans remain suspended in midair, dependent on the good will of the bureaucrats.

It is true that bureaucratic privileges had begun to be publicly denounced in the period preceding the Congress. Special shops, the existence of which had previously been denied, were mentioned by Yevtushenko in his famous speech to the Congress of Writers.[19] Timid allusions were made to this issue at the Party Congress. Gromyko brushed these aside in his own intervention, turning the criticism of a social layer into a criticism of individual morals and working patterns. This is the typical response of bureaucratic ideology. According to Gromyko, although the criticism is acceptable in principle, one should not criticize 'honest Communists'. And if the honest Communists enjoy the kind of special privileges that the workers resent? Here, the moralist Gromyko has nothing to say.[20]

At a press conference at the time of the 27th Party Congress, Aliyev, member of the Politburo and apparently number five in the bureaucratic hierarchy, was asked about the special shops. His reply was characterized by the kind of cynicism and lack of sensitivity which is a feature of the bureaucracy, totally lacking, as it is any kind of Communist conviction: 'Leaders work twenty-four hours a day. It is essential that they have shops which are open for twenty-four hours.'[21] And what of the miners, the lorry-drivers, the women workers in the textile factories who, in addition to their factory work, have to also look after the household, in the sexist climate that prevails in the Soviet Union? These women have to work literally sixteen hours a day. And what a contemptible piece of demagogy it is to speak only of the hours of opening, when the issue is the availability of goods, the quality and the low prices in these special shops. The existence of the *nomenklatura* is now officially recognized. But our prognosis is that their privileges are not about to be done away with.[22]

All of Gorbachev's reforms attempt to link workers' income to individual performance. This performance, however, is less a function of effort, discipline, or physical or technical qualification than it is of economic factors over which the workers have no collective control. These factors are: regular supplies of raw materials, the quality of machinery, the facilities to carry out repairs, the choice of technologies, the organization of work, etc. Workers are systematically penalized in their wages for the malfunctioning of the economic system for which they bear no responsibility. They resent this state of affairs as a profound injustice and they are expressing this resentment more and more openly. The more Gorbachev insists on individual calculation of salaries, invoking the typically Stalinist 'struggle against petty bourgeois egalitarianism', the more the demand for workers' control over production, even for workers' self-management, will also begin to be heard.

Some of the examples provided by workers are particularly scandalous. In *Pravda* of 1 March 1986, A.S. Suchanov, a member of the workers' brigade building the extension to the Moscow underground, not only denounced the irregular supplies of building material, which was the main cause of delays in construction, but also revealed that the proportion of purely manual labour on the site was exactly what it had been half a century earlier, just about 40 per cent. They used pneumatic drills similar to those produced in 1935, but of inferior quality. Two years later, not much had changed. The following complaint from one of the managers on the site appeared in *Moscow News* on 22 November 1987:

> We are without working tools. We have no means of transporting them to the site where the new station will soon be established. We have to move large blocks but have no means of doing so. We have to put up the frames by hand. We carry cement in shovels. We still use the pickaxe. This is not modern work, this work is from the stone-age.

A woman worker in a flax mill, V.N. Pletnyova, revealed in a letter published in *Pravda*, 27 February 1986, that in her combine, which specialized in the manufacture of domestic linen, it was becoming increasingly difficult to sell their products because of poor quality and unattractive design. She added:

> There is constant talk of the need to renew the machinery in the factory, but this has been delayed for many years. Fewer and fewer workers are willing to work in the sections where the cloth is made because of the lamentable sanitary conditions and the amount of dust.

If we follow attentively these workers' disputes in the Soviet Union, what we see is a slow resurgence of a class reaction which is more important than the immediate demands or complaints. The negative reaction of numerous workers to the brigade system, revealed in an article in *EKO* which caused quite a stir, was explained, according to the article, by the cohesion and collective solidarity of the workers on the assembly line, a cohesion and solidarity which the brigade system tended to undermine but which the workers valued highly.[23]

The speeches at the Party Congress, including the speeches from high officials, reveal that the social complaints of the Soviet workers are very serious indeed. They revealed that the provision of good quality food is irregular and inadequate. Housing conditions are poor and there are many problems with health and security at work. The indifference of many factory directors to the needs of the workers was emphasized. In *Pravda* of 1 March 1986 a miner, I.A. Shatalov, complained that although 150 million roubles had been invested in production at his mine, 'not a single rouble was invested in cultural or sports facilities for the miners'.[24] Two days later, another worker, G.S. Kostenko, pointed out that during the course of the twelfth five-year plan it had been decided to build 10,000 apartments for the workers of Glavbammstroi who were constructing a new railway line in Siberia. Only 1,000 were built and the result was a very rapid turnover of labour. A third of the workers changed their job each year because they were unhappy with the living conditions. Numerous speakers at the Congress revealed that social spending was considered non-priority or 'residual', i.e. it was considered by factory directors only after so-called economic spending had been decided.

All of these contradictions in the attempt at bureaucratic self-reform under bureaucratic control – which is how Gorbachev himself presents his project – boil down to the proposition: 'satisfy the demands of the workers without touching the power or privileges of the apparatus.' But it is precisely this power and these privileges which are the source of the workers' discontent.

At this Congress, Yeltsin, who was at the time party chief in Moscow, asked:

Why, at every congress, do we hear the same problems? Why has the word stagnation, a foreign word, made its appearance in the vocabulary of the party? Why have we not succeeded, after so many years, in eliminating the roots of bureaucratism?

Then he answered: 'Because some party officials lack the courage to recognize correctly and on time their situation and their proper role.'[25] A massive country of 280 million inhabitants is faced with stagnation, large-scale corruption, and social injustice, simply because 'some party officials' lack courage!

Gorbachev began by implementing some limited and gradual reforms, in order not to upset the apparatus, in order not to appear as an adventurer, in order to avoid the fate of Khrushchev. He is relatively young and he may survive. But his reform attempts have awakened public awareness. The people are less afraid to criticize, and the potential objects of criticism are innumerable. It is not just individual criticism that is at stake. In his speech to the Congress, Gromyko recognized that the critical letters published in the press were often signed by hundreds of workers. These are not then just letters of complaint but collective petitions which constitute a form of political or para-political activity. Gorbachev's complaints are but an echo of a much more massive complaint rising from the depths of Soviet society.

The greater this pressure becomes, the more it will be obstructed and passively resisted by a section of the apparatus. As this resistance develops, the reformers will become impatient and will insist more loudly, encouraging an even greater echo in society at large. Gorbachev and his modernizing team will begin to oscillate between *realpolitik* – always unrealistic in a period of growing social, economic, and political crisis – and radicalization. They will find themselves more and more in a position of having to make impossible choices.

Elected head of the party and representing the bureaucracy whose power and privileges he wishes to consolidate, Gorbachev will undermine this power and privilege the more he attempts to rationalize it. This is the principal contradiction in his orientation of radical reform.

# 5

# Perestroika and Gorbachev's Economic Reforms

The main objective of the Gorbachev team is to overcome the continuing decline in economic growth and to avoid stagnation. Economic reforms are at the centre of Gorbachev's new course. This is *perestroika*, the restructuring of the Soviet economy. And it is by the results of this restructuring that he will be judged. He will remain in power only if the balance sheet of his economic reforms is positive.

What is this perestroika? Part of the difficulty in answering this is due to the fact that the Gorbachev team have been very prudent in proclaiming their goals. They began step by step, not formulating their central or global objectives, to the point where many saw Gorbachev simply as a pure pragmatist. Another difficulty in defining perestroika derives from the fact that it contains contradictory elements: decentralization accompanied by the creation of new hyper-centralist structures.

Talk of the need for a transition from extensive to intensive industrialization is somewhat banal and anachronistic. This necessity was already stressed at the time of the Liberman reforms – twenty-five years ago! Talk of modernization, of the need for a 'scientific–technical revolution' is likewise nothing new. This is a need which has been stressed for at least two decades.

A definition of perestroika, however, is possible. The most acceptable definition is that of Catherine Samary, who describes it as a major utilization of market mechanisms in an economy dominated by central planning (i.e. a 'Socialist market'), as opposed to 'market socialism' where market regulation is dominant. It is the case that for a number of economists and ideologues, the first is merely a transition to the second. But it is unlikely that this will happen in the Soviet Union.[1]

The 'radical restructuring' called for by Gorbachev could also be summarized in the formula 'rationalization and profitability'. The pursuit of these objectives has strongly reinforced other goals: modernization; economic use of equipment, raw materials, and energy; increased use of robots and modern information technology in priority sectors; true prices; increased autonomy for enterprises; workers' income related to performance; better integration into the world market; resolution of the problem of grain and meat; resolution of the housing problem; and so on.

The list could be extended at will. It demonstrates the complexity of the problems which perestroika has to deal with and, therefore, the ambiguous, if not confused, character of the concept of perestroika itself.

On 11 June 1985, before a plenary session of the Central Committee, at which were assembled all the high Soviet dignitaries, with the exception of Gorbachev's principal rival, Romanov, Gorbachev enunciated a list of requirements with respect to the economy and the state. His audience was called on to understand and to put into practice 'radical changes'. The reforms were urgent: 'We don't have very much time.' There was, indeed, cause for alarm. After a brief respite as a result of the disciplinary measures introduced by Andropov, the rate of growth of industrial production had fallen again in 1984. According to official Soviet sources, industrial production grew by only 3.1 per cent during the period January to June 1985, compared with 4.5 per cent during the same period in 1984, and 4.1 per cent in 1983.

The complaints were significant, but rather routine. There was a new sense of urgency. The conclusion: renewal of growth with less investment. Investment itself had to be rationalized. The accent was on two factors: modernization and discipline. Gorbachev is the herald of the 'scientific technical revolution': automation, information technology, robotics – these are the central themes at the heart of the official ideology.

Discipline is to be achieved in a more economic use of raw materials and energy, a more rational use of equipment and labour, and a reduction in the demand for additional investment to achieve plan objectives. All of this is traditional, abstract, and unrealistic, in view of the material interests of the bureaucracy that runs the economy.

The only concrete proposal was for a substantial reduction in the construction of new factories and a concentration on modernizing existing factories and equipment. The 27th Party Congress, which met nine months later in February/March 1986, didn't add much in the way of precision to the contents of perestroika. The goals for the year 2000 were known in advance: production is to be doubled; all families are to have adequate housing; agricultural production is to be increased tremendously. The Congress simply confirmed these goals.

The principal means envisaged to achieve success in the promotion of economic and social growth, as defined at the Central Committee plenum in April 1985, remain:

1. The simultaneous strengthening of the central organs of planning and of the powers of enterprise directors, with a reduction in the powers of intermediate organs such as the ministries.

2. Greater work discipline and income related to individual performance.

3. The extension of the market in agriculture and services.

4. The creation of agro-industrial committees to stimulate the modernization of agriculture.

5. Giving priority attention to technology; robotics, electronics, electrical machines, lasers, biogenetics, etc., with a view to overcoming the Soviet Union's backwardness in these fields relative to the imperialist countries.

6. Modernization of existing enterprises rather than construction of new ones.

7. Moves against corruption, the black market, etc.

None of this is new. It falls far short of the two previous economic reforms, that of Liberman in the sixties and Kosygin in the seventies. Some of the things revealed, however, were new. In an article which caused quite a sensation, the economist O. Latsis condemned the excessive accumulation of stocks in all sectors of the Soviet economy. Penury was more apparent than real, at least in the sector of means of production. He revealed that these stocks had grown by more than 184 per cent between 1977 and 1985.[2]

A little later, the academician Abel Aganbegyan, principal economic adviser to Gorbachev, gave a complete account of the poor use of equipment in the Soviet Union and stressed the fact that the Soviet Union produced less grain than the United States but used four times as many tractors. He might also have added that the Soviet Union had nine times as many people employed in the agricultural sector. In other words, the productivity of labour in the Soviet agricultural sector is 10 per cent of what it is in the United States.[3]

How then is perestroika to be achieved, including as it does all those projects mentioned in Gorbachev's reports? There were the traditional and routine allusions to 'material interests' and to the 'mobilization of the workforce'. But everyone knows that these are mere words, which produced very little at the time of the Liberman and Kosygin reforms in the sixties and seventies. The Novosibirsk report in 1983 was similar in that Tatiana Zaslavskaia formulated a pertinent critique of the structural problems of the Soviet economy but ended up with extremely vague and limited reform proposals.[4]

Her ideas were in part the inspiration for Gorbachev's economic reform project, just as they were in the case of Andropov.[5] The Novosibirsk report contains the same emphasis on the need for strengthening both central planning and the powers of the directors of enterprises, with a reduction in the power of the intermediate layers of the bureaucracy.

We find there, too, another reform proposal, which only came to the fore after the 27th Congress, namely, the extension of the private sphere in agriculture and services. An interview with Zaslavskaia in *Izvestia* (1 June 1985) explicitly mentions such an extension in the field of agriculture, so long as it stayed 'within the limits of the law'. One must recall here that Mikhail Gorbachev was for seven years the secretary at the Central Committee responsible for agriculture. The least that one can say is that his management of agriculture was not brilliant. Soviet agriculture continues to stagnate. The shortage of animal fodder leads to a reduction in meat production, which has levelled off at about 60 kilos per head of population. The comparable figure in France is 100 kilos and in East Germany 92. Cereal production was around 195 tons in 1985 and 215 tons in 1986, still short of the annual objective of 240–50 tons foreseen in the 1981–85 plan.[6]

It seems that Gorbachev wants to stimulate private production by kolkhoz workers (those on collective farms) and sovkhoz workers (those on state farms), on private plots as well as in co-operatives. This private production represents today 25 per cent of all agricultural production in the Soviet Union, with an even higher percentage in animal breeding and fruit and vegetables (see table 16).[7]

The system of 'brigades under contract' has been introduced as an experiment on kolkhoz land. Brigades (which can all be members of the same family) are given the right to exploit a portion of kolkhoz land, keeping part of the profit and giving the rest to the kolkhoz. *Business Week* (7 December 1987) gives the example of a kolkhoz near Moscow where the family of a lorry driver had tripled its monthly income by raising cattle privately on kolkhoz land. This is, in reality, a reappropriation of collective land by private labour, an extension of the system of private plots without changing the proprietary status. It is a system half way between the Chinese reform model (based on private labour) and the restrictive system introduced under Khrushchev and Brezhnev.[8]

**Table 16**    *Private production as percentage of gross production*

|  | 1940 | 1965 | 1982 |
|---|---|---|---|
| Grain | 11 | 2 | 2 |
| Potatoes | 65 | 63 | 63 |
| Vegetables | 48 | 41 | 31 |
| Fruit | 70 | 54 | 41 |
| Meat | 72 | 40 | 30 |
| Milk | 77 | 39 | 30 |
| Eggs | 94 | 67 | 31 |
| Wool | 39 | 21 | 24 |

In a general way, perestroika should overcome or at least diminish the fundamental disproportion between industry on the one hand, and agriculture and services on the other. This is a disproportion which has characterized the Soviet economy since the first five-year plan. It is a disproportion which has inflicted severe – and avoidable – sacrifices on the workers and peasants in the form of inadequate supplies of consumer goods. It led to a general level of labour productivity inferior to what there could have been with a more equitable distribution of available resources. The level of consumption of the peasantry was below that of the workers because of the lower level of labour productivity in the countryside, as demonstrated in Figure 2.

Some of the more innovative reforms are in services where an experiment has been carried out in republic of Estonia. According to an article in *Izvestia* (19 August 1985), the service and repair sector in the Soviet Union today is among the sectors that give least satisfaction to Soviet consumers. In Estonia the firm Elektron, which repairs radio and television sets, rented one of its sections to a brigade of technicians on the basis of 650 roubles per month per individual technician. The latter were to pay the costs of materials, electricity, heating, etc. In return, they were permitted to charge their customers whatever they considered a fair price. Prices were, in fact, determined by the play of supply and demand. The technicians were allowed to keep 70 per cent of their revenue; 30 per cent went to the state enterprise.

The result seems to have been sensational. The waiting list in Tallin used to be two weeks – much shorter than in Moscow or Leningrad. Soon it was reduced to two days and goods were often available on the same day. What's more, the quality of repairs was better and bribes had disappeared. Prices stabilized very rapidly.

It was after this initial success that the law on private labour was promulgated in May 1987, giving the first concrete content to perestroika. It authorized individual commercial activity but did not permit

**Figure 2**    *Soviet living standard 1913–85 \**

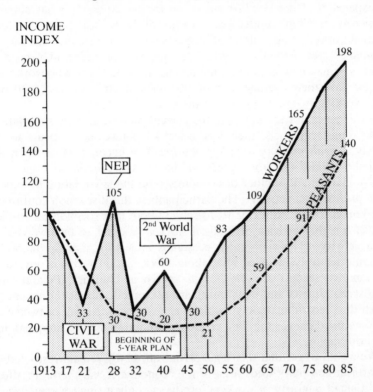

\*1913 taken as base; social services not included. This table overestimates the rise in real income in recent years. *Economica.*

*Source*: Jovan Pavlevski, *Le Niveau de vie en URSS. Economica.*

the employment of wage labour. According to Aganbegyan, local organs were given quite a large scope of regulating private labour. Wherever the local organs encouraged this activity, there was perceptible success. Taxis appeared in the streets of numerous towns: there were private doctors and clinics; there was a large expansion in the service sector.[9]

This is still on a relatively small scale, however. *Business Week* estimated 200,000 persons engaged in private activity, with 8,000 new co-operatives established, involving 80,000 members (7 December 1987). This is, of course, relatively small in an active population of 135 million. In addition, we see in the case of Hungary the difficulties in extending this type of reform into industry itself, except for the agro-food business.

The extension of private production to the kolkhozes should lead to an expansion of the kolkhoz market in the big cities. This has already happened in China under the reforms of Deng Xiaoping. Another 'rationalization' of agriculture also affects the sovkhozes, the state farms. Around 30 per cent of the agricultural produce of both kolkhozes and sovkhozes may now be sold on the private market. Those who work well can increase their average monthly earnings of 200 roubles by 30 per cent, working two days a week on their own initiative.

If we ignore, for the moment, the current rhetoric and the speculation about long-term goals, then this aspect of perestroika appears to be merely a *legalization of the black market*. This becomes clear when we read the debate that took place in the journal *Kommunist* (no. 18, 1986), involving a number of economists, on the law relating to 'individual professional activity'. The participants in this discussion confirmed well-known facts. Professor R. Lifschitz wrote that sociological studies had shown that at least 50 million workers wanted to be involved in extra activity. (The economists Kostakov and Rutsgaiser speak of 17 million effectively involved in a labour black market.) This is obviously the famous 'second economy', well known in Hungary, Poland, and Yugoslavia. Jurists and economists are not precise about the extent to which this 'second economy', which implies a working day of twelve or more hours, damages the 'first economy', undermining the campaign for labour discipline.

We would wager that this 'legal privatization' will remain restricted to the artisan and petty-trade area of the economy. It will therefore affect only a small minority of workers, producing only a small percentage of national revenue, with less scope than the NEP under Lenin, and it will not lead to a restoration of capitalism, in spite of the fears of certain 'leftists' and the hopes of the bourgeois sycophants of Gorbachev.

In fact, the thirty or so private activities legalized by the law of 19 November 1986 are strictly limited to the area of services and small-scale trade and commerce. Private taxis, restaurants, cafes, translators, musicians, and doctors are tolerated.[10] Forbidden are the private production of furs, jewellery, arms of all sorts, private education, clubs, baths and saunas, the production of cosmetics, the manufacture of photocopiers and all sorts of reproduction equipment, etc.

According to a report in the German newspaper *Die Zeit* (15 May 1987), these private artisans make little profit, perhaps two to three times the average salary per family, much less than can be made on the black market, not to speak of corruption and bribery which can bring in thousands, if not tens of thousands, of roubles per month. So it isn't capitalism that Gorbachev wants to introduce in the Soviet Union.

Prices in this private sector are exorbitant. A dinner for two in the private restaurant *Kropotkinskaia* in Moscow costs as much as 800 roubles (100 dollars – 40 per cent of the average worker's monthly wage). A small private shop sells locally made blue jeans for the same price. For the mass of workers this new commercial sector is out of reach. According to *Moscow News* (22 November 1987), there have already been protests against the excessive revenues in the private sector. In general, the protesters demanded higher tax on incomes and more competition to lower prices.

Here we can put our finger on the sociology of perestroika. The intelligentsia and the mass of the middle layer of the bureaucracy were dissatisfied with the system of distribution which barred them from the more exorbitant advantages of the *nomenklatura*. They were obliged to satisfy their needs with the time-consuming and laborious mechanisms of the black market. They supported with enthusiasm the extension of the legal market mechanism, which corresponded to their needs and their financial abilities. It is in this sector of the bureaucracy that perestroika has its greatest support.[11]

But, at the same time, Gorbachev aims to cut price subsidies from basic goods and services. It is true that these subsidies are a great strain on the Soviet economy, representing 20–25 per cent of global spending. According to Aganbegyan, subsidies to meat and dairy products account for fifty million roubles per year. One kilo of meat sold in a state retail outlet for 1.8 roubles per kilo has a state subsidy of three roubles. For a litre of milk, sold for an average of thirty kopeks, the subsidy is twenty-five kopeks. Prices on the kolkhoz market are two to three times the prices in state shops.[12]

The elimination of subsidies risks reducing the buying power of the wage-earner, especially the average wage-earner. Aganbegyan adds:

> In our socialist economy, an increase in the retail price should be completely compensated for.... After the war, when ration cards were finished and retail prices rose, a 'bread bonus' was introduced, depending on the size of income. It is very likely that, when the price of meat and dairy products is increased, there will also be a bonus of this type. At the same time, the price of other consumer goods may fall. [13]

But Soviet workers are worried about this. In other words, they are sceptical that the compensation will be adequate to deal with the increase in the cost of living. There are also worries about increases in the cost of housing and health, worries which are quite frequently expressed in the press. According to the *Observer* (28 June 1987), Gorbachev has decided to postpone the abolition of housing subsidies.

This expansion of the sphere of 'real prices' not only corresponds to certain social interests. It also has an economic objective: *the expansion of the market mechanism within the framework of the nationalized and planned economy.* A new system of enterprise management and financial responsibility was due to be initiated on 1 January 1988. This is the cornerstone of perestroika in the long term, although *Gosplan* and the ministries have resisted it up to now. This system increases the autonomy and the risks of management in forty-eight thousand Soviet enterprises. As in China and Yugoslavia, they risk bankruptcy if they operate at a loss over a longer period. In return for taking this risk, they will be permitted to keep a major part of the profit in the case of success, a portion of which will be distributed as bonuses to the workers and, of course, to the managers.

What is not at all clear, however, is the intended scope of 'real prices'. For the moment, it is only a question of eliminating subsidies on elementary consumer goods. It has not been resolved to eliminate subsidies from raw materials and equipment. If enterprises are not to be free to negotiate the price of their *inputs*, their freedom to decide the price of *outputs* is severely limited. All the talk about 'market Socialism' reduces itself to a turning of the screw at the cost of consumption in order to stimulate investments and increase labour productivity. In other words, what it amounts to is a Soviet version of austerity.

It is true that the number of prices set by the central authorities will be reduced in a draconian manner. Previously this was the case for two hundred thousand products. From now on the only prices centrally determined will be those applying to about a thousand raw materials and basic goods. But it is precisely these that enter into the production of practically all manufactured goods. This will be a severe restriction on the 'freedom of choice' of enterprise directors.

Aganbegyan emphasizes what he calls the 'substitution of direct trading relations for material and technical allocation' in the nationalized industries, in other words, for direct and centralized allocation of means of production.[14] This means that a supplier–customer relation will be extended to industry. But there is no guarantee that this will lead to 'real prices'. First of all, there are numerous situations where the existence of a de facto monopoly will allow the supplier to impose exaggerated prices. The existence of interconnected bureaucratic cliques will allow managers to overestimate the costs of production, incorporating into them the costs of wastage. The only measure which would reduce such risks would be workers' control and public accountability (the right to open the books). But, of course, there is no question of this.

At the same time the state itself, i.e. the central planners, are increasing the mechanisms of control. In fact, new super-centralist structures have been created, for instance, the 'State Agro-Industrial Committee' or *Gosagropom SSSR* which merged into one consolidated body most of the ministries which dealt with agriculture and departments in other ministries which related to agriculture. Similar super-ministries have been created in the areas of machine manufacture and energy. Enterprise autonomy in decision-making has also been severely restricted in the area of techological innovation since the policy is to create complex departments dealing with research and production which will be in charge of technological innovation.[15]

What exists here is, in fact, a hybrid system far removed from the 'market economy'. A constant accompaniment to perestroika is the worry that rationalization and profitability will lead to the reappearance of unemployment. The precedent of the Shchekino model has produced scepticism about the possibility of achieving mobility of labour.[16] In addition, the managerial bureaucracy has a material interest in opposing rationalization when it begins to threaten managerial income. Yuri Petrov, Communist Party secretary in Sverdlovsk, sums up the contradiction in the following way:

> Political and administrative methods are inadequate, especially when economic incentives are pulling in the opposite direction.... That which is good for the consumer and for the state, is bad for the producer.... We have discovered that, without any changes or renewal of equipment, the factory [at Sverdlovsk] can produce pipe line which is the equal of the best in the world. But if we actually manufactured them, the volume index (which determines the size of the bonus), as well as the incentive fund, would diminish.[17]

Will those measures be effective in practice? It would appear that in the construction industry, at least, there has been a measure of success. According to Kathy Rousselet (*Le Courrier des pays de l'Est*, no. 321, September 1987), after years of stagnation, low investment, and delays in the supply of building materials, radicals decentralization measures have been implemented and enterprises have joined together at local level, leading to a significant improvement in the situation. A new set of rules in force since December 1986 imposes a system of fines for later delivery.

Above all, there has been a rapid expansion of independent construction initiatives by enterprises and by smaller units such as enterprise sections and work brigades. This accounted for 11 per cent of all construction work in 1985 and will soon account for as much as 20 per cent. This is, in reality, a legalization of black-market labour, where the workers earn more money but use the materials and equipment of the enterprise. The social security status of this legalized black-market labour, as well as the norms of health and safety, are not in the least dealt with by the decree of 15 May 1986. It was, however, approved by the unions, which says a lot about the true nature of Soviet unions!

The case of the construction industry also illustrates the *social implications of perestroika*, already apparent in the issue of price subsidies.

Price rises will be compensated for by adjustments in social payments and in the wages of those on low incomes. The majority of wage-earners will receive no compensation. The extra income to be had from legalized black-market labour will lead to an increase in working hours and a decrease in bonuses as well as to an increase in productivity norms which will be to the detriment of the mass of workers. The deterioration of health and safety measures will have negative consequences for the whole labour force.

The only conclusion that we can draw from all this is that perestroika will not benefit the mass of the Soviet workers, at least not in its initial stages. To sweeten the medicine, therefore, there will be political changes. Apart from any consideration of the link between 'economic restructuring' and 'economic transparence', this is the reason why perestroika – Gorbachev's number-one goal – also involves glasnost, which is the essential means, if not for achieving perestroika, then at least for making it acceptable to the majority of Soviet society.

For the working class, the compensation takes the form of a *democratization of enterprise management.* Directors are to be elected by the workforce every five years, with the state having the right to veto candidates. This has the added advantage for the regime that it gives a certain legitimacy to the directors without, at the same time, instituting a genuine workers' control, not to speak of workers' management.

Tatiana Zaslavskaia had understood this much earlier and had proposed something similar, covering up her proposal with prudent and vague sociological verbiage:

> Under such conditions, it is particularly important that the different interest groups have a real and equal opportunity to openly express their interests, to defend them at the highest levels of administration, and to receive clear and precise answers to their requests and to their demands.[18]

There was no question of the workers having the *power* to impose their collective interest.

Professor Marcel Drach has expressed the view that there are three possible 'models' for reform of the Soviet economy, in other words, three possible outcomes for perestroika: a decentralized model *à la* Hungary; a dual model, which juxtaposes a rationalized state sector and a limited private sector, *à la* East Germany; a coercive model, *à la* Czechoslovakia. According to Drach, Gorbachev, after much hesitation, has opted for the decentralized model with greater autonomy for enterprises as well as self-financing.

But there is a *tertium datur*, and this is democratically centralized workers' self-management within a system of political pluralism, in other words, Socialist democracy.[19] There is an opposition, a manifest contradiction between Socialist democracy and workers' self-management on the one hand and market economy on the other, which the more intelligent defenders of a 'Socialist market economy' do not contest.[20] This is the real choice. But this choice is not merely a technical one; it is a social, political, even moral choice, in other words a class choice.

# 6

# Glasnost and Gorbachev's Political Reforms

A restructuring of the economic system will not succeed without democratization: this is the conclusion which the Gorbachevites have drawn in the Soviet Union, in Eastern Europe, and in the West, against the growing resistance to perestroika manifest among conservative sectors of the bureaucracy. This is also the conclusion reached by Gorbachev himself.[1]

If one starts from a Marxist analysis of the specific crisis of the sytem which underlies all the deficiencies so strongly condemned now by Gorbachev, it is evident that no fundamental renewal is possible in the economic sphere, not to speak of society as a whole, without ending the monopoly of power in the hands of the privileged bureaucracy. There is nothing reprehensible in presenting this elimination of bureaucratic monopoly as a thorough 'democratization' of Soviet society. This corresponds by and large to the nature of the process of renewal that is necessary: the birth (or rebirth) of a genuine (soviet) socialist democracy.

The real problems arise when one examines Gorbachev's designs and projects in the political arena, not only in view of the objective needs of Soviet society, of its working people, especially the Soviet proletariat, which constitutes the vast majority of the Soviet population, but also in view of the specific interests of the bureaucracy itself. It would be naive to believe that the members of the bureaucracy would be content genuinely to look for the best path of development for the country, in a disinterested manner, using all the information and skills at their disposal. What matters for the bureaucracy is the improvement of the economic situation without endangering their power or privileges. Throughout history this is how dominant classes and layers have always acted.[2] The Soviet bureaucracy is no exception to this rule.

In any case, the democratization of society which the Gorbachev team proposes has rather precisely limited goals: overcoming the immobility at every level of the ruling apparatus, in other words opening the way for perestroika in the upper levels of society; linking this process with a mobilization and partial repoliticization of the lower levels of society in order to liberate the necessary creative energies and allow the kinds of initiatives which are essential to the success of perestroika itself; making sure that the whole process doesn't end as it did in Czechoslovakia, in other words keeping the party firmly in control of the 'renewal'.[3]

Experience points in the same direction as this theoretical analysis: the reforms will certainly be difficult to put into effect. They trigger off contradictory mechanisms, awakening desires which oppose and contradict each other. They run counter to too many material interests.

After decades of dictatorship, to begin now to open the doors and windows, to liberate the media and the world of literature, to begin scientific debate and critical analysis of daily life, of social and political structures, will shake up the whole of society. This is the risk involved in glasnost. It represents a colossal change in the situation in the Soviet Union, far greater in scope and more profound than the destalinization begun by Khrushchev. It would be an unpardonable mistake on the part of Marxist analysts, not to speak of proletarian revolutionaries of both East and West, to underestimate the dyamic and the possibilities inherent in this situation for the masses to advance along the road of expressing and defending their own interests.

Gorbachev, and that wing of the bureaucracy that he represents, are taking considerable risks in setting in motion this dialectic between openings at the top and the possibilities of self-activity at the base. But they have no choice. To understand the factors which pushed them to take this risk, one has constantly to remember the gravity of the economic crisis, the infinitely greater risks to their power and privilege were society to get stuck in the rut of real economic stagnation or go into a downward spiral of decline in the manner of the Hungarian or Polish economies. One must remember that at the end of the Brezhnev era there was widespread discontent within Soviet society. 'A demoralized society was speaking openly of *razrukha* or devastation of the economy.'[4]

Gorbachev and his supporters give the impression that they are literally sitting on a time bomb. Inertia and opposition to the radical measures necessary to defuse this time bomb are increasing. These have to be neutralized by countervailing pressures. Hence the choice of glasnost on the part of the 'modernizing' bureaucracy. One factor which limits the risks involved, at least in their eyes, is the fact that a long period of depoliticization will make it less likely that the masses would enter the scene as they did in Czechoslovakia, at least in the short and medium term. Whether or not this is true, only time will tell.[5]

One can distinguish three distinct axes of reform initiated by the Gorbachev team: the 'liberalization' of the media and of discussion and criticism even outside the media (this is the real significance of glasnost); a purging and modernization of the apparatus in all its branches (state, cultural institutions, economy, armed forces, mass organizations such as Komsomol and the Womens' Union, the party, and the unions); greater flexibility in the institutions and mechanisms which directly exercise power.

The aspect of glasnost which has most attracted public attention, whether in the Soviet Union, in Eastern Europe, or in the West, is the liberalization of the media and of cultural creation. Films kept under wrap in the previous period are now being shown in Soviet cinema and on television. Plays previously blocked by the censorship are now playing in Soviet theatres. What were underground manuscripts are now being published. The associations of writers, cinematic artists, or actors are all under new, more liberal leaderships after conferences of those associations which were held openly and which brought real conflicts out into the open.

It would be a mistake to view this blossoming of activity as something orchestrated from the top. It is the explosion itself, i.e. the amplitude of the phenomenon, which is astonishing. What is perhaps more significant is the fact that most of the works considered representative of the Gorbachev era were, in fact, created three, four, and five years ago, if not earlier.

It would also be a mistake to view this liberal opening in the domain of culture and literature as exclusively an affair of intellectuals and artists, to which the mass of the workers are either indifferent or hostile. In his report to the 27th Party Congress, Gorbachev, paraphrasing Trotsky without knowing it, stated that:

Society's moral health and the intellectual climate in which we live are in no small measure determined by the state of *literature and art*. While reflecting the birth of the new world, our literature has been active in helping to build it, moulding the citizen of that world – the patriot of his homeland and the internationalist in the true meaning of that word.... When the social need arises to form a conception of the time one lives in, especially a time of change, it always brings forward people for whom this becomes an inner necessity. We are living in such a time today. Neither the party nor the people need showy verbosity on paper, petty dirty-linen washing, time-serving and utilitarianism.

What society expects from the writer is artistic innovation and the truth of life, which has always been the essence of real art.[6]

In fact, the Soviet people are one of the most creative in the world. The sale of books, including poetry, and literary and scientific reviews far exceeds that of the capitalist countries per head of population. For decades, Soviet readers have had to accept a mediocre production, boring, hypocritical and untruthful literature, from which the 'truth of life' was absent. To find this truth again in authentic works of value is as important for the Soviet people as finding spare parts for televisions or adequate supplies of meat on the market.

The liberalization of cultural–literary creation has an institutional dimension, the exemplary impact of which on the whole of Soviet society should not be underestimated. The congress of the Writers' Union, and then the congress of Cinematographic Workers threw out the conservative apparatchiks who controlled these organizations, even if they failed adequately to democratize their legal structures.[7] The liberalization of literary–cultural creation and of the mass media also has a directly political dimension which only the blind could refuse to recognize. It is not only the form which has changed, but the content as well.

We admit, of course, that the masses do not always recognize the aesthetic significance of the decline of the ossified, academic, stereotyped, dogmatic, and boring forms of literary expression. But could one believe that these same masses would remain indifferent when the privileges, the abuse of power, and the arbitrariness of the bureaucracy are being denounced, in films, novels, plays, on television, and in the daily papers, especially when these criticisms are not presented as applying to individual or exceptional cases but rather to the social structures and political institutions as a whole?[8]

Glasnost leads to criticisms of this scope and significance. Under such circumstances it becomes part of a *rebirth of general social debate* and a *gradual repoliticization of society*, including the working class, although it is not possible to predict the precise rhythms of this development or its scope in the different classes and groups. Although the debate at the moment seems to be monopolized by 'experts' – journalists of press and radio/television, economists and sociologists, historians and technocrats – all indications are that students, youth, defenders of national minorities, feminists, pacifists, and ecologists are beginning to participate in larger numbers. It would be very unusual if this debate also didn't begin to include the more independent trade unionists and the more articulate workers.[9]

An example of the political impact of literary–cultural liberalization is provided by the 'Baikal and Biva Conference', held in Irkutsh from 1 to

5 August 1987, bringing together seven Japanese and six Soviet writers to discuss the problems of pollution in those two major lakes in Japan and Russia. They decided to organize co-ordinated political action by ecologists in both countries against the ecological disaster which threatens humanity. Some Soviet writers, among them Viktor Rasputin, have declared themselves against the 'peaceful use of the atom', in other words, in favour of closing down all nuclear power stations.[10]

The most striking illustration of the mass impact of glasnost is the phenomenal success of the weekly *Moscow News*, which is today the most daring paper in Moscow, the real vanguard of glasnost. This began as a regular weekly for foreigners and was printed in English, French, German, Spanish, and Arabic. The regular print-run was 750,000. One must assume that it was also read by a number of Russians who knew foreign languages. But the director, Yegor Yakovlev, saw the usefulness of producing a Russian-language edition of the paper. The 250,000 copies printed each week disappear in a matter of hours. They are even sold for higher prices on the black market. Yakovlev had to double the print-run of the Russian edition. Half a million copies sold each week – of a paper that has little reverence for the authorities, in a city the size of Moscow – signifies an enormous reawakening of political interest on the part of the population in one of the main proletarian concentrations in Europe.

The breakthrough of glasnost in the media has been accompanied by a veritable revolt on the part of journalists against the self-censorship and bureaucratic control which conservatives have exercised over the press. At the congress of the Union of Journalists in March 1987 this revolt led to a spectacular victory. On the last day of the congress the 760 delegates present prepared to vote for the list of 200 persons who would make up the new leadership of the union. Voting was to be by show of hands. But suddenly a journalist from *Izvestia* expressed his dissatisfaction with the list – he thought it was too 'administrative' and had too few real journalists on it – as well as with the procedure of election. He called for a secret ballot. Many journalists spoke in his support. By show of hands the majority voted for a new list of candidates and a secret vote. And this was what happened.

It is also significant that the number of letters sent to the press continues to grow. Obviously, the people see in the press a possibility of achieving something which they do not see in the recall of delegates, although the Constitution gives them the legal right to do this.[11] At *Pravda* five hundred journalists work in the letters department. The richness and diversity of these letters is amazing.[12] The letters are even beginning to influence local soviets. According to *Moscow News* of 25 October 1987, the letters arrive at the Moscow Soviet not in piles but in sacks.

Although the *Moscow News* and the weekly *Ogonyok* (circulation: 1.5 million) are the vanguard of glasnost, their circulation is lower than the daily newspapers that defend a more 'moderate' line. Among the latter are *Trud,* the unions' paper (circulation: 18.5 million), *Izvestia* (circulation: 7 million) and *Komsomolskaia Pravda* (circulation: 13.5 million). *Pravda,* and the weekly *Literaturnaia Gazeta* (circulation: 3 million) often defend more conservative positions.

Jean-Marie Chauvier, from whom we have taken those statistics, says that the circulation of the more 'advanced' papers and journals only satisfies a tiny fraction of the potential readership in Moscow.[13] An attentive study of the Soviet media confirms that one should never confuse the beginning of a process with its final outcome. The provincial newspapers lag far behind the Moscow papers in terms of their openness. Taboos continue to exist. Any questioning of the 'organs of security', to which Gorbachev pays continuous homage, is rare. Questioning of bureaucratic privileges as a whole advances only one step at a time. Any raising of this issue is followed by months of silence. The real subjects of workers' discontent have little place in the criticisms and protests of the opposition. The liberal opposition, and even the nationalist, pan-slav, reactionary opposition have greater opportunity of expressing themselves than the Socialist, Anarcho-syndicalist or Communist opposition.

One should have no illusions about the implications of glasnost at the present time. But one must understand the nature of what is happening and what are its possibilities. It has to be understood as a conflict, a growing contradiction, a struggle between different social forces and different political currents rather than as a project in the hands of Gorbachev and his advisers.

The purging of the apparatus has taken on greater dimensions since Gorbachev came to power. It is greater in the upper than in the intermediate layers of the apparatus. There are precise figures for this. Since he became First Secretary of the Central Committee, and at the time of the 27th Congress, Gorbachev has placed 5 new members in the 12 member Politburo, replaced 10 of the 24 heads of departments in the Central Committee, 30 of the 80 ministers in the Council of State, 4 of the 15 Republican party secretaries, 50 of the 150 regional first secretaries of the party and 138 of the 320 members of the old Central Committee. Table 17 gives the dates of the nomination and election of the principal leaders of the Soviet Communist Party, demonstrating clearly how Gorbachev has changed composition of leading bodies in that country.[14] Table 18, published by *Le Monde* (18 February 1987), gives the same impression.

Gorbachev has succeeded in extending little by little the purge of the

**Table 17**    CPSU Politburo and Secretariat (as of 1 February 1987)

| Name | Date appointed |
|------|----------------|
| Politburo Full Members: | |
| | |
| GORBACHEV, Mikhail Sergeevich | October 1980 |
| ALIYEV, Geidar Alievich* | November 1982 |
| CHEBRIKOV, Viktor Mikhailovich | April 1985 |
| GROMYKO, Andrei Andreevich | April 1973 |
| KUNAYEV, Dinmukhamed Akhmedovich* | April 1971 |
| LIGACHEV, Yegor Kuz'mich* | April 1985 |
| RYZHKOV, Nikolai Ivanovich | April 1985 |
| SHCHERBITSKY, Vladimir Vasilevich | April 1971 |
| SHEVARDNADZE, Eduard Amvrosevich | July 1985 |
| SOLOMENTSEV, Mikhail Sergeevich | December 1983 |
| VORONTNIKOV, Vitali Ivanovich | December 1983 |
| ZAIKOV, Lev Nikolaevich | March 1986 |
| | |
| Candidate Members | |
| | |
| DEMICHEV, Petr Nilovich | November 1964 |
| DOLGIKH, Vladimir Ivanovich | May 1982 |
| SLIUN'KOV, Nikoly Nekitovich | March 1986 |
| SOKOLOV, Sergei Leonidovich | April 1985 |
| SOLOV'YEV, Yuri Filippovich | March 1986 |
| TALYZIN, Nikolai Vladimirovich | October 1985 |
| YAKOVLEV, Aleksandr Nikolaievich | January 1987 |
| YELTSIN, Boris Nikolaievich* | February 1986 |
| | |
| Secretariat | |
| | |
| GORBACHEV, Mikhail Sergeevich | 1978 |
| BIRIUKOVA, Aleksandra Pavlovna | 1986 |
| DOBRYNIN, Anatoly Fedorovich | 1986 |
| DOLGIKH, Vladimir Ivanovich | 1972 |
| LIGACHEV, Yegor Kuz'mich | 1983 |
| LUKIANOV, Anatol Ivanovich | 1987 |
| MEDVEDEV, Vadim Andreevich | 1986 |
| NIKONOV, Viktor Petrovich | 1985 |
| RAZUMOVSKY, Georgy Petrovich | 1986 |
| SLIUN'KOV, Nikoly Nikitovich | 1987 |
| YAKOVLEV, Aleksandr Nikolaevich | 1986 |
| ZAIKOV, Lev Nikolaevich | 1985 |
| ZIMIANIN, Mikhail Vasilevich | 1976 |

*Since removed from office

**Table 18**   *Composition of CPSU*

| Functions in February 1987 | Total | Occupied same position, October 1982 |
|---|---|---|
| Politburo: full members | 11 | 3 (30%) |
| candidate members | 8 | 2 (25%) |
| Secretariat | 12 | 2 (16%) |
| Heads of Central Committee departments | 19 | 2 (10.5%) |
| Republican first secretaries | 14 | 5 (35.7%) |
| Regional first secretaries | 157 | 61 (38.8%) |
| Vice-presidents of Council of Ministers | 12 | 1 (8.3%) |
| Ministers | 87 | 25 (28.7%) |
| Titular members of Central Committee | 307 | 175 (57.7%) |

state and economic[15] apparatus, as well as the military apparatus. When the young German pilot, Matthias Rust, landed his light plane on Red Square, demonstrating the incompetence and negligence of the military high command, Gorbachev seized the opportunity to install his own man, General Yasov, over the heads of all the marshals. Within the armed forces as well as within the military hierarchy, 'modernizers' confront conservatives, the former by and large supporters of Gorbachev.[16]

The administrative purge has also been accompanied by a campaign against corruption, the abuse of power, and violations of 'Socialist legality' – all of which are regularly exposed in the press. It is at this point that glasnost and political reform reinforce each other. Bureaucratic arbitrariness has been revealed in all its magnitude. Not less than 60,000 administrative actions were annulled in 1986 due to irregularities and violations of laws and rules, and, in general, as a result of a complaint from the persons affected. Fourteen judges were dismissed altogether, 76 were transferred elsewhere, and 837 were officially reprimanded.[17]

A 'court of administrative recourse' was established in January 1987 to deal with complaints and reviews. But the decisions of higher state bodies, as well as the activities of the KGB, remain outside the realm of such procedures. This appeals procedure was consolidated when the Supreme Court, on 30 June 1987, adopted a 'law concerning the procedure of appeal against illegal actions of officials which damage the rights of citizens'. This law came into force at the beginning of 1988.

Do these administrative reforms come to grips with judicial and police arbitrariness? For the moment, the few cases of abuse of power on the part of the KGB which have been condemned in the press could be counted on one hand.[18] The most spectacular case of judicial abuse which has come to light concerned the first secretary of the party in the autonomous Bashkir republic in the Urals. He had systematically persecuted the second secretary of the party in the city of Ufa and had caused him to be wrongly condemned on the basis of false accusations. The unfortunate Safronov, in spite of his innocence and, according to *Pravda*, his merits, spent three years in prison.

The deputy head of the department at the ministry of justice, Leonid Nikolaev, recently revealed that judges maintain a direct 'red telephone line' with the political leadership in their region for 'urgent consultation' pertaining to trials and sentencing. A case is known of another 'red line', this time direct to Moscow, which allowed the acquittal of a Ukrainian journalist who had been wrongly arrested and was at the point of being sentenced for having investigated corruption in high places in the local bureaucracy (*Sunday Times*, 3 May 1987).

Even the abuse of psychiatric internment has begun to be denounced. The *Komsomolskaia Pravda* of 11 November 1987 revealed the case of a young worker who had been interned in 1986 because he had protested against the poor ventilation in his factory. The *Moscow News* of 29 November 1987 told of the case of a young medical student interned in a psychiatric hospital because he had attempted to send a letter to the American consul encouraging contacts between Soviet and American students. Some weeks previously, an ex-lieutenant of the KGB, Vladimir Titov, had held a press conference in Moscow describing what he had undergone during a period of psychiatric internment between 1982 and 1987 (*The Times*, 21 October 1987).

The 'Friends of the Soviet Union' in the capitalist and post-capitalist countries have apparently learned nothing from their past or present misadventures. The Moscow correspondent of the French Communist party newspaper *L'Humanité*, Gérard Streiff, felt obliged to write:

At one time, there was talk also of psychiatric internment. At the time of the first conference of psychiatrists of the Socialist countries, held in Moscow in September 1985, the famous Czechoslovak specialist, Joseph Pogadi, described this campaign about the use of psychiatry against dissidents as a 'monstrous myth'. The president of the executive committee of the World Association of Psychiatrists, Jean–Yves Gosselin (Canada) has recently written that 'not a single example [*sic*] of the political use of psychiatry in the socialist countries has been confirmed'.[19]

Unfortunately, these words had hardly been written when the Soviet press began to admit precisely this and began to reveal cases of psychiatric abuse. The press has also written about the official theory which allows this psychiatric abuse to take place: the so-called 'creeping schizophrenia'. This condition is characterized by the following symptoms: inflexibility and obstinacy; a tendency to oppose authorities, to reject tradition, and to question official political orientation; very strong doctrinaire convictions; excessive notions of one's own importance; a tendency to draw attention to oneself.

With such a definition there would be many schizophrenics who deserved to be locked up. These would include: Marx, Lenin, Trotsky, Rosa Luxemburg, Auguste Blanqui, Plekhanov, in fact all the great revolutionaries of the past, all the great anti-fascist leaders of the thirties, all the leaders of the anti-apartheid movement in South Africa, not to mention the Communist Party leaders in the capitalist countries.

Apart from the police-state logic which underlies the corruption of justice in the Soviet Union, there is also a grotesque application of the planning principle to the problem of delinquency and its suppression. The judges have to fulfil a certain 'plan' with regard to convictions. If the planned number of convictions or the planned penalties have not been achieved, then the judges are under pressure to deliver disproportionately heavy penalties to meet the 'objectives of the plan'. There was a case in the district of Orel where a judge condemned a 'thief' to one and a half years in prison for having stolen two jars of cucumbers ... from his mother-in-law's cellar. At the same time, the urban militia (the police) are encouraged by the same plan to reduce the amount of crime in their neighbourhood and therefore the number of arrests!

Demands for a substantial reform of the judicial system continue to be made. Proposals have been made public to liberalize the penal code (it is currently being revised), even to abolish phone-tapping[20] and the death penalty.[21] But the extent of these reforms, whether radical or moderate, is still not known.

At the Central Committee meeting of 27–28 January 1988, certain political and institutional reforms were proposed. They concerned:

1. The selection of candidates (more than one candidate per post) for elections to local and regional soviets. (It is not certain whether this reform also extends to elections for the Supreme Soviet.)

2. A method of secret ballot for the election of party officials. (It is not certain whether this secret ballot will apply to the election of delegates to the congresses of the Communist Party or to the Central committee.)

3. The selection of candidates for the election of trade union delegates within enterprises.

4. The establishment of new mechanisms for worker participation in the management of enterprises.

The practical consequences of these reforms seem to have been very modest. In the local elections of 21 June 1987 there were multiple candidates in seventy-six districts, i.e. in about 0.4 per cent of all constituencies. All of them were approved beforehand by the party. The Moscow correspondent of *Le Monde* wrote at the time (23 June 1987):

> A visit to the polling station in a Moscow suburb showed that very little had changed in the constituencies. None of the voters we saw made use of the polling booth. Voters who were questioned knew nothing about the candidates they were voting for.... As had been the case previously, it was possible for one person to vote on behalf of the entire family, simply by showing the internal passport of all family members.

The political reforms, however, are by no means at an end. Jean Radvanyi lists a number of statutes which have already been adopted or which are being prepared by the Supreme Soviet.[22] The following statutes have been adopted:

1. A law of referendums.
2. A decree concerning the kinds of issues wherein social organizations will have the right to veto administrative decisions.
3. A law concerning the right of citizens to have legal recourse against arbitrary administrative decisions.
4. A decree on the periodic review of the competence of cadres and specialists.
5. A decree on the disciplinary responsibilities of subordinates.
6. A law concerning the national archives.
7. A law on state security.

The following are in the process of preparation:

1. A law on the press and information (i.e. on censorship).
2. A law concerning the holding down of more than one office or one job at the same time.
3. A law on the status of ministries.
4. The famous review of the penal code which should re-examine Article 190 ('anti-Soviet propaganda') and Article 142 (religious affairs), among others.

All of these legal changes are undoubtedly movements forward in the struggle against an arbitrary and repressive bureaucracy. Radvanyi gives the example of Article 58 in the 1977 Constitution which promised citizens the right of appeal against decisions or actions by public bodies. This, however, remained a dead letter since the necessary legislation to implement it had not been brought forward. In spite of a continuous polemic since that date, the minister of justice and the entire administrative apparatus succeeded in putting off the implementation of this article for ten years! The law finally came into force in June 1987. It complements the new Article 139 of the penal code, promulgated in 1986, which *Izvestia* described as 'anti-bureaucratic' (16 May 1987). *Izvestia* immediately added, however, that in the year since its promulgation there had been only one case where it had been applied.[23] One of the deputies to the Moscow Soviet, Ilina, wrote with a certain feeling of bitterness in *Moscow News* (11 October 1987) that:

> A strange situation has been created.... Every day the government grants more rights and prerogatives, and removes all sorts of injunctions, but at the lower echelons of society all of these new possibilities remain untouched. I don't know whether this is a result of bad will or inexperience.

The fundamental reasons for this passivity and scepticism of the ordinary people are social and economic, not ideological; still less are they the result of some 'Russian tradition'. The rebirth of activity on the part of the mass of the people demands a certain space and objectives. They need more and not less glasnost, more and not less democracy. As the editor of *Novy Mir*, Streliannyi, said, paraphrasing Marx: 'One cannot jump across a precipice by making two leaps. And we are on the edge of a precipice.' Only the working people can make the revolution which Gorbachev says is necessary to take the Soviet Union out of the crisis. But how does one mobilize the masses against the bureaucracy while, at the same time, keeping the masses under bureaucratic control? This is Gorbachev's real dilemma.

There are three essential contradictions – but these are not the only ones – in the policy of perestroika which Gorbachev himself has described in his recent book, *Perestroika*. They concern the exercise of power, the plurality of parties (and organized currents), and the material roots of bureaucracy.

On the subject of the exercise of power, he writes:[24]

> We are obviously not going to change the system of Soviet power or its fundamental principles. (p. 54)

> True, the perestroika drive started on the Communist Party's initiative, and the Party leads it. The Party is strong and bold enough to work out a new

policy. It has proved capable of heading and launching the process of renewal of society. (p. 55)

Naturally, Party organizations worked and the overwhelming majority of communists did their duty to the people sincerely and selflessly. (p. 23)

But, on the other hand, he states that:

An educated and talented people committed to socialism could not make full use of the potentialities inherent in socialism, of their right to take a real part in the administration of state affairs. (p. 47)

A breach had formed between word and deed, which bred public passivity. (p. 22)

All honest people saw with bitterness that people were losing interest in social affairs, that labour no longer had its reputable status. (p. 24)

Therefore we attach priority to political measures, broad and genuine democratization, the resolute struggle against red tape and violations of law, and the active involvement of the masses in managing the country's affairs. All this is directly linked with the main question of any revolution, the question of power.... Hence we must – if we want perestroika to succeed – gear all our work to the political tasks and the methods of the exercise of power. (p. 54)

There then follow two incredible admissions:

On the whole, society was becoming increasingly unmanageable (p. 23)

When the command–economy system of management was propelled into existence, the soviets were somehow pushed back. Quite a few issues were decided without their participation, or just left undecided to grow into problems. This lessened the prestige of the soviets. From that moment the development of socialist democracy began to slow down. Signs appeared that the working people were being alienated from their constitutional right to have a direct involvement in the affairs of state (p. 111)

It is clear that the first set of quotations flagrantly contradicts the second set. If society is unmanageable and the workers are alienated from the exercise of power – the view of revolutionary Marxists for decades, which they express with the formula 'political expropriation' – how is it possible, for a Communist, to deny the necessity of changing this political system? If party organizations accomplish their tasks and if the overwhelming majority of Communists carry out their duty with respect to the workers, how does one explain the fact that those workers have become politically passive and have lost all interest in social affairs? If 'the original meaning of the concept of socialism [is] an ideological and political movement of the masses, a grass-roots movement' (p. 54), how can one approve of the fact that 'the revolution' is to be carried out by 'the highest organs in the party'?

The incoherence becomes even more flagrant when Gorbachev, in the most daring section of his book, proclaims: 'we faced a formidable task – the need to restore completely the role of the soviets as bodies of political power and as the foundations of socialist democracy'. (p. 112) Fantastic! But this daring proclamation is immediately qualified, if not rendered completely void, when Gorbachev adds that the decisions of the Central Committee plenum of January 1987 'let the soviets arrange their work in such a way as to become the true bodies of popular government' (p. 113). The decisions to which Gorbachev refers dealt with the *local* soviets. But can the 'complete restoration' of the role of the soviets as organs of political power be achieved only at local and enterprise level? Is it here or is it not rather at the central level, at the level of the state, that real political power is exercised? But Gorbachev doesn't have a word to say about the exercise of direct power by the soviets at this level. And for good reason. He only mentions in passing the 'replacement of the functions and activities of government and administrative agencies by those of party agencies' (p. 112).

But almost immediately after this condemnation of the 'institutional' cause of the political expropriation of the working class, there is an emphatic reaffirmation of the ideological–political reasoning and the institutional mechanisms which underlie this expropriation:

> The prestige and trust in the party has been growing. Although we are still at a stage of transition from one qualitative state to another, the party bodies are trying not to assume the duties of economic and administrative organizations. This is far from easy: it seems such a well-trodden path – exert party pressure and the plan is fulfilled. But the party's goal is different: above all, to theoretically analyse processes, to sense critical points in the development of contradictions in time, to introduce corrections into strategy and tactics, *to elaborate policy* and define methods and forms for its realization, *to select and place personnel* [the precise definition of the nomenclature!] and to provide for perestroika both ideologically and organizationally. *Only the party coud do all this.*
>
> Management and economic matters *are the job of government and other organizations that are responsible for these matters....* The party must do its job. And all others must do theirs. When this doesn't happen, party guidance, party ideological work and work with the cadres proves inadequate. (p. 122–3; my emphasis)

Where are the soviets in this scheme? They have completely disappeared! What has happened to the exercise of power by the working people? It is true that Gorbachev distinguishes between the direct exercise of administration by the party and the work of professional managers. But this is a functional division of labour within the bureaucracy. It is the party, and the party alone, that chooses the managers and decides the political line (policy, strategy) that is to be followed. No one else has the right to do it: 'Official opposition does not exist in our country' (p. 123).

This confirms once again the thesis defended by revolutionary Marxists that real Socialist democracy, real exercise of political power by the working masses, genuine soviet power are incompatible with the single-party regime.[25] The soviets will become sovereign and real organs of 'popular power' only when they are freely elected, only when they are free to decide on political strategy and political alternatives. All of this presupposes the existence of a recognized legal opposition (the only requirement being actual respect for the Socialist constitution, regardless of ideological position). It also presupposes the right of workers and peasants freely to elect those whom they wish to elect, independent of political orientation and ideology, and without the party, not to speak of the KGB, having the right to veto candidates. It presupposes, in other words, a plurality of parties and political currents.

In spite of all the daring formulations, political perestroika as Gorbachev describes it remains within the framework of a political system based on a single party, a party which is the political expression of the bureaucracy, a party which controls the apparatus of management, which can consider political policy in its totality, which can elaborate overall political solutions. Under such circumstances, there can be no exercise of political power by the soviets. Under such circumstances, it should come as no surprise that the mass of the working people remain to a large extent passive, sceptical, and depoliticized.

Gérard Streiff quotes a phrase from a play by Yuri Marakov: 'Tell me, Papa, are you a Communist or are you a member of the party?' Jean Radvanyi, nonetheless, concludes quite happily that 'the leading role of the Communist Party, clearly formulated in the 1977 Constitution, has in no way [!] been questioned by the changes that are taking place.'[26]

The same contradiction reappears when it comes to determining the *social roots of bureaucracy.*[27] Gorbachev reiterates the fundamentally self-justifying thesis of the bureaucracy itself – the evil is basically psychological and ideological:

> The greatest difficulty in our restructing effort lies in our thinking, which has been moulded over the past years. Everyone, from General Secretary to worker, has to alter his thinking. And this is understandable, for many of us were formed as individuals and lived in conditions when the old order existed.

*We have to overcome our own conservatism.* Most of us adhere to correct ideological and political principles. But there is a substantial distance between a correct stand and its realization. (p. 65)

For a Marxist, an 'order' (old or new) is determined above all by the structure of economic and political power; it is social existence which determines social consciousness. But no, says Gorbachev: it is conservative thinking (i.e. social consciousness) which determines the 'order' (old and new). In the light of the facts which any study of social conditions in the Soviet Union would reveal, this is an untenable thesis. When dealing with the 'years of stagnation', Gorbachev did not hesitate to explain that:

Public property was gradually fenced off from its true owner – the working man.... Ever increasing signs appeared of man's alienation from the property of the whole people. (p. 47)

The only people to resent the changes are those who believe that they already have what they need, so why should they readjust? ... And then glasnost, or openness, reveals that someone enjoys illegal privileges (p. 31)

He quotes from a letter he had received from Lithuania:

What do people think about your policy? I shall not lie to you, Mikhail Sergeevich, because that could only harm our common cause. I'll tell you the whole truth. I shall not speak about the privileged section of society. Everything's clear here. Many would like to continue living as if in a drug-induced sleep, in a land of milk and honey. I want to speak about the proletarians, the people for whom this perestroika was started. Unfortunately, there is no deep understanding of your policy among them and there is still little trust in it (p. 70)

He continues elsewhere:

We also took into consideration our past experience, in which repeated attempts to reform upper management levels without support from below were unsuccessful *because of the stubborn resistance of the management apparatus, which did not want to part with its numerous rights and prerogatives.* We have recently encountered this resistance, and still encounter it now. (p. 85; my emphasis)

Today, when social justice is the point at issue in our country, much is said about benefits and privileges for individuals and groups of individuals. (p. 101)

The quality of the services provided to the entire population is much lower than at the aforementioned organizations and institutions [special shops, etc.]. Such phenomena are naturally criticized by the working people. (p. 102)

But if there are privileged layers and those who are without privileges, if there are special rights and privileges for those who manage public property while the workers feel alienated, then there is clearly a difference in social status and opposing interests between the workers and the bureaucracy, and surely these differences in social status and material interests are what underlie the differences in mentality.

Behind the opposition between 'conservatism' and 'revolutionary policy' (i.e. perestroika pushed to its limits) lies another opposition, that between the 'privileged layers of society' and the workers, those 'proletarians' that Gorbachev's Lithuanian correspondent spoke about.[28]

However, having revealed this opposition, he then proceeds to deny it and concludes with (false?) naivety (or dissimulation): 'The restructuring concerns all, from rank-and-file communist to Central Committee secretary, from shopfloor worker to minister, from engineer to academician. It can be brought to a successful end only if it is truly a nationwide effort' (p. 56). But this unanimity evaporates when the same Gorbachev tells us that: 'During my trip to the Kuban region, I reproached trade union leaders for pandering to managers, sometimes going so far as dancing to their tune.... Trade union committees should have teeth, and not be convenient partners for management' (p. 114). So there is indeed an *opposition of interests* between workers and managers. He both denies and admits this opposition at the same time.

These essential contradictions of political perestroika are not purely theoretical – a partial, incomplete democratization which is emasculated by the refusal to question the monopoly of power and the privileges of the bureaucracy, a refusal to struggle for the direct exercise of power by the soviets based on a plurality of parties. These contradictions lead to practical political problems and to political crises, as was evident at the time of the Yeltsin affair.

# 7

# Gorbachev and the Limits of Destalinization

Outside of the Soviet Union there is a tendency to underestimate the importance of destalinization in the political, intellectual and emotional lives of the Soviet people. As glasnost develops, this will be a key question animating hundred of thousands of people, if not vastly more. There are a number of reasons for this.

First, the number of victims of the purges in the thirties was eight million.[1] In addition, there was the forced collectivization – the 'elimination of the kulaks'. Those are the two principal crimes of Stalin and his henchmen. The number of victims was so great that a large portion if not a majority of families in the Soviet Union today are affected by it. The descendants of the victims, especially the descendants of Communists eliminated in the purges, still energetically defend their fathers and mothers.[2] Little by little, the stories about these courageous battles for rehabilitation are beginning to appear in the Soviet press.[3] The old political prisoners, released from the camps by Khrushchev, are joining the battle with their memories and with their demands for justice.[4] Such people are numbered in their millions. Although quite a number of them have died in the past thirty-two years, the number of survivors is not insignificant. And they are all passionate partisans of destalinization. The number of people directly concerned is already a considerable section of the Soviet population.

To this large mass of people one must add those from the other side of the barricade: the old torturers, jailers, guards, informers, agents of the GPU responsible for the arrests and interrogations, etc. Here also, of course, time has taken its toll. The number of survivors now is much smaller than in 1956 at the time of the 20th Congress. They, too, intervene in the debate, which is freer now than it was under Khrushchev, but their intervention is, of course, in defence of Stalin. The resistance to destalinization, motivated by purely individual fear, is more restrained now than it was in 1956.

The moral or, if one wishes, the political–moral aspect of destalinization is a prominent theme in this debate, and quite rightly so. This is a kind of supreme test of the credibility of glasnost, because the crimes of Stalin were the greatest secret and the major shame of the regime. If the regime is now not willing to reveal the truth about its own past, how can it be relied on to reveal the truth about the present? Numerous intellectuals have expressed this view, and they are not the only ones. Ordinary people are saying the same thing. The novelist Yuri Nagibin wrote in *Komsomolskaia Pravda* on 23 April 1986: 'Culture cannot exist without memory, without each one of us realizing that we are a link in the chain of history. The person ignorant of his origins is without culture.' There is also the song of Vladimir Vysotsky:

> Hidden in our memory forever
> Are dates, and incidents, and faces . . .
> If in the minefield of the past you dig
> It's better that you never make mistakes[5]

The Soviet people are too cultured, the number of politicized intellectuals, young people, and workers is already too numerous, to allow such a major hole in the national memory, which would become a blot of national identity. Martin Walker is right when he writes:

> Gorbachev's first year in power was remarkable for the frankness with which he spoke of the problems of the present, and the failures of the immediate, Brezhnev-ruled past. But there were other truths to tell, of Khrushchev's time, and of Stalin's; and without the readiness to tell them, Gorbachev's hopes of a brave new Soviet future will be built on so much spiritual sand.[6]

Numerous Soviet writers express the same view. The poet Yevtushenko writes: 'To hide the truth is a sign of weakness. Public silence is a hidden form of anarchy.'[7]

In an article entitled 'The Truth Heals – Notes on the Recasting of Conscience appearing in *Moscow News* (21 June 1987), the novelist Alexander Neiny writes:

> Our moral education loses all its qualities if deprived of the vitamins of truth. The masters of silence, the magicians of demagogy, the false guardians of public morals existed and still exist. It is largely thanks to their efforts that our best workers have been banned and defamed, in small committees, without publicity. . . . They have invented a multitude of instructions, open and secret,

some of them imposing an automatic veto on all information about the true state of the environment, or allowing archive officials to check notes made by researchers and to suppress them if, in their view, they aren't useful for the historian or the novelist.

Stalin 'has inflicted greater defeats on the revolutionary movement in Russia than all of our adversaries', said the pro-Gorbachev writer Mikhail Shatrov in the review *Ogonyok* (quoted in *Le Monde*, 6 July 1987). 'There is no perestroika without a perestroika of the memory', added the poet, Yevtushenko. 'If we turn to the past', said *Literaturnaia Gazeta* on 22 October 1986, 'it is to answer questions that torture us.'

The completion of the destalinization process is also necessary for the free development of science, especially the science of history. Without revealing the truth about the past, without publishing the archives and documents of the epoch, it will be impossible to liberate history from being manipulated in the service of this or that fraction of the leadership, impossible to write history with the necessary minimum of objectivity and impossible to assemble all the facts which make the writing of history *possible* in the first place.[8]

But the interest in the past is not reduced to the furnishing of materials for books on history. The results of an objective study of the past have to be appropriated for the purpose of developing a scientific analysis and scientific theories concerning the key problems of the construction of Socialism in the present. The big debates of the twenties, the less well-known debates of the thirties – echoed in the pages of the *Bulletin of the Opposition* – provide incomparable material for dealing with such problems as the relations between plan and market; the parameters of the rhythm of industrialization; the correctness or incorrectness of the 'priority of heavy industry'; the links between the level of consumption of the masses (as well as the size of the consumption fund) and growth in the productivity of labour; not to mention the central question of the social composition of the peasantry and the conditions for maintaining the worker–peasant alliance. On the question of the transition to Socialism (the construction of Socialism), no theoretical advance is possible until the results of this debate have been assimilated.

Finally, it is obvious that there are links between the terms of this past debate, as well as the manner in which it was stifled by Stalin, and the political problems currently being debated in the Soviet Union. In other words, destalinization concerns not only the scope and credibility of glasnost. It is of equal concern to the content and the dynamic of perestroika.

The completion of destalinization has for a long time been the subject of an intense political struggle inside the Soviet Union. This struggle develops on two fronts: first, the struggle for the rehabilitation of all the victims of the Stalinist purges, especially the old Bolsheviks, the party leaders involved in the Moscow trials of 1936–38 who were executed or deported in large numbers; second, a struggle to come to terms with Stalinism itself and to determine the causes of this real degeneration of power in the Soviet Union.

The rehabilitation of the victims of the purges began in the first phase of destalinization under Khrushchev. Its scope at the time was considerable. According to Dmitri Yurassov of the Institute of Historical Archives, there were 612, 500 rehabilitations between 1953 and the end of 1957, of whom 48,000 were rehabilitated by the Military Council of the Supreme Tribunal, 200,000 by other military tribunals, and around 200,000 by regional and local tribunals. Of the rehabilitations ordered by the Supreme Tribunal, 31,000 were posthumous, in other words they had been condemned to death and executed.[9]

Nonetheless, there were numerous victims of the purges who were not rehabilitated under Khrushchev. In particular, the majority of the Bolshevik leaders who had been victims of Stalin were not rehabilitated. There were exceptions, which made the process itself as well as the outcome quite incoherent. Seven of those charged at the third Moscow trial were rehabilitated in 1958 by decision of the Supreme Court. These were: Krestinsky, Khodzhaev, Ikramov, Ivanov, Chernoc, Grinko, and Zelensky.[10] Krestinsky, the most prominent among them, had been a member of the Politburo under Lenin, as well as people's commissar for finance and ambassador to Berlin. He had been close to Trotsky for a long time but had never joined the Left Opposition.[11] Unlike the rehabilitation of Tukhachevsky and the other Red Army leaders executed in 1937, the rehabilitation of Krestinsky was done very discreetly. At a time when the military chiefs were publishing books with memories and pictures of their old comrades executed by Stalin, the name of Krestinsky was hardly mentioned in the Soviet Union.[12]

Two other close friends of the founder of the Red Army, old Bolsheviks and heroes of the civil war, Smilga and Muralov, both condemned at the time of the second Moscow trial, were rehabilitated by the Supreme Court in 1986 according to *Sotsialisticheskaia Industria* (reported in *El Pais*, 17 July 1987). On 16 July 1987 the Supreme Court also rehabilitated the great Russian economist, Nikolai Kontratiev, condemned to prison in 1930 and executed in 1937.[13] One of his co-workers condemned with Kontratiev was Alexander Chayanov, one of the principal theoreticians of 'non-market peasant agriculture' in Russia.[14]

Kontratiev had been a minister under Kerensky. His condemnation in 1930 and his execution in 1937 were linked with the fact that his research, as well as that of his friend Chayanov, strengthened the arguments of Bukharin and his political allies for greater moderation in the collectivization drive. But, having rehabilitated Kontratiev, they continued to refuse to rehabilitate Bukharin.

The rehabilitation of Bukharin had been refused for a very long time. His son Yuri and his wife Larina had carried out a long campaign and had made numerous appeals to leading party bodies. In 1958 the Praesidium (as the Politburo was then called) discussed the demand for Bukharin's rehabilitation in the presence of M. Thorez and Harry Pollit, of the French and British Communist Parties respectively. Khrushchev argued in favour of rehabilitation, but Thorez and Pollit objected. Their objections seemed to carry significant weight among the rest of the Politburo members who feared a loss of prestige for the Soviet party and for the other Communist parties. Khrushchev was unable to secure a majority and the outcome was against Bukharin.[15]

Larina and Yuri, however, continued their campaign for the rehabilitation of the man whom Lenin, in his testament, had called 'the favourite son of the party'. They presented petitions in 1961 and in 1976–77. The petitions were rejected. At the time of the petition in 1976–77, the head of department at the Control Commission of the party, G.S. Klimov, told Yuri explicitly that the accusations of criminal activity against his father, for which he had been executed, would not be withdrawn. When asked by Yuri if he really believed that Bukharin had tried to poison Gorky, Klimov replied that this was a question for the tribunal to decide and the decision had been made already in 1938.[16] Yuri could begin a legal procedure to overturn this decision but Klimov advised against it in view of the 'complexity' of the case.[17]

Finally, in March 1988, fifty years after they were condemned, Bukharin was rehabilitated, along with the other Bolshevik leaders condemned at the same trial. Among those rehabilitated in March 1988 was Christian Rakovsky, close friend of Trotsky who had been prime minister of Ukraine, ambassador to Britain, and one of the earliest leaders of what became the Left Opposition. After Trotsky's exile in 1928, it was Rakovsky who became the leader of the Left Opposition inside the country. He was sentenced on 12 March 1938 to twenty years in prison and was shot in 1941.[18]

One can see that the root of the problem is political. The leaders of the Soviet Communist Party have, for a long time, refused to make the distinction between the *legal* rehabilitation of the old Bolsheviks and their *political* rehabilitation. The first concerns the infamous accusations, the obvious lies used in the course of the trials to justify deportations, imprisonment, and executions: sabotage, terrorist acts, mutiny, conspiracy with foreign espionage services (in particular, the Gestapo and the Japanese espionage service), plotting the territorial dismantling of the Soviet Union, etc. The second concerns a political judgement on the policies and orientations of the various opposition currents (not the policies falsely attributed to them in Stalinist texts).

This second issue is obviously a question of political judgement. It belongs to history. As far as we are aware, none of the persons demanding rehabilitation for the victims of Stalin are demanding the approval of all their political policies. This would be logically impossible, since many of them held policies which were diametrically opposed.

On the contrary, this is a demand for *openness*, for glasnost, a demand that elementary justice be re-established, that the accusations against these victims for crimes which they obviously did not commit should be withdrawn. The fact that the leaders of the Communist party have continued deliberately to maintain this confusion between the two types of rehabilitation explains why the battle for complete rehabilitation for all of Stalin's victims continues both in the Soviet Union and abroad.[19]

This political battle around the question of rehabilitation has had a resonance throughout the whole of Soviet society. There have been dramatic public confrontations. The Austrian journal *Profil* recently reported (13 July 1987) on two public meetings held in Moscow. The first, discreetly announced by a small notice on the door of the Institute of History and Archives, attracted thousands. The lecture was given by Professor Yuri Borisov and the title of the lecture was 'Stalin – Politician and Man'. It was, in general, an apology for the dictator, while admitting that there had been abuses.

The majority in the audience were indignant and questions were hurled at the speaker. How many victims? How many had been rehabilitated? Many speakers said that their fathers had died in the camps or that their mothers had been deported. There was a more serious disturbance when Borisov gave a second lecture on 13 April 1987 to an audience of writers in the Central House of Culture. On this occasion members of the audience confronted him with precise facts. One historian working on the archives cited the case of the interrogation of the great director, Meyerhold, one of the victims of the purges. Meyerhold had been tortured, as had been admitted by the GPU lieutenant who carried out the interrogation. His left hand was broken and he was forced to drink his own urine (report in the West Berlin newspaper *Tageszeitung* 27 July 1987).

At the beginning of January 1988 some hundreds of people met in the large hall at the Writers' Union in Moscow. The occasion was a lecture by Afanasiev. The writer Mikhail Shatrov also spoke at this meeting and said that he was very unhappy with the balance-sheet 'of perestroika as far as the question of history was concerned' in the past year of 1987. The historians continue to give out half truths, he said. The evaluation of Leon Trotsky which appeared in the journal *Sovietskaia Rossiia* in the autumn of 1987 had removed the stigma of being 'an agent of foreign powers' but it had still treated him as an 'enemy of the people'. The same partial rectification had taken place with respect to the other comrades of Lenin–Zinoviev and Kamenev.

At this meeting almost a hundred written questions were sent to the speaker from the audience. To one question he gave a reply which led to enthusiastic applause: he stated his view that not only Bukharin, Tomski, and Rykov, but also Trotsky, Kamenev, and Zinoviev should be rehabilitated. Afanasiev has also criticized the historian, Volkogonov, author of the first official biography of Stalin. This historian reduced the phenomenon of Stalinism to a psychic illness and deficiencies of character in Stalin, but continued to defend the coercive command structure of the system. 'It is time to analyse the social and mental structures which made the Stalin phenomenon possible' (*Frankfurter Rundschau*, 12 January 1988).

It is clear, therefore, that the question of the legal rehabilitation of the victims of the Stalinist terror is being linked more and more with the question of the overall assessment of Stalin and Stalinism. The resistance of the bureaucracy to the recognition of the scope of Stalin's crimes[20] is not just a question of 'moderation' or of 'seeking the right opportunity'. In hiding the real extent of the terror, they are continuing to lie to the people, in spite of the admonition of Lenin that only the truth is revolutionary.

The real problem concerns the two variants used by the bureaucracy in explaining Stalinism. The first version, the 'psychological–subjectivist' one, explains Stalinism in terms of 'cult of the personality', personal perversion, paranoia, 'dogmatic thinking', and so on. The second variant explains it in a more objectivist–historicist manner: the international context, the threat of fascism, the need to speed up the industrialization of the country in view of the approaching war, the lack of culture of the masses and the need to secure all those processes by means of an extremely centralized leadership. But what is unfortunate about both those explanations is the fact that neither individually nor together do they explain the crimes of Stalin, or the massive extent of those crimes, or the disastrous consequences for the Soviet people and for the country's national defence, or the whole political orientation of the Stalin faction.

Purging and breaking up the Red Army; depriving it of its principal commanders – of Tukhachevsky, who had brilliantly foreseen the military strategy needed to fight off the nazi attack; imprisoning the designers and builders of Soviet airplanes and weapons; bringing about a terrible famine which demoralized a large part of the armed forces: can all of this be explained in terms of 'the needs of national defence'? In what sense was the murder of millions of Communists 'necessary for industrialization', especially when among those murdered was one of the leading constructors of the new Soviet industry, Piatakov?

This is all manifestly incoherent and absurd. In the climate of glasnost, of openness, of democratic debate, of a return to sources, this incoherence will become even clearer to an important sector of public opinion. This is the real fear of the bureaucracy, this is what explains its hesitation, its unwillingness to complete destalinization.

Because there is a true and alternative explanation of Stalin and destalinization. If one rejects as inadequate the subjectivist/objectivist explanations already mentioned, one is led to admit a *social* (*sociopolitical*) *explanation*: the purges and the terror were only the final step in the elimination, by the Stalinist faction, of all the Communist cadres of the Soviet proletariat. They represented the culmination of the political expropriation of this same proletariat by the Soviet bureaucracy. They represented a political counter-revolution, completing a whole series of measures of expropriation on the social level: one-man management in the enterprises; the forbidding of strikes; the total and servile subjection of the unions to the orders and interests of the managers; the introduction of the most severe labour code in the world. Through the implementation of all these transformations, the Communist Party of the Soviet Union changed from being a party of the workers, albeit increasingly bureaucratized, into a party of the bureaucracy and its political instrument against the working class.

The advantage of the explanation of Stalin and Stalinism which we have just outlined is that it is coherent and it enables one to account for all the essential features of that epoch. It is also in perfect conformity with Marxist methodology and with the principal concepts and principal working hypotheses of historical materialism. It has had and will continue to have an increasing attraction for the new generation of critical Marxists that is emerging in the Soviet Union. But for all the bureaucrats, including the most liberal and Gorbachev himself, it has the terrible disadvantage that by and large it is identified with the analysis of Stalinism and of Soviet history formulated by Leon Trotsky.[21]

The cunning of history reveals itself again when, after the blind fury with which the Stalinists persecuted Trotsky and 'Trotskyism', it has become impossible to deal with Stalin and Stalinism without, at the same time, dealing with Trotsky and Trotskyism – in other words, with the alternative to Stalinism offered by the Left Opposition, later by the United Opposition, and finally by the Left Opposition alone. Glasnost should signify the freedom to discuss all those alternatives without restriction or discrimination, with access to all the documents.

Gorbachev and his allies are confronted with a real dilemma in this question of destalinization. It is not only the loss of credibility of glasnost itself which is at stake if they repress once again the demands for complete destalinization, as happened under Khrushchev. They are also confronted with immediate problems for instance a new edition of the history of the Communist Party. They can try to evade some of the issues by feigning a certain 'impartiality' towards the events of the thirties: Stalin is guilty of 'excesses' but not everything he did was bad. But these manoeuvres won't go very far. Too many people, among them more and more experts, are passionately interested in seriously examining the archives of the period.

For the moment, they seem to have recourse to two options. The first consists in conjuring away, if not physically destroying, some of the proofs of Stalin's crimes. According to a report in *Le Monde* (23–4 August 1987)

> The legal archives of the thirties, forties and fifties are actually being destroyed at the rate of five thousand dossiers a month under the pretext that there is a 'lack of space' to preserve them, according to the latest edition of the dissident journal, *Glasnost.*
>
> According to this journal, published by ex-political prisoners, among them Sergei Grigoriants, the documents concerning millions of Soviet victims of the terror are preserved in the archives of the Military Tribunal and of the Supreme Court of the USSR. 'Documents of this sort were *cleaned* from the archives of the ministry of justice in the sixties and seventies. As far as the archives of the KGB are concerned, nobody knows where they are.' For a number of years, writes *Glasnost*, two presidents of the Supreme Court managed to save the archives from destruction. But, 'when the minister of justice, Vladimir Terebilov, became head of the Supreme Court, with Sergei Gussev as his deputy, the cleaning out of the archives began again.'
>
> At first the archives were burned in the furnace at the Supreme Court building. But, reveals *Glasnost*, 'this caused too much smoke in the city. Now they are burned outside of Moscow.'

This allegation was denied, but in such ambiguous language that it seems likely that a section of the legal archives have indeed been destroyed. The interest of those of the *nomenklatura* who were personally involved in the terror, and especially those who have defended the purges throughout the sixties and seventies, and who continue to justify today the elimination of the Bolshevik leaders, is obvious.

The other option of the bureaucracy is to abandon the most infamous accusations against the old Bolsheviks and Trotsky, while maintaining, in a more sutle way, all the historical falsifications and distortions concerning their political positions. This is how Ligachev operates, the official in charge of ideology in the party leadership and an old hand at this trick. But Gorbachev makes it easy for him. He did it once again in his speech of 2 November 1987 commemorating the seventieth anniversary of the October revolution.[22]

This line of reply takes us back once again to the calumnies and falsifications of the years 1924–29 against the Left Opposition and against Trotsky in particular.[23] Unfortunately for them, all the defamatory statements made against Trotsky by Ligachev, Gorbachev, and their ideologues such as Afanasiev, the editor of *Pravda* directly contradict statements made by Lenin himself in texts which are becoming more widely available.

According to official statements by party leaders, Trotsky's negative characteristics prevailed over his positive ones. According to Lenin, 'Trotsky is, to be sure, the most able man in the present Central Committee' (Testament,[24] p. 6). Party leaders today say that Stalin deserves credit for the way in which he carried out the struggle against Trotsky. But, according to Lenin ( *Testament*, p. 7):

> Stalin is too rude.... This circumstance may seem an insignificant trifle, but I think that from the point of view of preventing a split and from the point of view of the relation between Stalin and Trotsky which I discussed above, it is not a trifle, or it is such a trifle as may acquire a decisive significance.

Trotsky, repeat the leaders of the party today, was never a Bolshevik. Lenin ( *The Stalin School of Falsification*, p. 105):

> As for conciliation [with the Mensheviks and Social Revolutionaries] I cannot even speak about that seriously. Trotsky long ago [in the spring of 1917] said that unification was impossible. Trotsky understood this and from that time on there has been no better Bolshevik.

Trotsky was a narcissistic egoist, animated by extreme ambition, abandoning his wife and children in Siberia, 'living comfortably in emigration', 'constantly changing his political positions'. Lenin (note addressed to Trotsky during the civil war; *The Stalin School of Falsification*, p. 49)

> Comrades, knowing the harsh character of comrade Trotsky's orders, I am so convinced, so absolutely convinced, of the correctness, expedience and necessity for the good of our cause, of orders issued by comrade Trotsky, that I give them my full support.

Unfortunately, a writer as serious as Zhores Medvedev has contributed to this enterprise of character assassination, in an interview with the West German news magazine *Der Spiegel* (no. 5, 1987):

Medvedev: In the third place, Trotsky in the twenties was a left oppositionist; what he called for in 1926, Stalin implemented in the thirties.
*Der Spiegel*: The centrally administered economy, the militarization of labour.
Medvedev: Trotsky never had, unlike Bukharin, an alternative programme; the rivalry between him and Stalin was a rivalry between two authoritarian figures.

It is enough to read Trotsky's *New Course* of 1923 or the other opposition documents of that year, but especially the opposition documents of 1926–27, including the *Platform of the Opposition* of 1927, to realize how unfounded those accusations and calumnies are.

Not only were the criticisms and proposals of Trotsky and of the other Communist leaders who supported him eminently political, having nothing whatsoever to do with his 'authoritarian' character, they were opposed also to the policies of Bukharin, supported at the time by Stalin. Those policies of Trotsky went to the heart of the matter, dealing with the need for a fundamental democratization of social and political life and with the need to combine planned industrialization on the one hand, with protection of the small and middle peasants on the other.

In fact, there is an obvious similarity between some of Trotsky's proposals and the things that are being condemned by Gorbachev today, with the difference that Trotsky also condemned bureaucratic abuse, waste, and corruption, and this at a time when they were only beginning, whereas Gorbachev is doing this fifty-five years later when they have caused the deaths of millions of Soviet people and brought about immense and avoidable suffering as well as military, economic, and social catastrophes.

During the most serious moments of the civil war, the system of nomination [of party officials from the top] didn't reach 10 per cent of what it is today. The appointment [and not the election] of secretaries of provincial committees has become the rule. This puts the secretaries in a position where they are independent of their local organizations.... 

This is a fact which is known to every member of the party. Members of the party who are dissatisfied with this or that decision of the central committee or even of the provincial committee, who have this or that doubt in their minds, who privately note this or that error, irregularity or disorder, are afraid to speak about it at party meetings, and are even afraid to talk about it in conversation.... Free discussion within the party has practically vanished, the public opinion of the party is stifled.

Why are we unanimous about going over to a regime of workers' democracy? We, as a party, reflect the processes developing in the working class. The working class feels the strength of the enemy which it can see in the shop windows, an enemy which lives in the same city as ourselves. This is the most important factor and when we speak about workers' democracy it is a reflection of a process taking place in the working class....

Every unit of the party must return to collective initiative, to the right of free and comradely criticism – without fears and without turning back – and to the right of organizational self-determination. It is necessary to regenerate and renovate the party apparatus and to make it feel that it is nothing but the executive mechanism of the collective will.

The party press has recently presented not a few examples that characterize the already ossified bureaucratic degeneration of party morals and relations. The answer to the first word of criticism is 'Let's have your membership card!'[25]

In the third appendix to the *New Course*, it is said that the economic orientation which would allow the maintenance of *smychka* (the worker–peasant alliance) would proceed 'not by suppressing the market but on the basis of the market'. In his work of 1925 entitled *Toward Capitalism or Socialism*, Trotsky wrote: 'Our present comparison with the prewar level is made entirely from the point of view of quantity and price.... The comparative production coefficients must also include quality; otherwise thay may become merely a source or instrument of self-delusion' (in *The Challenge of the Left Opposition*, p. 349). This is like reading Gorbachev or Aganbegyan – fifty-five years earlier!

The most scandalous accusation is that concerning the 'militarization of labour' which Trotsky and the opposition – anticipating Stalinism of the thirties – are alleged to have put forward in 1926. To refute this calumny, here are two extracts from documents of the opposition which state exactly the contrary. In the 'Declaration of the Thirteen' to the plenum of the Central Committee and to the Control Commission in July 1926, we read:

The bureaucractic regime penetrates like rust into the life of every factory and workshop. If party members are denied in fact the right to criticize their district committee, province committee or the Central Committee, in the factory they are denied the chance to voice criticism of their immediate superiors. Party people are intimidated. An administrator who is able to assure himself the support of the secretary of a higher party organization, because he is 'a loyal man', thereby insures himself against the criticism from below and often even from responsibility for mismanagement or outright petty tyranny.

In a socialist economy under construction a basic condition for the economic expenditure of national resources is vigilant control by the mass, above all by the workers, in the factories and shops. As long as they cannot openly criticize and oppose irregularities and abuses, exposing those responsible by name, without fear of being called oppositionists, 'discontented elements' or troublemakers, or of being expelled from the party cell or even from the factory – as long as they cannot do that, the struggle for a 'regime of economy', or for higher productivity will inevitably travel down the bureaucratic path, i.e. more often than not will strike at the vital interests of the workers. This is precisely what we see happening now. Inefficiency and sloppiness in setting pay rates and work norms, which make life hard for the workers, are nine times out of ten the direct result of bureaucratic indifference to the most elementary interests of the workers and of production itself.

Is this an illustration of a tendency towards the 'militarization of labour'? In 'The Platform of the Opposition', the whole of chapter 2 deals with the situation of the working class and the unions. It would be good to read it in its entirety but we must content ourselves with the following extract:

> The decisive factor in appraising the progress of our country along the road of socialist reconstruction must be the growth of our productive forces and the dominance of the socialist elements over the capitalist – *together with improvements in all the living conditions of the working class.* This improvement ought to be evident in the material sphere (numbers of workers employed in industry, level of real wages, the kind of budget appropriations for workers' needs, housing conditions, medical services, etc.); in the political sphere (party, trade unions, soviets, the Communist youth organization), and finally, in the cultural sphere (schools, books, newspapers, theatres). The attempt to push the vital interests of the workers into the background, under the contemptuous epithet of 'narrow craft professionalism', to counterpose them to the general historical interests of the working class, is theoretically wrong and politically dangerous.[36]

Faced with the statements of Medvedev and the 'Gorbachevites', according to which the 'bonapartist tendencies' of Trotsky, fear of his 'dictatorship', frightened the Communist cadres and facilitated the victory of Stalin, we demand that the whole truth should be made known, that all the documents of the period, starting with the *New Course*, the 'Platform of the Forty-Six', and the *Platform of the Opposition* of 1926, be published so that the readers of today can form their own independent and critical opinion about the real debates of that period – especially in the light of what has happened since then.

The *legal* rehabilitation of Bukharin and of the other leaders condemned in the Moscow trials automatically implies the *legal* rehabilitation of Leon Trotsky and his son, Leon Sedov. According to the verdict of the first trial (19–24 August 1936):

Trotsky, Lev Davidovich, and his son Sedov Lev Davidovich, living now abroad, have been found guilty, on the basis of the declaration of the condemned, N. Smirnov, E.S. Golzman, V. Dreitser, F.D. Olberg and Berman-Jurin, as well as on the basis of material of this court, of having directly prepared and personally directed the organization of terrorist actions in the USSR, against the leaders of the Communist Party of the Soviet Union and against the Soviet state. If they are found on the territory of the USSR their immediate arrest and transfer to the Tribunal of the Military College and to the Supreme Tribunal of the USSR is ordered.[27]

In the statement of 5 February 1988, announcing the rehabilitation of Bukharin, Rakovsky, and twenty leading Bolsheviks condemned in March 1938, the Supreme Court said that the condemnations were a 'gross violation of Socialist legality', based on 'falsifications' and 'illegally obtained confessions'. What possible argument is there now for the continued refusal to rehabilitate Trotsky?

There is, however, an immediate political dimension to this whole affair. What is at stake here is a judgement on the use of falsifications and calumnies as an instrument of discussion and political polemic. This concerns not only the past, but also the present. Four leading historians, among them L. Chirikov of the Academy of Social Sciences, sent a letter to *Moscow News* protesting against the article by Yuri Afanasiev which gave favourable mention to Trotsky and which appeared in the same paper (*Moscow News*, 11 January 1987). In this letter (*Moscow News*, 10 May 1987), they state:

Y. Afanasiev refers only to letters of Lenin to the Congress (i.e. the 'testament' of Lenin), while ignoring the long and hard struggle which Lenin carried out both before and after October against Trotsky and the Trotskyists on the question of the character of the motor forces of the revolution and its perspectives, and the victory of Socialism in our country....

After the victory of fascism in Germany in 1933.... Trotsky aimed at an overthrow of the Soviet government by force, using for his key objective the possibility of defeat in the future war against fascism ... Trotsky's line was to restore capitalism in the Soviet Union.

In his reply, which appeared in the same issue of *Moscow News*, Afanasiev evaded the question of what were the real positions of Trotsky, evaded the issue of the falsifications, the lies on which the trials and the verdicts were based, the massacre of the old Bolsheviks and of hundreds of thousands of Communists. In this evasion are revealed all of Gorbachev's contradictions and dilemmas.[28]

There was a rather grotesque follow-up to this neo-Stalinist offensive. On 17 June 1988 *Rude Pravo*, the organ of the Czechoslovak Communist Party, published an article on its front page which contained a vitriolic attack on the well-known Czech socialist revolutionary, Petr Uhl, as well as an attack on Ernest Mandel but, above all, on Leon Trotsky. All the old Stalinist calumnies, already thrown out by the Soviet Supreme Court, were restated:

> In his book *Permanent Revolution,* published in 1930, he asserted that the full implementation of the socialist revolution was unthinkable within a national framework. Therefore [!] he was for the elimination of socialist power at the place where such power had prevailed.... The advocates of Trotsky literally outlined, as one of their first and foremost tasks, the struggle against anti-fascist forces in conformity with the transparently provocative idea according to which fascism has to prevail because, allegedly, its later downfall would enable a worldwide revolution.... The Trotskyites even presupposed the formation of internal fronts that were to be targeted against individual left-wing oriented sections of the French liberation movement. Perhaps this was the reason why the Trotskyites could legally [sic] convene their conference in France at the time of the occupation of this country.

There would be no point in refuting this miserable tissue of lies which contains not a single word of truth. The date of publication of this article, however, is very significant. A conservative faction in the Czechoslovak bureaucracy was persuaded to mount an attack on Mikhail Gorbachev on the eve of the 19th Conference of the Soviet Communist Party through the device of an attack on Trotsky, the Fourth International, Petr Uhl and Ernest Mandel. Times have certainly changed.

# 8

# The Ideological–Moral Crisis

Perestroika is presented as a response to the economic crisis. Glasnost is an attempt to surmount the political crisis. But no attempt has been made to elaborate an overall response to the ideological–moral crisis which affects Soviet society. The inability of the Gorbachev team to complete the process of destalinization is the most obvious demonstration of this fact.

This ideological–moral crisis is an extremely profound one. It encapsulates, in a certain manner, the whole crisis of the system. The more clear-headed among the Soviet leaders are well aware of this even if their manner of speaking about it is often contradictory and indirect.

Dev Murarka states that Mikhail Gorbachev is motivated by a profound conviction that 'if Soviet society is to be regenerated, this can only come about through the party and, for this purpose, the ethics of the party have to be redefined.'[1]

It's true that he stated in 1985 that 'it is essential to understand that a new stage has begun and that a psychological restructuring (perestroika) is called for ... After all, restructuring always begins with a restructuring of people's mentality.'[2]

This is, of course, very vague and far from being a definition of a new Communist ethic. It is also an attempt to evade responsibility because, apparently, it is the whole population which is called on to change its mentality, although this population is not responsible for the impasse created by those who rule over Soviet society.

The diagnosis has, of course, developed with time. At the 27th Congress, prepared before the Brezhnevites were reduced to a minority on the leading bodies of the party, Gorbachev defended manifestly incoherent positions. For instance, in his report to the Congress, he stated:

A new way of life has taken shape, based on the principles of social justice, in which there are neither oppressors nor the oppressed, neither exploiters nor the exploited, in which power belongs to the people. Its distinctive features are collectivism and comradely mutual assistance, triumph of the ideas of freedom, unbreakable unity between the rights and duties of every member of society, the dignity of the individual, and true humanism.[3]

Almost every word is a half truth and a half lie, if not a complete lie. Social justice when there exist the kinds of phenomena we described in chapter 1? No oppressors or oppressed? But what of the facts described in chapter 2? The power belongs to the people when they can't even elect whom they choose to representative bodies, still referred to inappropriately as soviets, which in any case have no power to decide on political line or to choose between economic, social, or cultural alternatives? Comradely mutual assistance when it's impossible to obtain medical assistance or pharmaceutical products without bribery?[4] Triumph of freedom when Gorbachev himself justifies censorship,[5] when mentally healthy people are interned in psychiatric prisons as a way of dealing with their non-conformist ideas?

But in the same report Gorbachev says:[6]

> If private-owner parasitic sentiments and levelling tendencies begin to surface, this means that something is wrong about the choice of ways and means in our work, and has got to be rectified. (p. 135) We must admit today that owing to a slackening of control and for a number of other reasons groups of people have appeared with a distinct proprietary mentality and a scornful attitude toward the interests of society. (pp. 137–8) We feel just indignation about all sorts of shortcomings and those responsible for them – people who neglect their duties and who are indifferent to society's interests: hack worker and idler, grabber and writer of anonymous letters, petty bureaucrat and bribe-taker. (p. 176)

> The party must declare a determined and relentless war on bureaucratic practices. Vladimir Ilyich Lenin held that it was especially important to fight them at moments of change, during a transition from one system of management to another, where there is a need for maximum efficiency, speed and energy. Bureaucracy is today a serious obstacle to the solution of our principal problem – the acceleration of the country's socioeconomic development and the fundamental restructuring of the mechanism of economic management linked to that development. This is a troubling question and appropriate conclusions are required. Here it is important to bear in mind that bureaucratic distortions manifest themselves all the more strongly where there is no efficiency, publicity, and control from below, where people are held less accountable for what they do. (p. 183)

In practice, purposeful education work was often replaced by artificial campaigns leading propaganda away from life with an adverse effect on the social climate. The sharpness of the contradictions in life was often ignored and there was no realism in assessing the real state of affairs in the economy, as well as in the social and other spheres. (p. 187)

Having spoken of these most flagrant contradictions, Mikhail Gorbachev concludes as if none of them even existed: 'People should constantly see and feel the great truth of our ideology and the principled character of our policy. Work and the distribution of benefits should be so organized ... that every Soviet citizen should have firm faith in our ideal and values' (p. 186). Is this naivety or cynicism? A year later, Gorbachev went much farther in revealing the extent of the social malaise. Speaking to the congress of trade unions, he said: 'Today we want to radically change the situation in society, because we don't want to go on living as we have lived, nor go on working as we have worked' (*Pravda*, 26 February 1987). But what does this mean?

No longer work as we have worked, no longer live as we have lived, when there are no oppressors or oppressed, no exploiters or exploited, when 'collectivism and comradely mutual assistance' have already triumphed? He continues: 'Workers are legitimately indignant when they see the behaviour of those leaders ... who allow the abuse of power, stifle criticism and enrich themselves.'[7]

The bourgeoisie profit immensely from this ideological–moral crisis of Soviet society. But what is of greater importance is the deception, the disenchantment, the depoliticization of the Soviet workers which the Gorbachev regime has as yet failed to overcome.

A communist worker from the city of Minsk has summed up in admirable fashion the causes of this depoliticization of the Soviet working class:

I think that the main cause of all this is the indifference shown towards the working class.... The worker will agree to sacrifices for the sake of the common good, if he is convinced that these sacrifices are really necessary. But if these sacrifices are only used to pay for lack of ability, of professional awareness or of idleness of someone else, then the worker begins to slow down his rhythm even in carrying out what is directly his duty.

The negative attitude to work, which has increased a lot recently, is a sort of 'strike', a perfectly natural response to the bureaucracy, to the severity and even rudeness shown towards those who produce all the material wealth of society. The worker repays indifference with indifference. This indifference is profoundly anchored in our lives. It is not something which affects only individuals, it affects the whole of the working class.

He ends his description of the situation with a call for justice, equality, and democracy:

> One could say that this is all neither here nor there, that this is not what matters. What matters is technical progress, self-financing, democratization, etc. Fine, I agree. But if there is no justice, no elementary justice in the distribution of goods, then nothing will change. String-pulling, speculation, unequal rights – these things humiliate the ordinary worker, they injure him. The worker who is humiliated and offended is not a good worker. He will never really believe that he is working for himself ... Only a worker who respects himself and is respected can be a good worker and a true citizen. I am convinced that true socialism is a society in which people can think independently.[8]

Such sentiments continue to exist after three years of glasnost for the simple reason that the day-to-day reality has not changed and because the working class can see the continued existence of injustice and inequality.

Gorbachev himself has become more precise in his descriptions of this social evil. In his latest book, *Perestroika*, he writes:

> Propaganda of success – real or imagined – was gaining the upper hand. Eulogizing and servility were encouraged; the needs and opinions of ordinary working people, of the public at large, were ignored. In the social sciences, scholastic theorization was encouraged and developed, but creative thinking was driving out from the social sciences, and superfluous and voluntarist assessments and judgements were declared indisputable truths. Scientific, theoretical and other discussions, which are indispensable for the development of thought and for creative endeavour, were emasculated. Similar negative tendencies also affected culture, the arts and journalism, as well as the teaching process and medicine, where mediocrity, formalism and loud eulogizing surfaced, too.
>
> The presentation of a 'problem-free' reality backfired: a breach had formed between word and deed, which bred public passivity and disbelief in the slogans being proclaimed. It was only natural that this situation resulted in a credibility gap: everything that was proclaimed from the rostrums and printed in the newspapers and textbooks was put into question.[9] Decay began in public morals: the great feeling of solidarity with each other that was forged during the heroic times of the revolution, the first five-year plans, the great patriotic war and post-war rehabilitation was weakening: alcoholism, drug abuse and crime were growing; and the penetration of the stereotypes of mass culture alien to us, which bred vulgarity and low tastes and brought about ideological barrenness increased.[10]

One could not formulate a more severe indictment of the ideological–

moral crisis of Soviet society during the Stalinist and post-Stalinist period. This is a long way from the 'new way of life'. A purely logical analysis of Gorbachev's statements and of the absence of positive solutions would be inadequate. Above all, it is essential to explain the striking contrast between on the one hand the coherence of the economic and political discourse, and on the other the incoherence of the ideological discourse.

In our view, the ultimate explanation of this contrast is to be found in the social material interests of the bureaucracy which Gorbachev continues to represent. These interests do not hinder the formulation of radical economic and even political reforms which would make the system function better. But they do hinder any attempt to get at the roots of this ideological–moral malaise because this would involve exposing the nature and function of the bureaucracy. Without stating precisely the nature of the problem, no substantial remedy can be proposed.

That is why, for the *n*th time, and in completely typical manner, Gorbachev identifies 'bureaucracy' with 'bureaucratism', a move which was already quite common under Stalin. *He reduces the phenomenon of social stratification to a question of bad habits and dishonest morals.* Bureaucracy is routine, it is operational slowness; it is not the monopoly of power in the hands of a privileged elite. The cause of this is to be found in the loosening of control, so the solution is obvious – the re-estabishment of control. Stalin already set the pattern in the case of the Workers and Peasants Inspectorate: the bureaucratic struggle against bureaucracy!

The state has to be tougher, its organs more severe. 'Discipline' has to be reinforced. The bureaucratic nature of Gorbachev is revealed in this orientation. This is the quintessence of bureaucratic philosophy.

From a Marxist point of view, the material roots of the ideological–moral crisis of the Soviet Union are easy to lay bare. The 'proprietary mentality', the parasitism, the nepotism, the corruption, the desire for private enrichment – all of those things which recur constantly, in spite of all the propaganda and all the official exhortations, are the result, in the final analysis, of the survival in the Soviet Union of the market and of money. They are reinforced by the appeals to 'material interests' and to 'the struggle against levelling' and against 'egalitarianism'. All the appeals against 'proprietary mentality' are, and will remain, without effect as long as the ordinary people can see in their day-to-day lives that those in high places live better, consume more, and have more pleasures and greater freedoms than they do.

We will not examine here the question of why the rapid abolition of market categories is not possible in a society in transition from capitalism to Socialism. Nor will we examine the extent to which the survival of market categories and of money has been reinforced and deformed by the bureaucratic dictatorship and its principal concomitant – social inequality. But what we insist on is the analysis which Marxists have always made, beginning with Lenin, in recognizing the effects of this reality on the consciousness of the masses, even though they regarded the survival of these categories as inevitable. In connection with the higher salaries paid to 'bourgeois experts', Lenin wrote:

> The corrupting influence of high salaries – both upon the Soviet authorities ... and upon the mass of workers – is indisputable. ... To conceal from the people the fact that the enlistment of bourgeois experts [and, even more so, of 'communist' experts!] by means of extremely high salaries is a retreat from the principles of the Paris Commune would be sinking to the level of bourgeois politicians and deceiving the people.[11]

The bureaucracy has concealed this from the masses for the past fifty-five years, since the time of the Stalinist campaign against 'egalitarianism' and 'levelling'. Gorbachev continues to conceal it. Without a scientific analysis and an open and honest recognition of these contradictions, it will be impossible to develop a systematic education to at least limit their effects. Without a constant effort to fight the scale of social inequality, defending in theory and in propaganda the virtues and advantages of egalitarianism, the continuous erosion of Socialist values is inevitable.[12]

Under those circumstances it was inevitable that a 'profit' mentality would develop in the working class, a tendency to seek individual advantages by means of black-market labour, theft, complicity with bureaucratic corruption, etc.[13] But one cannot combat this mentality by means of an appeal to 'material interest' or higher productivity. It can only be combatted by a true Communist praxis, especially by a systematic return to co-operation, solidarity, self-activity, democratic self-organization, and control in the hands of workers' collectives.

Sensing obscurely the need to offer new values to the masses, one wing of the bureaucracy, led by Suslov, deliberately encourages the development of Russian nationalism, especially in art and literature.[14] We would wager, however, that with the partial re-establishment of freedom of research, of political discussion and political action, important sections of youth will find these new values in a return to authentic Marxism. Mark Frankland is quite wrong when he portrays Marxism as a combination of scientific pretensions and blind faith.[15] Marxism combines scientific rigour in analysis (which implies a permanent 'constructive doubt') with a *moral imperative* to combat inequality, oppression, and injustice, in all its forms. This combination commands attraction and credibility the moment the practice of those who espouse it corresponds to the theory.

Conservatives sense this instinctively, hence their promotion of strong authority, even of authoritarianism. Hence also their fierce attacks on 'Trotskyism'.[16] The Gorbachev team has no overall solution to this ideological–moral crisis. They do, however, offer partial solutions to very specific phenomena which are an expression of the crisis. Gorbachev's three main targets, in this respect, have been corruption, alcoholism, and prostitution.

Corruption is universal in the Soviet Union.[17] We examined its origins, its scope, and its evolution in chapter 1. Soon after coming to power, Gorbachev began an offensive against corruption, relying essentially on the police and the courts. The Soviet press has published numerous examples of convictions for corruption. One of the most well-known cases was that of Valid Usmanov, minister responsible for the cotton industry, who was condemned to death for having systematically falsified harvest figures, receiving bonuses and other financial rewards for 4.5 million tons of cotton that never existed.[18] More than two thousand officials in the republic of Uzbekistan were fired from their posts as a result of this affair. At the same time, Uzbek deputies were accused of using state funds to build large dachas for themselves and their families. As a result of the same inquiry, the party head in Bukara, A. Karimov, was sentenced to death and executed.[19] According to *Pravda* (23 January 1988), the Uzbek mafia stole four thousand million roubles from the state.

The limited effectiveness of this 'bureaucratic–repressive struggle against the bureaucracy' was revealed in a most striking manner by the events that followed. After the execution of Usmanov and Karimov, and after the elimination of thousands of corrupt and incompetent officials, 40 per cent of Uzbek enterprises returned false reports to Moscow for the 1986 plan. Of 211 collective farms that had been examined, 147 were found to have lied about the production of animal fodder. In the words of the vice-president of the executive committee of the soviet in Tashkent, Ernest Rizaev: 'One of the most serious problems that we have to face up to is the problem of personnel, the problem of the cadres who direct perestroika.'[20] Too true!

In Kazakhstan the situation was no better. It was said that four thousand officials were either suspected or accused of corruption. They all enjoyed the protection of Kunayev, member of the Politburo until December 1986. In chapter 6 we looked at the ethnic–political implications of this affair.

The vice-minister for foreign trade in the Soviet Union, Vladimir S.

Suskhov, was caught at Sheeretetievo airport at the beginning of 1986 illegally importing jewellery and video cassettes. In his dacha, police discovered 2.3 million dollars worth of gifts from foreign firms looking for trading contracts in the Soviet Union. His wife, Valentina, member of the State Committee for Science and Technology, accused of corruption in dealings with an Italian firm, was sentenced to eleven years in prison. Suskhov himself was sentenced to thirteen years.[21]

The battle against alcoholism has been the most spectacular of Gorbachev's reforms. On 17 May 1985, after two entire sessions of the Central Committee devoted to this problem, 'measures against alcoholism and drunkenness' were promulgated, coming into effect on 1 June of that year. Alcoholism is a terrible scourge in the Soviet Union, affecting four million people, according to a report from the Academy of Sciences. Its effects on the economy (absenteeism) and on public health are disastrous. It is undoubtedly the main cause of the fall in life expectancy which has taken place in the Soviet Union in recent years, the only industrialized country to experience such a regression.

The least one can say is that the campaign against alcholism has not been supported by the entire population. Like prohibition in America in the twenties, it has produced a whole host of illegal activities: private distillation, home-made 'vodka' using sugar bought in the shops or stolen from the kolkhoz, black-market sales which bring in enormous profits, and so on.[22] The list could be extended. The response of the Gorbachev team has been a typically bureaucratic one: a combination of new punitive measures and moralizing exhortations. A decree of the Supreme Soviet of 2 June 1987 introduced, for the first time, a penalty of up to twenty years hard labour for the illegal production of alcohol (*Le Monde*, 4 June 1987).

The scale of the problem is reflected in the scale of the repression. In 1986 the police confiscated two million litres of *samogon* (home-made alcohol). In 1987 there were a hundred thousand arrests (*Observer*, 12 July 1987). According to the deputy procurator general, Viktor Naidenov, this is only the tip of the iceberg. According to a report published in *Pravda* at the beginning of July 1987, the sale of sugar in the shops had gone up 11 per cent, an increase of one million tons!

If the essentially repressive struggle against alcoholism has been ineffective, and if the results of the education campaign have been disappointing, this is because the whole campaign bypasses the *social nature of the problem*. The cause of large-scale alcoholism is not the 'Russian cultural tradition', as some Western observers maintain, but rather the demoralization, the lack of social and political perspectives, the atomization of society and individual isolation. Boredom and the absence of hope and ideals are drowned in vodka or samogon. It is an elementry thesis of Marxism, if not of the whole of scientific sociology, that four million cases of drunkenness are not simply four million individual psychological cases. They are four million proofs of the existence of a profound social malaise.

The same remark applies to the phenomenon of prostitution in the Soviet Union and to the purely repressive manner in which the Gorbachev team has attempted to deal with this problem. For decades, official propaganda denied that there was prostitution in the Soviet Union or in the other 'Socialist countries'. This, however, was flying in the face of the evidence. The existence of this phenomenon is now recognized, a phenomenon which extends far beyond the hotels used by foreigners and the 'hostels' used by the KGB. The response, however, has been purely repressive. According to the *Literaturnaia Gazeta* of 22 July 1987, a law in force in the Russian republic, and about to be introduced in the other 14 republics, lays down a fine of 100 roubles for the first offence, and 200 roubles for any subsequent offence, in a country where the average monthly salary is 200 roubles.

In the press, the problem is treated in a most superficial manner. There's talk of loss of 'moral values', of 'a generation turned bad', etc. The most elementary fact is ignored: the difference between the income of a prostitute and that of an average worker couldn't help but encourage prostitution, especially in a country where 'material interest' and money play such a large role. The problem of the profoundly sexist character of Soviet society is passed over almost completely: the pressure of superiors demanding sexual services from their subordinates, sexual abuse in offices and by the police, etc. This sexist background to the extension of prostitution in Soviet society is reflected in the new legislation. Typically, only the prostitute is punished, and not the buyer of services. The latter is, in most cases, a man, while the former is almost always a woman. In a sexist society, this makes a big difference.

The new programme of the Soviet Communist Party, adopted at the 27th Congress, is a reflection of the inability of the Gorbachev team to offer a solution to the overall ideological–moral crisis of Soviet society. The programme marks a new stage in the theoretical degeneration of the party, yet another more overt break with Marxism.

This programme marks a retreat even in relation to the Khrushchev programme adopted in 1961. Its main characteristic is the total disappearance of any kind of overall historical objective. Socialist society, as understood by Marx, Engels, Lenin, Trotsky, Luxemburg, Plekhanov, and all the other Marxist theoreticians up until the late twenties, was the first stage of Communist society, and as late as 1928, was described by Stalin in the following manner:

We say quite often that our republic is a socialist republic. Does that mean that we have already achieved socialism, eliminated classes and the state, since the achievement of socialism means the disappearace of the state? Does it mean that classes, the state, etc. survive under socialism? It obviously doesn't mean that.[23]

In the *Critique of the Gotha Programme*, Marx stated most clearly that in the first phase of Communism (Socialism), as it emerges directly from capitalism, the associated producers do not exchange commodities and do not produce value. Within the logic of the Stalinist theory of Socialism, a theory which says that Socialism can be constructed in a single country, the 1961 programme of the Communist Party puts off the disappearance of market production until the establishment of Communism. But at least the goal remained. Khrushchev's programme promised that by the 1980s the Soviet people would have achieved Communism. They would have surpassed the production of the United States and all basic products would be free. The 1980s have come and the Soviet Union is still far from having achieved the level of production of the United States, not to mention surpassing it. The new programme adopted under Gorbachev doesn't even promise to surpass the United States by the year 2000. The goal of the disappearance of market production has completely disappeared from the new programme.

The issue is no clearer with respect to the question of the state. Except for one obscure phrase, the programme adopted at the 27th Congress does not envisage the disappearance of the state. On the contrary, it calls for its reinforcement. It mentions a 'state of the whole people' which has replaced the dictatorship of the proletariat, as did the 1961 programme. This state, like the 'leading role of the party', does not disappear but is rather strengthened as 'Socialism' develops and as 'Communism' is constructed.[24] Classes and different social layers will continue to exist – the working class, the peasantry, and the intelligentsia (as the bureaucracy are called). We are now told that classes and social layers will continue to exist even under Communism! It is only in a 'higher stage of Communism' that society will become 'socially homogeneous', in other words, classless.

One would search in vain in Marx or Lenin for any suggestion of a 'lower stage of Communism' in which the state and social classes continue to exist. In reality, a Socialist society, a society without classes, does not exist in the Soviet Union.[25]

Classes continue to exist, says the new programme, but they are not antagonistic. But, in this case, why the state? Why is it necessary, as Gorbachev demanded in his report to the 27th Congress, to reinforce the secret police, the KGB? Why does not society organize its own affairs directly, instead of delegating management to a separate apparatus, the state?

Engels was very precise:

> In contrast to the old gentile organization, the state is distinguished by ... the institution of a public force which is no longer immediately identical with the people's own organization of themselves as an armed power. This special, public force is needed because a self-acting armed organization of the people has become impossible since the cleavage into classes ... This public force exists in every state; it consists not merely of armed men, but also of material appendages, prisons and coercive institutions of all kinds, of which gentile society knew nothing.[26]

Is there such a public force in the Soviet Union, consisting of an army, police, prisons, coercive institutions of all kinds? Obviously, yes. Does this not, in itself, bear witness to the fact that in this country there must exist profound social contradictions? The 'state of the whole people' demonstrates precisely that the 'people' are not 'whole' but socially divided. If not, then the 'people' would have no need of a state.

The new programme seeks to avoid this contradiction in a Stalinist manner:

> From the point of view of internal conditions, our society has no need for an armed force. But as long as the danger exists that imperialism will launch wars of aggression and military conflicts, the party must devote continuous attention to reinforcing the defensive force of the USSR, consolidating its security and the capacity of its armed forces to destroy any aggressor. The armed forces and the security organs of the state must demonstrate a high degree of vigilance and be always ready to undo any attempt on the part of imperialism against the USSR and its allies.

In the light of the Marxist theory of the state, as summarized by Engels, this argument does not hold up. A society which is not divided into socially antagonistic forces has no need of a separate armed force to adequately defend itself against external aggression. Its own internal cohesion is adequate guarantee that a general arming of society is superior and more effective than some specialist armed force. In reality, the authors of the new programme do not themselves believe that the armed forces and the state security are to deal exclusively with some potential external aggressor. Elsewhere, the same programme states that:

> The state organs are obliged to do everything necessary to guarantee the protection and the extension of socialist property, the honour and the dignity

of citizens, and to carry out a determined struggle against crime, drunkenness and the abuse of alcohol, to punish all violations of the law and to eliminate their causes.

The same programme also states:

The party attaches the greatest importance to eliminating violations of work discipline, drunkenness and hooliganism, the private property mentality and the search for gain,[27] servility and sycophantism. In the struggle against these phenomena, it is essential to use both the authority of public opinion and the force of the law.

The force of the law – does this not refer to precisely the 'material appendages' that Engels spoke of, in other words, the police, the judges, the prisons, if not the torturers. In this respect, Lenin's conception was absolutely clear:

During the transition from capitalism to communism suppression is *still* necessary, but it is now the suppression of the exploiting minority by the exploited majority. A special apparatus, a special machine for suppression, the 'state', is *still* necessary, but this is now a transitional state. It is no longer a state in the proper sense of the word; for the suppression of the minority of exploiters by the majority of the wage slaves of *yesterday* is comparatively so easy, simple and natural a task that it will entail far less bloodshed than the suppression of the rising of slaves, serfs or wage-labourers, and it will cost mankind far less. And it is compatible with the extension of democracy to such an overwhelming majority of the population that the need for a *special machine* of suppression will begin to disappear. Naturally, the exploiters are unable to suppress the people without a highly complex machine for performing this task, but the *people* can suppress the exploiters even with a very simple 'machine', almost without a '*machine*', without a special apparatus, by the simple *organization of the armed people* ...
  Lastly, only communism makes the state absolutely unnecessary, for there is *nobody* to be suppressed – 'nobody' in the sense of a *class*, of a systematic struggle against a definite section of the population. We are not utopians and do not in the least deny the possibility and the inevitability of excesses on the part of *individual persons*, or the need to stop such excesses. In the first place, however, no special machine, no special apparatus of suppression, is needed for this; this will be done by the armed people themselves, as simply and as readily as any crowd of civilized people, even in a modern society, interferes to put a stop to a scuffle or to prevent a woman from being assaulted. And, secondly, we know that the fundamental social cause of excesses, which consist in the violation of the rules of social intercourse, is the exploitation of the people, their want and their poverty. With the removal of this chief cause, excesses will inevitably begin to *wither away*.[28]

If, in the Soviet Union, there are hundreds of thousands of members of the 'state security organs' (the KGB), if the prisoners in the prisons and Gulags number in their millions, is this not a proof that the people themselves are not 'armed', that it is not a case of the minority of old exploiters or of individual excesses, but that it is a massive social phenomenon, arising out of a 'profound social cause' – the misery, the unsatisfied social needs, the deception, and the profound ideological disarray of the ordinary people? Is this not a proof that not only Communism but also Socialism has not been achieved in the Soviet Union?

The majority of prisoners in the Soviet Union, contrary to a false view current in the West, are not political but ordinary common-law prisoners, commonly known as 'zeks'. The existence of a prison society so vast confirms, as Lenin stated, the existence of a profound social problem, of serious social contradictions which are the opposite of what one would expect in a classless Socialist society.

There are also many political prisoners in the Soviet Union. There are many hundreds of people in Soviet prisons, not because they offended against the common law but because of what they have written or said, in other words, on account of their opinions. One such example was the poetess Irina Ratushinskaya, who was condemned to seven years hard labour followed by five years of exile for having written several poems which 'aimed at subverting or weakening the Soviet regime'. Seven years for having written poems judged subversive! And this barbarism exists in a society which, according to the programme adopted at the 27th Party Congress:

> creates and develops a genuine democracy ... in which the ideas of freedom, human rights and the dignity of the human person are given a real content which guarantees the unity of rights and obligations, in which the same laws and ethical norms, the same discipline applies to everyone, in which conditions are constantly improving for the multi-dimensional development of personality.

Freedom, human rights, humanism, the multi-dimensional development of the human personality, the freedom of culture and artistic creation which lead to seven years hard labour for some poems which displease the censor and the procurator – could one imagine a more striking example of hypocrisy, of duplicity, of double-talk which could only lead to general cynicism throughout the whole of Soviet society? Is the Soviet Union, then, in a state of civil war, in which Socialism is under attack and its adversaries are attempting to restore capitalism, armed to the teeth and using apparently innocent poems to incite millions of citizens to rebel against the 'power of the soviets'? Not at all, says the new programme, with a large amount of cynicism. The Soviet Union is today a country in which 'a socialist way of life has developed based on comradely mutual support', in which 'the exploiting classes have been eliminated ... and the need to repress them has gradually disappeared'. Repression, then, is no longer necessary against the bourgeoisie and its acolytes, since these have disappeared. It remains necessary, however ... against a poet!

The new programme assures us that, in the Soviet Union, the exploitation of man by man has disappeared. At the same time, it affirms that the exploiting classes have long ago disappeared. There is no possibility of their reappearance in the Soviet Union. To the extent that these affirmations conform with reality, the restrictions on political and civil liberty which continue to exist in the Soviet Union are a flagrant violation of the Leninist party programme of 1919.[29] Not only the spirit but also the letter of this programme require that one demand the suppression in the Soviet Union of all those paragraphs of the penal code which criminalize 'anti-Soviet agitation', 'slander of the Soviet state', and the free formation of political groups, which authorize censorship and the prohibition of publication, and which limit free access to the press and media.

It is not just the political reality of the Soviet Union today which stands condemned by the party programme of 1919, but also the social and economic reality. In 1919 the Russian party set as its goal the six-hour day and the thirty-hour week. In 1986, seventy years later, the party has not even set such a goal for the year 2000. In the capitalist countries, many unions are engaged in the struggle for a shorter working week, since the possibilities for this have been created by the new technology. The new programme talks a lot about these new technologies, but there is no mention of the potential for shorter working time.

In 1919 the party set as one of its goals the achievement of free medical care and pharmaceuticals. It also called for a whole series of other measures, such as the prohibition of overtime, the provision of free clothing, food, and books to school pupils, eight weeks pre-natal and eight weeks post-natal maternity leave, a living wage for all those unable to work, etc. In 1986 the programme of the party calls for the free distribution of pharmaceuticals to children under three years of age by the year 2000. The other goals of 1919 are not even mentioned.

In *State and Revolution* Lenin insisted that the salary of state officials should be at the same level as that of skilled workers. This was seen as one of the main guarantees against the bureaucratic degeneration of the workers' power. But the programme of 1986, in true Stalinist fashion, attacks 'egalitarianism', presenting it not as a goal to be achieved but as a 'deviation' to be avoided at all costs.

The suppression of the division of labour is seen by the new programme only in the form of the disappearance of manual labour in production. Manual labour is identified with 'traditional manual labour'. But what of working on a computer, supervising the work of robots and repairing automatic machines – are not these examples of manual labour? However, the *social* division of labour, which Marx and Engels envisaged as disappearing, concerned above all the different functions of production and administration, in other words the disappearance of the bureaucracy in the social sense of the term, without which the disappearance of the state has no real content. There is no question of this in the new programme, and for good reason: the bureaucracy could hardly envisage its own disappearance.

Foreign policy is the continuation of domestic policy.[30] If the Soviet bureaucracy openly abandons the programme of the proletarian world revolution in favour of peaceful coexistence with imperialism, this is not because it is 'revisionist', or has made a mistake or has illusions, etc. It is because the defence of its own social interests lead it in this direction. This 'revisionism' is the product of the social situation of the bureaucracy, of its material privileges and its monopoly of political power, and not its cause.

The most spectacular difference between the programme of 1919 and that of 1986 is to be found in its international dimension. The programme of 1919 proclaimed that:

> Only the proletarian communist revolution is able to lead humanity out of the blind alley which was created by the imperialists and the imperialist ways. In spite of all the difficulties the revolution will have to face, temporary failures, waves of counter-revolution – the final victory of the proletariat is inevitable. To attain the victory of the world proletarian revolution, the fullest confidence, the closest unity and co-ordination of all the revolutionary activity of the working class in all advanced countries are necessary.

In the new programme the terms 'world revolution' and 'proletarian revolution' are not even mentioned. The international section of the proramme has four central themes: the reinforcement of the unity of the 'Socialist camp'; coexistence and peaceful competition with the 'imperialist camp'; the 'consolidation of relations with the liberated countries': i.e. with the bourgeoisie of the so-called third world; fraternal collaboration with the Communist parties of the 'non-Socialist countries', even where there are differences of opinion.

The substitution of 'campism' for international proletarian class struggle as the motor force of historical progress is obviously not fortuitous. If one abandons any revolutionary perspective for the imperialist and semi-imperialist countries, if one eliminates the world proletariat as the main revolutionary subject, no other recourse is left, except to the 'Socialist camp', whether it be to 'preserve peace', to resolve the problems of the third world, or whatever.[31] The overthrow of capitalism is no longer seen as the solution to the problems of the advanced capitalist countries.

In addition to this total change from the programme of 1919, there is also a significant change from the Khrushchev programme of 1961. The Khrushchev programme had put forward two ideas, still within the general framework of a 'campist' ideology: the idea of struggle between the two world systems (now 'competition' has replaced 'struggle') and the idea of a 'non-capitalist road of development' for the countries of the third world.

The 'non-capitalist road of development' has utterly failed in countries like India and Egypt, two countries specifically mentioned in the 1961 programme. Nonetheless, the perspective of a disappearance of capitalism was still part of Khrushchev's rhetoric. Mikhail Gorbachev, the realist, has abandoned it entirely. Since what remains is economic competition with imperialism, a competition in which no early victory is promised, the survival of capitalism is an underlying assumption of this whole ideology. A Communist programme which implies that capitalism will survive indefinitely!

The most depressing aspect of the new programme is the total absence of any kind of historical perspective. Apart from the goal of abolishing all nuclear weapons, something which can't be achieved in the Soviet Union alone, the only concrete tangible objective is to provide housing for every Soviet citizen by the year 2000. This objective alone, even if it is something positive in a country still marked by poverty in the field of consumption, is not something which can satisfy the thirst for ideals and for justice on the part of youth everywhere, including youth in the Soviet Union.[32]

The Soviet Union today is one of the most culturally advanced countries in the world. It is also one of the most advanced in the field of technological potential. Against such a background, the greyness and dullness of the new programme is striking. There is nothing here which could inflame the imagination, for instance, half-day work, free distribution of basic consumer goods, higher education for everyone, the elimination of hunger in the third world, victory over cancer and other serious illnesses, participation of all workers in the management of enterprises, participation of all citizens in local soviets, 50 per cent women membership in all organs of social leadership, abolition of the political police, etc.[33]

The abandonment of all the classical objectives of Socialism – not to speak of Communism – in the new programme of the Soviet Communist Party is not just a function of the greater realism of Mikhail Gorbachev, who knows quite well that under the existing regime the greater part of these objectives cannot be achieved, neither before the year 2000 nor beyond.[34] What we are concerned with here is the impossibility of achieving these goals in their totality, not the impossibility of achieving any given one of them taken separately. To set the goal of achieving some particular one of these objectives would, in fact, be a worthwhile inspiration for the working class and youth of the Soviet Union. The real obstacle to setting any particular one of these goals, in a realistic manner, is not the relative backwardness of Soviet society and certainly not the problems arising from hostile capitalist encirclement. The material interests of the bureaucracy and its monopoly of political power – these are the real obstacles.

The fact that these objectives, in their totality, are not capable of being achieved in the Soviet Union as it is, taken separately, is simply another way of saying that Socialism is not achievable in a single country. But where it is stated that the USSR and the world have to remain as they are today? Underlying the apparent realism of Gorbachev is a profoundly conservative vision of reality, which corresponds perfectly to the social and ideological conservatism of the Soviet bureaucracy, but not at all to the real dynamism of the world in which we live.

The revolutionary vision of the world which inspired the authors of the Communist programme of 1919 was infinitely more realistic. This vision was based on an understanding of the profound contradictions of capitalist production and bourgeois society. It is understood that these contradictions periodically lead to explosions. This vision was firmly based on the inevitability of the revolutions and counter-revolutions which would flow from this underlying tendency of capitalism. It saw militarism and war as another inevitable product of this same tendency.

This analysis, which matches the real history of the twentieth century, leads to a strategic orientation towards the world revolution. The goals of this revolution, some of which we have already outlined, are a significant force for mobilization. But this presupposes an identification with the working class and with the oppressed and exploited of the world. The positions of the Soviet bureaucracy, expressed in its 'campist' ideology, are opposed more and more to the interests of the world proletariat, above all because of the revolutionary potential of the workers, a potential which we have already seen in Poland in 1980–81. This is why the bureaucracy cannot return to the strategy of world revolution, nor can they inspire or stimulate the working class and youth of the Soviet Union. Hence the greyness of the new programme of the Soviet Communist Party.

# 9

# Gorbachev's Foreign Policy

Out of all of Gorbachev's initiatives, his proposals for partial nuclear disarmament in Europe have had the greatest impact on the rest of the world. This was characterized by an exceptionally successful media effort and it called NATO's bluff on implementing its own 'double zero option'. It also represented a spectacular reversal of the positions previously defended by Soviet diplomacy. It led to the signing of the treaty with the United States in December 1987.[1] As a second step, the Gorbachev team have proposed a 50 per cent reduction in strategic weapons, in fact a complete elimination of all nuclear, biological, and chemical weapons by the year 2000.

This can only be welcomed. The positive character of this turn of events is beyond doubt. The whole international labour movement, as well as all the mass anti-imperialist movements, can only gain from the decline in the credibility of Reaganite propaganda about 'the evil empire'. The infantile manichaeism of the most reactionary circles of imperialism – by no means limited to the Republican Party in the United States and its allies, Mrs Thatcher and company – has no objective basis in the history of the twentieth century. Neither Communism nor the Soviet Union, even during its worst period under Stalin, were responsible for the Second World War, nor for the first, nor for Hiroshima or Auschwitz, nor for the numerous colonial wars which have brought death to more than a hundred million people this century, not to speak of the human catastrophe which famine and underdevelopment have caused and are still causing in the third world.

Hysterical anti-Soviet propaganda has a political purpose, a purpose which is inhuman, namely, to accustom public opinion little by little to the idea that a nuclear war would be a lesser evil; better dead than red.

There is some doubt that this propaganda was effective even during the worst moments of the Reagan era. There is no denying the fact that, by means of a highly effective public relations effort, Gorbachev and his team of advisers have, in a very short time, by and large neutralized the effects of ten years of Rambo hysteria.

It is true that the imperialist milieu which opposes the 'double zero' treaty is feeding a new hysteria about the alleged 'massive superiority' of the armies of the Warsaw Pact in conventional weapons. This propaganda is based on misinformation and mystification,[2] since it refuses to take into account the qualitative superiority of NATO forces and weaponry and since it refuses to recognize also the specific character of the armies of the East European 'people's democracies'.[3] Of course, the imperialists are taking a risk here, since the Soviet leaders may take them at their word and initiate a process of conventional disarmament.

At the same time, the political space for an anti-war movement has expanded. By not subordinating itself to diplomatic negotiations, by safeguarding its independence with respect to all governments, by maintaining its fundamentally unilateralist orientation, the anti-war movement has undoubtedly increased its capacity for mass mobilization.

It's a pity that the Soviet bureaucracy had to await the arrival of Gorbachev to take this initiative, because its positive and stimulating effect on the anti-war movement in the imperialist countries would have been greater when this movement was at its peak in the early eighties. We called for such an initiative at the time, including unilateralist measures which the Soviet Union could have and should have taken as a way of reinforcing the mass movement in favour of unilateral nuclear disarmament in the West. Nevertheless, the rule still applies that 'better late than never'.

One should not exaggerate the practical effects of this treaty. This is not yet real disarmament. It is not even a substantial step towards nuclear disarmament. Europe and the rest of the world remain under the threat of strategic nuclear weapons, the use of which would destroy human civilization, if not physically destroy the human race itself. World military spending has increased, not diminished – a gigantic waste of resources, literally criminal in view of the most elementary needs which are not being satisfied, and not only in the southern hemisphere. Military spending has also increased in the Soviet Union, under the constant pressure of American remilitarization.

Under those circumstances, the battle against the arms race and the threat of war remains a priority task for the international labour movement. Neither Gorbachev nor the Soviet Union, nor the 'Socialist camp', can act as substitute for this movement in attempting to carry out this task. The notion that real world disarmament could be the result of negotiations and treaties between East and West is as utopian today as it was before the acceptance of the 'double zero option'.

From this point of view, there has been no progress in the positions of Gorbachev or of his allies East and West. The notion that the threat of war can be removed definitely and once and for all without the overthrow of capitalism in its principal bastions remains the basis of Soviet policy in the matter of war and peace.

This is certainly an advance on the notion that the Soviet Union or the 'Socialist camp' could win a world nuclear war. Such a war would destroy the human race, if not all life on the planet. Soviet military doctrine has undergone important developments in this respect. The Soviet marshals, Sokolovski and Gretchko, had both claimed victory in a nuclear war as a possibility and as a goal.[4] This position has now been abandoned,[5] especially by the present chief of staff of the Soviet armed forces, Marshal Sergei Akhromeyev.[6]

In defending the idea that nuclear parity with the United States is indispensable – the new Gorbachev doctrine – Soviet diplomacy and the Soviet military leaders are, in fact, defending the doctrine of 'mutual deterrence'.[7] One finds, from time to time, among the spokesmen for the Soviet armed forces, allusions to the Sokolovski–Gretchko policy. But this is obviously the position of a minority and it does not determine the policy of the bureaucracy as a whole.

The new doctrine was stated by Gorbachev in his recent book:

> The fundamental principle of the new political outlook is very simple: *nuclear war cannot be a means of achieving political, economic, ideological or any other goals* [emphasis in original] ... Nuclear war is senseless; it is irrational. *There would be neither winners nor losers in a global nuclear conflict* [our emphasis]: world civilization would inevitably perish. It would be a suicide rather than a war in the conventional sense of the word.[8]

He accepts, in other words, the position defended by revolutionary Marxists and by numerous pacifists for many decades: the strategic goal of the workers movement, in fact, of the whole of humanity, cannot be the defeat of a nuclear aggressor or victory in a nuclear war, but rather *the avoidance of nuclear world war*. It is a question of physical survival, in the most literal sense of the term.

Although commented on very little in the West, or not at all, there has been a significant development of public opinion on this issue in the Soviet Union. Spontaneously, and in spite of official propaganda and militarist indoctrination, the Soviet people have adopted an attitude similar to that found among the ordinary people in Western Europe and Japan, in other words, they are opposed to any use whatever of nuclear weapons. According to the Communist Party journal, *Kommunist* (no. 5, 1987, p. 119), a poll carried out in the factories and offices in Moscow revealed that 83 per cent of the Soviet people are convinced that, regardless of its outcome, nuclear war would destroy human civilization; 93 per cent are of the view that there is *no justification whatsoever* for the use of nuclear weapons, not even 'defence of the fatherland' or 'defence of socialism'.

We believe that Gorbachev the politician has taken account of this majority current of public opinion in order to change both his diplomatic offensive and Soviet military doctrine. Those who continue to oppose him demonstrate not only a lack of mental clarity but also of elementary political sense. The doctrine of the Soviet bureaucracy remains tied, however, to the notion that nuclear war is avoidable without the overthrow of Capitalism. They remain wedded, in other words, to a campist view of world destiny, a view which is unrealistic and utopian.

In a world bristling with nuclear installations, even a purely conventional war would run the risk of a catastrophe on a similar scale to a nuclear war. Who could doubt this after the experience of Chernobyl? Some experts, one-time advisers to the White House, are advocating 'selective deterrence' with the use of conventional or so-called 'antiforce' weapons, designed to hit enemy military installations, 'with the same effect' as nuclear weapons (Michel Tatu in *Le Monde*, 19 January 1988).

It is impossible to deny the broad connections that exist between the economic interests of imperialism and the military operations in which it becomes engaged. A Soviet author wrote, at the time of the publication of Gorbachev's book:

There is another factor which helps to explain the desire of the United States to maintain a military presence in the Gulf for as long as possible, even if this only intensifies the Iran–Iraq conflict. In the USA itself, the reserves of oil are in decline. Armand Hammer, a prominent representative of business interests in America, president of the board of directors of Western Petroleum, said at the beginning of this year that: 'the United States has oil reserves which will last for only seven years. Without commenting on the exactness of this prediction, we must remember that the extraction of oil in the Gulf has become cheaper and that its reserves are practically inexhaustible. ... In other words, the United States will have to increase its imports from this region. Could it not be for this reason that the United States is unwilling to see its force in the Gulf replaced by a United Nations force?[9]

Finally, the idea that only that sector of imperialism directly engaged in the manufacture of arms has an interest in remilitarization is contradicted by the whole experience of the twentieth century. The production of weapons constitutes a guaranteed 'substitute market', as was formulated firstly by Rosa Luxemburg and developed by us in our book *Late Capitalism*. This 'substitute market' is of importance for capital as a *whole* when confronted by a crisis of market outlets and overaccumulation.

In addition, as long as nuclear weapons, nuclear installations, and the socio-economic potential for their creation remain, humanity remains at the mercy of a change of political regime in the capitalist countries, for instance, the coming to power of nazi-type desperadoes ready to launch a nuclear war.[10] The right-wing religious fundamentalist and presidential candidate in the United States, Pat Robertson, spoke in terms of such a scenario. The only guarantee against such a suicidal catastrophe is the suppression of the bourgeois state, going beyond national sovereignty and the capitalist mode of production, with the workers themselves taking control of all the factories, in particular those capable of producing weapons of mass destruction, prohibiting the manufacture of arms, with the workers having the *material and political ability* to enforce such a prohibition.

The only alternative solution to this materialist foundation for the suppression of the threat of nuclear war is the idealist thesis defended by Gorbachev in the passage quoted above: basing international politics on the moral and ethical norms common to the whole of humanity. But, as long as humanity is divided into antagonistic classes and competing states, such common norms will never be accepted. To base the survival of the human race on such a utopia is to take an enormous risk. This is playing Russian roulette with the physical existence of humanity.

The thesis that the nuclear destruction of humanity can only be definitely avoided by the establishment of a world socialist federation, democratic and pluralist, in which the freely associated producers effectively control all the factories and laboratories, in no way implies that nuclear world war is already inevitable. Such an idea, which would make any struggle for Socialism, indeed any political and social activity, pointless, has often been attributed to revolutionary Marxists, either as a result of ignorance or manifest bad faith.[11] What we say, however, is something completely different.

In our view, at this stage in history, we are engaged in a race between, on the one hand, the degeneration of bourgeois society and return to barbarism and, on the other hand, the advance of the working masses towards the construction of a socialist world. In this context, we demand and applaud concrete steps towards nuclear disarmament. In this race, victory is possible. This struggle is far less utopian than the idea that humanity will preserve itself from nuclear catastrophe while retaining a regime of aggressive competition based on private property and all the struggles that this engenders, on a planet bristling with more and more nuclear installations controlled by states that are in fierce competition with each other.

The Soviet bureaucracy cannot accept this Marxist thesis, so well-founded on the lessons of history, if not on the most elementary good sense. The obstacle is not a logical or intellectual one. Gorbachev is clearly not lacking in intelligence. The obstacle is the priority of material interests over purely rational argument in determining the behaviour of social groups. The attachment of the Soviet bureaucracy to the theory of 'peaceful coexistence' is a function of those material interests. Any decisive breakthrough in the world revolution, the taking of power and the democratic exercise of power by the workers in any imperialist country, would automatically stimulate a massive political reawakening of the Soviet proletariat. It would signify the end of the power and privilege of the Soviet bureaucracy. That is why the bureaucracy is interested in maintaining the *status quo* in the major countries of the world. This was the policy of Gorbachev's predecessors. It remains Gorbachev's policy.

This does not exclude periodic attempts to change the international relation of forces in its favour whenever the bureaucracy estimates that this can be done without too great a risk. This was particularly the case after the victory of the Indochinese revolution, when America suffered from its 'Vietnamese syndrome'. This, however, didn't last very long – long enough, however, for the Soviet Union to become involved in its senseless adventure in Afghanistan. Nevertheless, this does not undermine the fundamental orientation of 'peaceful coexistence'.

Our basic criticism of this orientation has nothing to do with any inevitability of nuclear war, or with any demand that the Soviet Union should launch 'revolutionary wars' or export revolution.[12] Those who criticize revolutionary Marxists in this sense, in reality share with the sycophants of the Kremlin, the campists, and the theoreticians of exterminism an unrealistic and serious underestimation of the autonomy of the revolutionary process.[13]

This process results from contradictions internal to the countries themselves. They are not provoked or organized by Moscow or by some conductor of the orchestra of subversion. A conspiracy view of history is contrary not only to Marxism but to the whole of scientific methodology in the social-historical sciences. The same applies to the revolutionary process in the post-capitalist bureaucratized societies, for instance the workers' revolt in East Germany in 1953, the Hungarian revolution of 1956, the Prague spring of 1968–69, and the rise of Solidarity in Poland in 1980–81.

Our opposition to peaceful coexistence as a strategy is an expression of a rejection of campism, of any attempt to reduce the social–political struggle on a world scale to a simple East–West confrontation. It is based on the right and duty of the workers of every country to defend their class interests and to struggle for power whenever they so wish and when conditions make this possible, quite independently of any so-called 'negative consequences' or 'risks' which this might entail for relations between the great powers.

In fact, the history of the twentieth century confirms that every victorious revolutionary struggle of the workers of any country has improved the conditions for emancipation at the international level and has by no means led to 'negative consequences', even where they have provoked a furious response on the part of imperialism, including military intervention. Not one such revolutionary victory has provoked a world war. On the contrary, it was the strangulation of potentially victorious revolutions which directly paved the way for world war. This was the case with the German and Austrian revolutions of 1918–19 as well as the Spanish and French revolutions of 1936.

What we criticize in the international behaviour of the Soviet bureaucracy is not their failure to intervene militarily in support of revolutions elsewhere. What we demand above all is that they should not be a *political* hindrance to the organic unfolding of the revolution in those countries, that they should not *subordinate* the workers movement of those countries to the diplomatic manoeuvres of the Kremlin, camouflaged with such phrases as 'the interests of the USSR, bastion of the world proletariat', or 'the Socialist camp, the chief conquest of the world proletariat'.

It is essential to underline that *every* conception of 'Socialism in one country', in other words, every conception of 'national Communist messianism', which sees in the 'Communist' power of any particular country the main, if not the only, 'bastion' of the world revolution, leads to disastrous consequences. An example of this was the rise of the powerful mass movement in Bangladesh, which was on the way to establishing the independence of that country from Pakistan. The Chinese government, which saw the military dictatorship in Pakistan as an ally against India, called on the Maoists of East Bengal to oppose 'secession', in other words, to act as counter-revolutionaries.

The strategic line of peaceful coexistence has to be rejected because of its counter-revolutionary implications for any country in the midst of struggles rising out of explosive social crises. The degree of material or political aid which the Soviet Union gives or should give to revolutionary movements either still in struggle or in the aftermath of victory, is another matter. This is no substitute for the more general right of the workers in every country to defend their interests and to make their revolutions without subordinating themselves to the interests of any state whatsoever.

Gorbachev's strategic orientation of peaceful coexistence represents a new and significant shift away from the bureaucracy's highly pragmatized version of the so-called 'doctrine of Marxism–Leninism'. A comparison of the Khrushchev programme of 1961 and the programme adopted at the 27th Congress demonstrates this very clearly. In place of the classical Marxist conception, shared by Lenin and the Communist International during the early period, of a world revolutionary process fundamentally determined by the internal contradictions of the capitalist mode of production, of imperialism, and of bourgeois society, the 1961 Congress had put forward the idea of 'peaceful competition between the two systems'. The perspective of proletarian Socialist revolution in the main capitalist countries was dropped.

But Khrushchev still proclaimed that capitalism would be 'buried' in this competitive struggle. The perspective of a world victory for Communism was based on a campist extension of the utopia of Socialism in one country. Production per head of population in the Soviet Union would exceed that of the United States, which would lead more or less automatically to the people of the West turning to Socialism, in a peaceful, electoral, non-revolutionary manner. The Soviet Union, said Khrushchev, would have achieved this goal by 1985. The date came, and went. The Gorbachev team no longer speak of burying capitalism, not even by means of peaceful economic competition. As we have indicated earlier, the new programme doesn't even mention the disappearance of capitalism.[14]

To give the semblance of an ideological basis to this massive theoretical capitulation, the Gorbachev team has invented a new concept, that of the 'globalization' of political solutions to the key problems facing humanity. In his report to the 27th Congress, Gorbachev stated:

The course of history, of social progress, requires ever more insistently that there should be constructive and creative interaction between states and peoples on the scale of the entire world. Not only does it so require, but is also creates the requisite political, social, and material premises for it.

Such interaction is essential in order to prevent nuclear catastrophe, in order that civilization can surive. It is essential in order that worldwide problems that are growing more acute should also be resolved jointly in the interests of all concerned. The prevailing dialectics of present-day development consists in a combination of competition and confrontation between the two systems and in a growing tendency towards interdependence of the countries of the world community. This is precisely the way, through the struggle of opposites, through arduous effort, groping in the dark to some extent, as it were, that the controversial but interdependent and in many ways integral world is taking shape.[15]

We find this idea again in his book *Perestroika*:

And we have not only read anew the reality of a multi-coloured and multi-dimensional world. We have assessed not only the difference in the interests of individual states. We have seen the main issue – the growing tendency towards interdependence of the states of the world community. Such are the dialectics of present-day development.[16]

The formula is a vague one, the thinking is very confused and the expressions are somewhat contorted. Various interpretations are possible. This piece of apparently dialectical thought contains quite a number of sophisms. There will undoubtedly be attempts to reconcile this with 'orthodoxy' on the question of class struggle. The invention of the formula of 'globalism' has been attributed to Anatoly Dobrynin, one-time ambassador to Washington, presently in charge of the international department of the Central Committee and one of the principal political advisers to Gorbachev.[17] Other important advisers lay stress on the 'restructuring', perestroika, of international relations.

Two recent publications have attempted to spell out what is meant by this. The widely circulated *Politicheskoe Samoobrazovanie* (which means 'political self-education') published in its third issue of 1987 an article with the title 'The Creative Character of the Marxist–Leninist Theory of Revolution'. The author, I. Plimok, states that:

Something else which is new, from the point of view of principles, is the thesis concerning the global unity of the world at its present stage of development. Marx thought of associated humanity only from the communist perspective. But the 'globalization' of forms of struggle at the end of the twentieth century, as well as the appearance of global problems, has led collective Marxist thought to the conclusion that although the world that is being gradually constituted is a contradictory world, it is, from many points of view, globally united and mutually interdependent.[18]

The 'mutual dependence' of Kremlin 'Socialism' and American capitalism has been elevated to the level of a thesis of 'Marxism': poor Marx would turn in his grave. This is obviously an attempt to rationalize, on the ideological level, the relation of mutual dependence between the American grain surplus and the Soviet Union's grain shortage.

A more important person than Plimok, namely, Georgy Arbatov, director of the Institute of American and Canadian Studies at the Academy of Sciences and one of Gorbachev's principal advisers, published an article in the party's theoretical review, *Kommunist*, entitled 'Militarism and Contemporary Society'. This article attempts to find the theoretical foundation for the concept of 'globalization' in the nuclear threat. After some ritual references to Lenin and some pertinent comments on the continuing threat of nuclear war, Arbatov performs a veritable *salto mortale* (*Kommunist*, no. 2, 1987):

> As in times past, militarism today is produced and reproduced by capitalism; it is a function of class at the international level as well as within capitalist society itself. But that doesn't exhaust the question. The elementary equation: 'capitalism equals militarism' doesn't enable us to advance a single step in the direction of finding effective ways of combating militarism.

The rupture with logic, both formal and dialectical, is obvious. The elementary equation: 'capitalism equals militarism' could just as easily lead to the conclusion: every effective struggle against capitalism, every real weakening of capitalism (not to speak of its overthrow) is, at the same time, a weakening of militarism. Is this true or not? One would have to examine the question in the light of historical experience. The academician continues:

> because it would follow that one couldn't abolish militarism and the danger of war until after the world victory of socialism. Such a view would condemn us to passivity in the struggle against militarism and hide the differences and contradictions within the dominant bourgeoisie.

The first part of this argument is a gross sophism. The view that the danger of war could only be *definitively* abolished with the victory of world Socialism, far from condemning us to passivity, would encourage us to redouble our efforts against both capitalism and against the dangers of war. In organizing concrete mass actions against the threat of war – for example, the preparation of a general strike in Britain in 1920 against the threat of British intervention against the Soviet Union – the labour movement was able to *combine* its struggle against capitalism, its struggle against war, and its Socialist convictions. In what way does this lead to passivity? What lies behind such a sophism is the bureaucracy's fear of mass action.

Arbatov's *real* motivation, as a representative of the Gorbachev team, is revealed in the second part of the quotation. *The exploitation of interimperialist contradictions takes the place of anti-capitalist class struggle as a means of resolving the key conflicts of our epoch.*

Hence the perilous jumps and hence the conclusion of Arbatov's fast-moving argument. The imperialist bourgeoisie as a whole is just as interested as the working class in maintaining peace and abolishing militarism. Only a small minority attached to the 'military industrial complex' profits from militarism.[19] Capitalism could survive without militarism. The two systems could collaborate in an increasing number of areas. The whole argument culminates in two sentences, the clarity of which leaves nothing to be desired:

> We would like to see the United States as a partner, in spite of all the differences which continue to exist and in spite of all the things which we don't like in that country and in that society. We don't need the USA as an enemy.

> Not to make points in the propaganda battle, not to conquer the other party in the arena, but to resolve by agreement the tasks which history has placed before us – that is how the situation is seen in Moscow.

Gorbachev, in *Perestroika*, echoes the same idea:

> My mission is, as I see it, not only to get across an understanding of our policy and our vision of the world, but to understand and appreciate more fully the American frame of mind, to learn better what the American problems are, and, in particular, the specific political process in the US. One cannot do otherwise. A scientific policy must be built on a strict assessment of reality. It is impossible to move towards more harmonious relations between the US and the USSR while being mesmerized by ideological myths.
>
> We do not communicate enough with one another, we don't understand one another well enough.[20]

The relations between imperialism and the Soviet Union are reduced to a problem of 'communication'. This is contrary not only to Marxism but to elementary socio-political science.

The whole lack of realism in reformism – and peaceful coexistence is merely another version – is evident in these formulations. The contradictions inherent in capitalism; the crises which flow from these contradictions; the laws of economic development which sustain militarism; the refusal of the dominant class to abdicate peacefully when faced with the attempts by the masses to overthrow it; the defence which this class makes of its private property and its enormous material resources – all of those are forgotten in view of the 'common interest' in avoiding nuclear war! And what about regional and local wars? They have gone on practically without interruption since 1945, in spite of the ever increasing stock of nuclear weapons. And what of civil wars? Of counter-revolutionary interventions against revolutions that have been victorious, such as we see in Nicaragua?

There is nothing surprising, of course, in the fact that the Soviet bureaucracy would prefer to see the economic crisis disappear as quickly as possible, rather than seeing it as an opportunity to educate the workers of the world in an anti-capitalist spirit.[21] It also comes as no surprise when we see adherents of a more dogmatic form of this 'Marxism–Leninism', such as Otto Reinhold, ideological chief in the SED, the East German Communist Party, expressing the view in *Die Zeit* (20 November 1987) that:

> It is perfectly natural for us that a series of questions are raised, for instance the question: what is the relation between our theory of imperialism and the affirmation that [the United States] is capable of adhering to peace? Does this imply that imperialism and the monopolies do not have an expansionist tendency?

Some SED theoreticians are going even further than their Soviet colleagues. For instance, Rolf Reissig, director of the Institute for Scientific Communism under the Central Committee of the SED has written that 'it is possible to have a capitalism oriented towards peaceful co-existence and competition between systems'. He has also written: 'While the military industrial complex is in conformity with monopoly capitalism, it is not under all circumstances necessary to this system' (*Tages Anzeiger Magazin* 10, Zürich 1988). In the SED's official theoretical magazine, *Einheit* (no. 2, 1988), the same Rolf Reissig wrote unabashedly that broad (!) strata of monopoly capitalism are interested in advancing the 'scientific technical revolution' outside of the military sphere and avoiding 'the waste of enormous resources for arms'. Because of East Germany's position as 'border guard of the camp' a whole generation of cadres has been educated in the idea of 'the revanchist aggressiveness of monopoly capital'. We can bet that there these ideas will provoke a general turmoil and deep political and ideological disarray. This picture should be completed by indicating that in place of the 'non-capitalist road of development' that Khrushchev projected for the main countries of the third world, the Gorbachevites write openly that, with a few minor exceptions (Angola, Mozambique, South Yemen and Ethiopia; Nicaragua, El Salvador and Guatemala are absent from the list) the development of the third world is, and will remain, capitalist for a long period, and that the USSR and the national liberation movements have to work within this framework. Deng Xiao Ping goes even futher, stating that socialism would be a hindrance in the third world.

The general meaning of all these theoretical revisions is that the Kremlin is engaged in negotiating a broad agreement with imperialism. Its objective is to establish a pattern of 'advanced peaceful co-existence', which involves its making manifold political concessions in exchange for economic advantages. The third world liberation movements and the unfolding revolutions in many key areas of Latin America, Africa and

Asia risk being left to pay the bill for this search for a global accord. To understand the reasons for this project, the starting point cannot be an idea that Gorbachev is taking his inspiration from a 'revisionist' ideology, or the ridiculous theory that the Soviet leader is trying to reintroduce capitalism into the Soviet Union. As under Stalin, Khrushchev and Brezhnev, the bureaucracy is operating essentially pragmatically, trying to resolve immediate problems in accordance with its own material and social interests. Doctrine and ideology are adapted to suit the need of *realpolitik*, rather than the *realpolitik* flowing from revisions of doctrine. Gorbachev's fundamental motivation, which is shared by most of the other tendencies or currents of opinion in the top echelons of every section of the Soviet bureaucracy, is that it is a matter of urgency to overcome the stagnation and dysfunctioning of the Soviet economy. A radical reduction in the senseless waste of material and human resources is urgent. Gorbachev, his main economic adviser, Abel Aganbegyan, and his main ideologues never stop repeating that if *perestroika* – understood in this way – is not put into practice, the USSR will become little more than a second-rate power, and will fall technologically and militarily so far behind the imperialists that it will not be able to catch up. Therefore the detente policy followed by Gorbachev has a twofold objective corresponding to this motivation.

The first aim is to reduce the cost of the arms race, which has become unbearable for the USSR. Parity in military spending between the USA and the USSR means a double burden for the USSR as compared with that of the US. Because its national income is only half that of the US, an equivalent military expenditure would represent 14 to 15 per cent of Soviet national income compared to 7.5 per cent for the US. Above all, the USSR wants to avoid the financial costs of a further militarization of space. This means neither disarming the USSR in the face of imperialism, nor dismantling the Soviet armed forces. Rather, the goal is to modernize as cheaply as possible by gradually de-emphasizing nuclear spending and by maintaining technological parity with imperialism in the area of conventional arms (or rather, regaining parity, because the Soviet Union seems to be already seriously behind in this area).

The second aim is to dismantle the trade and technological blockade that American imperialism imposed on the Soviet Union after its intervention into Afghanistan – if not since the beginning of the cold war – and to obtain large-scale credits from the imperialist countries for the modernization of the Soviet Union. Stalin sought in vain to get such credits at the end of the Second World War. The fact that Washington refused them at a time when the Soviet economy was very weak was undoubtedly one of the reasons for the 'structural assimilation' of Eastern Europe by the Soviet bureaucracy, and the division of Europe into two camps. This was scarcely something that Stalin decided after the victory of Stalingrad, as apologists for the cold war wrongly suppose. The amount of credit sought is very considerable, in line with the need of overcoming the Soviet Union's present technological backwardness. Stalin hoped for $5 billion from Roosevelt-Truman. Gorbachev is probably looking for ten times that amount from Reagan's successors, even if this is spread over a number of years (obviously the 1989 dollar is worth much less than the 1945 one). We should remember that West Germany just granted two billion dollars' worth of credit to the USSR. Joint ventures with imperialist multinationals are already quite advanced. According to a report in the British *Sunday Times* (3 July 1988), the modernization of the Soviet telephone system will involve spending of more than £1,000 million, twenty to thirty per cent of which will go to the British group GEC-Plessey. A large part of this spending will be financed by Western credits. So the objective cited above does not seem entirely fanciful.

The search for an overall accord with imperialism inevitably involves close collaboration between Washington and Moscow to settle what are commonly called 'regional conflicts'. Today, this concerns above all Central America, southern Africa (Namibia, Angola, South Africa), north-west Africa (Ethiopia/Eritrea), the Middle East (the territories occupied by the Israeli state, Lebabon, the Iran/Iraq war and its repercussions in the Persian Gulf), Afghanistan and Kampuchea. The concept of regional conflict is ambiguous, if not obfuscating. It haphazardly throws together phenomena as different as genuine people's revolutions with a permanent revolution dynamic (Central America); independent, stormy mass movements against national and social oppression (South Africa, Palestine); civil wars between petty-bourgeois nationalist governments and pro-imperialist reactionary forces (Angola, Mozambique); resistance to national oppression led by progressive petty-bourgeois forces (Eritrea) or politically retrograde forces (Afghanistan); wars between bourgeois states (Iran/Iraq) and so on. Moreover, this is not an exhaustive list of all the different phenomena in question.

So it is not possible either to make a peremptory and sweeping judgement about the Kremlin's gradual disengagement from these regional conflicts, nor to approve or disapprove of it en bloc without making any distinctions. We support the withdrawal of Soviet troops from Afghanistan and the withdrawal of Vietnamese troops from Kampuchea, for reasons that the Fourth International has explained for a long time. We do not challenge the negative consequences of this withdrawal from the point of view of the working class, but we are convinced that prolonging the presence of these troops would have even more negative effects than the withdrawal itself. Gorbachev has decided on this solution for Afghanistan not only to reduce the costs of a military operation that has no hopes of success, not only to make negotiations with Washington and Beijing easier, but above all undoubtedly because the Afghanistan war has become increasingly unpopular in the Soviet Union itself. A recent opinion poll there showed that fifty-seven per cent of the population supported the withdrawal of troops. The same applies to the occupation of Kampuchea by Vietnamese troops, which represents an unbearable political and economic burden for a society on the verge of famine and a government facing a growing crisis of authority among the masses. It seems certain that Moscow is exercising increasingly open pressure on Hanoi from this point of view. Moscow's change in attitude towards the civil war tearing north-west Africa apart is of a similar scope, even if it does not concern a conflict identical to those in Afghanistan and Kampuchea. The behaviour of the Mengistu regime in relation to oppressed nationalities, above all the Eritreans, is indefensible from any point of view, whether from Leninist principles or humanitarian concerns. Advancing the idea that safeguarding Ethiopian national unity takes priority over the fight against famine, cold-bloodedly running the risk of millions of people dying rather than allowing supplies to get through to the rebels, means acting like a bloodthirsty despot, not like a proletarian revolutionary or an anti-imperialist. If you compare this attitude with the one that Lenin took at the height of the civil war in Russia to the 'Nansen mission's' fight against famine, it becomes clear what a vast difference there is between a real communist and a narrow-minded nationalist like Mengistu. Again, in this case, the Kremlin's disengagement seems necessary and justified even from the standpoint of proletarian internationalism, if the aim is not simply to reduce the Soviet Union's unproductive military spending.

The Iran/Iraq war and the Gulf conflict is complicated, but the immediate and unconditional ending of this senseless, fratricidal war is manifestly in the interest of both the Iraqi and Iranian masses, and in the interests of both the Arab revolution and the Iranian revolution. If the Soviet Union throws its weight into the ring with this aim, in particular by stopping its supply of arms to both belligerents and putting pressure on the countries of Eastern Europe to do the same, we could only approve. (For the time being, the Soviet Union is directly or indirectly the main source of arms for Iraq.)

The case of the territories occupied by Israel is quite clear. For a long time, the Kremlin's aim has been to get the Zionist state to make some minor concessions to Syria and to the PLO in exchange for a definitive recognition of Israel by the Arab world, including the PLO. To achieve this end – which for the moment is unrealizable, in view of the Zionist establishment's resistance to making the slightest concession of this sort – Moscow has been putting forward the idea of an international conference including the Soviet Union. In this way, it hopes for nothing more than to recover some political influence in the region. However, the insurrection of the Palestinian masses is giving this policy of open collaboration with the imperialists in the Middle East a severe buffeting. Gorbachev, who is even more pragmatic than Khrushchev or Brezhnev, will therefore hesitate before committing himself fully to this course. He will wait to see how the events unfold.

On the other hand, a 'peaceful solution' of the conflicts in southern Africa and Central America has unquestionable counter-revolutionary implications. Through their merciless economic blockade and the military aggression they support, the imperialists have the Nicaraguan revolution by the throat. The Salvadorean and Guatemalan revolutions are facing massacres perpetrated by the local agents of imperialism. The internationalist duty to aid this revolution is clear. The argument that this is too expensive for the Soviet Union is hypocritical and dishonest, if you compare the amount of aid given to Nicaragua with what the Soviet Union gives to bourgeois governments in the third world. So the mounting pressure on the Sandinistas today – which will be put on Cuba in the future – to seek an accommodation with Washington reflects a definite political choice. It means that Gorbachev is giving priority to an overall detente agreement, rather than to the strategic advances that the bureaucracy could gain from an alliance with revolutions that are already victorious or that could be in the not-too-distant future. The clear signal that Washington is sending is: Drop any idea of extending the revolution in Latin America, or there is not going to be any lasting detente. If Dukakis becomes Reagan's successor, this is not going to change much. In response, Gorbachev has been sending more and more signals to the effect of 'Message received and understood'.

In Angola the original scheme for a compromise agreement that would couple withdrawal of Cuban and South African troops has been seriously put in question again by the fact that Pretoria seems to be moving towards an additional demand – inclusion of its stooges in the counter-revolutionary tribalist organization, UNITA, in the Luanda government. The Soviet government is actively trying to overcome the resistance of Fidel Castro and of part of the MPLA leadership to this proposal.

The southern African affair is more serious.The Nicaraguan and Salvadorean revolutions are besieged fortresses. But in Nicaragua, as weak and small as it is facing the imperialist giant, the revolution is armed and holds state power. These are not inconsiderable advantages. In El Salvador, while the revolutionists facing a bloodthirsty and merciless enemy, do not hold power, they are at least armed. But the oppressed black masses of South Africa do not have these advantages. They are not armed. They do not have a scrap of political power. But the impressive trade union self-organization that led to the success of the general strike of 6–8 June 1988 shows a very promising potential for struggle. Pressure from the Kremlin for a deal with the liberal wing of the South African bourgeoisie, the agent of imperialism in the country, could be a real stab in the back to a young and enthusiastic workers' movement if it won the trade union leaderships, in return for political concessions, to accepting the maintenance of capitalist super-exploitation through imposing self-limitation on workers' struggle.

However, in both cases – Central America and southern Africa – Washington and Moscow are not the only players. They cannot impose a counter-revolutionary 'normalization' that would maintain imperialist domination of these two regions through local agents. The autonomy from Washington of the local possessing classes in Central America is very marginal. The relative autonomy of the supporters of apartheid is much greater, but it still has its limits. On the other hand, the real autonomy from the Kremlin of the Nicaraguan and Salvadorean revolutionists, to say nothing of the South African mass organizations, would make it much harder for Gorbachev to carry through a capitulationist turn. The outcome of a 'global deal' will depend in the last analysis on the capacity of these organizations to maintain and increase their autonomy from all those social forces (including the international social democracy) that advise them to make rotten compromises and put pressure on them for that.

On the basis of all these data, can we conclude that Gorbachev's foreign policy represents fundamentally a right turn in comparison with previous Soviet foreign policy? Is his foreign policy as a whole negative? We should guard against over simplifications. Like his domestic and economic policy, the course that Gorbachev is following is made up of contradictory elements. To understand the reasons for these contradictions, it is sufficient to remember that Gorbachev is operating *from a position of weakness on two fronts.* He is coming under growing pressure both from imperialism and from the Soviet masses (or, if you prefer, from the mounting social crisis in the Soviet Union which is being at least partially aggravated by the beginnings of independent activity and consciousness among the workers.) Once you understand that, the elements of the puzzle that emerge successively in a disparate way become comprehensible. To this can be addded the no less contradictory evolution in the third world, where the liberation movement overall is on the defensive but retains a capacity for fighting back and above all an autonomy that are still remarkable.

In these conditions, condemning everything that is taking place in the Soviet Union as 'rightist' or even counter-revolutionary is indefensible. If Gorbachev is on the right, were Brezhnev, or even Stalin, on the left? If everything that Gorbachev is doing has to be seen as consistent 'treachery', are the rehabilitation of the Moscow trials defendants, or the de facto toleration of strikes then 'rightist', in comparison with the repression of Stalin and Brezhnev? What of his condemnation of the Hitler-Stalin Pact and of its implications for the Polish and German workers' movement, his implicit condemnation of the military intervention in Hungary and Czechoslovakia? But, on the other hand, an overall 'yes, yes', or even a 'yes, but', are likewise inadmissable from the standpoint of the interests of the Soviet and world working class. We cannot approve of economic measures that lead to the re-emergence of unemployment and a decline in real wages, or of rotten compromises at the expense of the Central American and South African revolutions. The only valid judgement then is a nuanced one, case by case, problem by problem, as I have formulated it throughout this chapter. Too bad for the over-simplifiers. They will be proven wrong by the events, as they were in the past and as they are today by what is happening in the Soviet Union and in the world.

# 10

# The 'Socialist Camp', the Communist Parties and the Social Democracy

Perestroika and, in particular, glasnost, took the pro-Moscow Communist Parties by surprise. For decades – ever since the crisis provoked by the 20th Congress and destalinization had been partly surmounted – they had been repeating the same line: everything is as it should be in the Soviet Union. But who could say that now? Even worse – Gorbachev and his team have put the blame for the profound problems and mistakes on the top leadership of the party and state. The lethargy of the Brezhnev ruling group was at the root of it all. Gorbachev and the more radical elements of his supporters denounce all those, whether at the top or bottom of the hierarchy, who are still inclined to defend the status quo. Can one still go on maintaining the myth that the party, the Leninist Central Committee, or the secretary general were always right? The 20th Congress made this thesis untenable, what with the terrible crimes that had been committed over a quarter of a century. Now we have a second explosion after two decades of lethargy have led to stagnation. But what a balance-sheet for a party that was 'always right'! Now it is admitted that for almost half a century – it was wrong!

The chief ideologist, Ligachev, tries in vain to limit the damage to the prestige of the party and to its leaders. One shouldn't, he says, 'excessively denigrate' the past. One must recognize the merits of the veterans of the Second World War and those who 'constructed Socialism' during the thirties. The conservatives who defend the heritage of Stalin, or even want to rehabilitate Stalin himself, hide behind this kind of argument.

The East European Communist Parties were taken even more by surprise than the pro-Moscow Communist Parties in the capitalist countries. The latter at least have the consolation that the Soviet Union is becoming a little more attractive for a certain number of workers and

*135*

intellectuals in the West. For the parties of Eastern Europe, however, Gorbachev is a double threat. Their own legitimacy is undermined at the same time as the social and economic crisis in these countries, a crisis which existed before Gorbachev came to power, continues to get worse.

One should not exaggerate the scale of the Gorbachev effect on the popular masses of Eastern Europe. The view of the Soviet Union as a foreign force, as a force of national oppression, has not disappeared. The (red) tzar remains a tzar, even if he has become liberal. Hostility to Communism is still prevalent (though less so in Czechoslovakia and in East Germany than in the other countries), even if this Communism begins to show a 'human face' (much less human, we must add, than that of the Prague Spring).

Nonetheless, among certain layers of the working class, who have learned from their experience over the past two decades, the words and actions of Gorbachev are being used to force concessions from the local bureaucracy. For instance, the residents of Prague acclaimed Gorbachev when he visited Czechoslovakia.[1] Youth in East Germany shouted 'Gorbachev, Gorbachev' when they demonstrated for the right to hold a pop concert in East Berlin.[2] Gorbachev's visit to Bucharest met with a quieter response from a population still traumatized by terrible economic conditions and harsh political repression.[3] The gerontocracy that rules Eastern Europe at the moment resent the fact that this upstart in Moscow makes it more difficult for them to control the popular movements. Zhivkov, Kadar, and Honecker are seventy-five and Husak was seventy-four when he resigned a short while ago. They resent, but they are unable to rebel. For this upstart represents the Kremlin, and the Kremlin remains the ultimate source of their power. There is also little they can do by way of intrigue in Moscow to moderate the line of the new boss or replace him.

The effect of Gorbachev in Eastern Europe is to amplify the movement which had already begun before he came to power. The slow rebirth of public opinion had already begun in Hungary, Czechoslovakia, and especially in East Germany. In Poland, a similar phenomenon preceded the explosion of Solidarity and it hasn't completely disappeared, in spite of the decline in the mass movement after the Jaruzelski coup. In Yugoslavia this process has been going on now for at least twenty years, and on a much larger scale than in the Soviet Union itself.

This rise in public awareness has reached the threshold of political activity, at least in East Germany, not to speak of Poland and Yugoslavia. We can see this in the case of writers and artists, in the ecology movement, and especially in the independent peace movement.[4] In Czechoslovakia there was an independent and spontaneous demonstration of young people even before the effects of Gorbachev were noticeable.[5]

There is a song by the Czech pop group The Plastic People, banned in Prague, which admirably sums up the political clarity attained by this new youth opposition in Czechoslovakia:

> They fear the old for their memories
> they fear the young for their innocence
> they fear the school pupils
> they fear the dead and their funerals
> they fear the graves and the flowers
> they fear the churches, the priests, and the nuns
> they fear the workers
> they fear the members of the party
> they fear those who are not in the party
> they fear science
> they fear art
> they fear records and tapes
> they fear plays and films
> they fear writers and poets
> they fear journalists
> they fear actors
> they fear painters and sculptors
> they fear musicians and singers
> they fear radio stations
> they fear the TV satellites
> they fear the free flow of information
> they fear foreign literature and journals
> they fear technological progress
> they fear printers, duplicators, and photocopiers
> they fear typewriters
> they fear phototelegraphy and telex
> they fear direct dialling abroad
> they fear letters
> they fear the telephone
> they fear letting people out
> they fear letting people in
> they fear the left
> they fear the right
> they fear the departure of Soviet troops
> they fear changes in the clique that rule in Moscow
> they fear detente
> they fear disarmament
> they fear treaties which they have signed
> they fear their own police
> they fear for their own spies

they fear spies
they fear chess
they fear tennis
they fear hockey
they fear women gymnasts
they fear St Wenceslas
they fear Jan Hus
they fear all the saints
they fear Christmas gifts
they fear St Nicholas
they fear the rucksacks before the statue of Lenin
they fear the archives
they fear the historians
they fear the economists
they fear the sociologists
they fear the philosophers
they fear the physicists
they fear the doctors
they fear the political prisoners
they fear the families of the prisoners
they fear the evening
they fear the morning
they fear each day
they fear the future
they fear old age
they fear heart attacks and cirrhosis of the liver
they fear the little conscience they have left
they fear being in the street
they fear being in their privileged ghetto
they fear their own families
they fear their relations
they fear their old friends and comrades
they fear each other
they fear what they have said
they fear what they have written
they fear losing their positions
they fear fire and water
they fear wet and dry
they fear snow
they fear wind
they fear the heat and the cold
they fear quietness and noise
they fear light and the shade
they fear joy and sadness
they fear jokes
they fear those who are right
they fear those who are honest

they fear those who are educated
they fear those who have talent
they fear Marx
they fear Lenin
they fear our dead presidents
they fear the truth
they fear freedom
they fear democracy
they fear the charter of human rights
they fear socialism
then why, in god's name, do we fear them?

Leaving to one side the aspect of paranoia in Stalinism, which, given what we know today, cannot be denied, there is a real material basis for this generalized fear, which is nothing other than the fear of losing power. This results from the origins of their power. Except in the case of Yugoslavia, they were not placed in power by a popular revolution but by the military–bureaucratic intervention of the Kremlin.[6] The framework within which the 'Gorbachev effect' operates is historically conditioned by this illegitimacy of the power of the different bureaucracies of Eastern Europe.

This illegitimacy and the constraint imposed by this historical framework are further reinforced by the practical effects of the Brezhnev doctrine of 'limited sovereignty',[7] the military interventions in Germany (1953), Hungary (1956), and Czechoslovakia (1968); by the presence of Soviet troops in most of these countries; by the bonds of diplomatic, commercial, and economic dependence which have been progressively tightened.

Of course, the Soviet bureaucracy are paying an increasing political and military price for their resolution to preserve this strategic glacis acquired as a result of the Second World War. The forces which they maintain in these countries, which act essentially as an 'internal police', are quite expensive.[8] The Soviets cannot rely on the loyalty of the local troops. The social and political tensions existing in these countries also threaten to have repercussions in the Soviet Union itself. The attraction of capitalist Western Europe in the East, especially in East Germany, is a constant source of aggravation in Moscow which affects Gorbachev too.[9] That is why perestroika also logically implies a restructuring of relations with 'people's democracies'.

But how far could they go in this restructuring? Gorbachev has spoken of the Prague Spring with a certain amount of sympathy. There are certainly quite a few common elements in his platform and in that which Dubček proposed at the beginning of 1968. On 4 November 1987, G. Smirnov, director of the Institute of Marxism–Leninism in the Soviet

Union, stated openly that it was necessary to 're-examine' the attitude adopted by Moscow to the Prague Spring (*International Herald Tribune*, 5 November 1987). When the head of the Czechoslovak Party at the same time disappeared from Moscow and didn't appear on the stand during the military parade on 7 November 1987, the rumour began to circulate that Gorbachev would openly condemn the intervention of Warsaw Pact troops in Czechoslovakia in August 1968.

But the real problem is not such an ideological–political revision. The real problem is the eventual revocation of the Brezhnev doctrine, the risk of losing control over a number of East European countries, even over this whole part of the continent. This is something which the majority of the bureaucracy or the military would never forgive. At the present moment, therefore, such a revocation is unlikely.

In view of the obvious concern in Prague, Gorbachev had to clarify where he stood. In Warsaw, he stated that 'any attempt to separate one or other country from the socialist community would signify not only a violation of the will of a nation but a violation of the whole international order established after the war, a violation of peace itself' (*Izvestia*, 1 June 1986). Of course there are ambiguities in this formula. Dubcek had no intention of separating Czechoslovakia from the 'Socialist community'. But would it be possible, in Gorbachev's view, within the framework of this community, for the 'national will' to express itself through a political regime which it had freely chosen, through a system of Socialist democracy based on the acceptance of party plurality?

The countries of Eastern Europe now seem to have a greater latitude in their domestic and foreign policies. At the Stockholm conference on disarmament in Europe, a formula was accepted which opposed measures of constraint within both blocs.[10]

When Jakes replaced Husak in Prague, Gorbachev emphasized the 'unity of views' between the Soviet and Czechoslovak Communist parties. Some days later, the press agency TASS rejected any parallel between perestroika and the Prague Spring. Taking up once again the Czech regime's official version of the Prague Spring, TASS stated that:

> the decisions of the plenum of January 1968 remained a dead letter, to the extent that the opportunist leadership of the right wing of the Czechoslovak Communist Party was unable to elaborate a real programme of action. The policies of Alexander Dubcek would have led to a 'weakening of the Czechoslovak CP' and would have 'prejudiced the foundations of socialism in that country.'[11]

Such a statement remains unproven and is a manifest calumny. Responding to statements of this kind, Alexander Dubček, in an interview with journalists of *Unita*, the paper of the Italian Communist Party, said that at no other time in its history did the Czechoslovak Communist Party enjoy greater support from the majority of the Czechoslovak people than during the period of the Prague Spring. He rejected categorically the suggestion that any so-called anti-Socialist elements could, in any way, have threatened 'Socialist power' in Czechoslovakia. He recalled that at the time of the occupation of Prague by the troops of the Warsaw Pact, these same troops did not occupy the headquarters of the 'right-wing Social Democrats', of the 'church groups' or other right-wing forces, nor did they arrest any elements from those groups. They occupied, however, the headquarters of the party, the unions, and the government, and arrested only Communists.

He described the contents of the Action Programme of April 1968 elaborated by the Central Committee of the Czech Party, a document the very existence of which was denied by TASS, and demanded three things: that the documents of the period be published, especially the Action Programme; that the 468,000 members expelled from the party during the 'normalization' be rehabilitated, that they be readmitted to the party and that they be permitted to practise in their professions;[12] finally, that a regime he installed in which the people had the right to elect and recall their own leaders.[13]

Dubček used a phrase which reminded one of the Gorbachevites and the problem of destalinization in the Soviet Union: 'The memory of a nation is hereditary.' One can see how the way of treating Stalinism and post-Stalinism in Eastern Europe rebounds on glasnost in the Soviet Union itself and undermines its credibility – just as the unfinished destalinization does in the Soviet Union. How can one speak of the 'Leninist demand for truth' while continuing to tell lies about the invasion of Czechoslovakia? How can one re-establish historical truth in the Soviet Union – but not the truth about the Soviet occupation of Czechoslovakia?

And this is true not only for Czechoslovkia. When M. Rakowski, one of the leaders of the Polish Communist Party, visited Moscow, he did an interview for *Moscow News* (24 January 1988) in which he emphasized the importance of the Gorbachev–Jaruzelski accord on 'co-operation in the fields of ideology, science and culture'. This accord says that it is the duty of Soviet and Polish historians to fill in the famous 'blank pages' in their common history. Rakovsky said: 'The Polish press is now publishing documents which, before this accord, would never have seen the light of day.' But will all the 'blank pages' be filled?

Undoubtedly, the truth will be told about Stalin's dissolution of the Polish Communist Party and about the murder of almost its entire leadership. The truth will eventually be told about Katyn and, perhaps, about the Warsaw uprising of 1944. But will they tell the truth about the arrest and deportation of the Social Democratic leaders of the *Armya Krajova*, in spite of the solemn assurances of safe conduct?[14] Will the truth be told about the massive repression of 1946–1947, about the falsification of the results of the election of 1947? Will the truth be told about 1956? About 1968? About Solidarity? About the military coup of Jaruzelski, co-signatory of this accord about filling in the 'blank pages'? Will a debate be allowed in Poland about all those semi-taboo subjects, a debate similar to the one currently taking place in the Soviet Union about Stalinist repression and the Moscow trials?

In addition to Czechoslovakia and Poland, there is also Hungary, 1956–57, East Germany, 1953, the whole history of repression after the Second World war, directed not only against the bourgeoisie but also against the workers throughout Eastern Europe. Glasnost, as a re-conquest of memory and historical truth, will certainly put the relations between the bureaucracies of Eastern Europe and Moscow to the test. And this cannot help but have repercussions in the Soviet Union itself.

The Gorbachev course in the Soviet Union objectively encourages the intelligentsia and some of the cadres and younger members of the Communist Parties in Eastern Europe to demand a similar reforms in their own countries, above all more glasnost, openness. This is already the case in East Germany, where such demands meet with obstruction and rejection from the leadership.[15] However, the practical effects of Soviet perestroika on the economies of the 'people's democracies' will not be sufficient for Moscow's representatives there to regain any kind of popular base of support.[16]

With the exception of the GDR, the countries of Eastern Europe are currently in the middle of a serious economic crisis which is having a severe effect on the living standards of the masses. The crises in these countries is aggravated by their greater degree of integration into and dependence on the international capitalist economy.

The main elements of this crisis are: foreign debts, growing charges on these debts and a growing balance of payments problem in relation to the West and the Soviet Union; increasing, if not galloping inflation; disastrous reductions in the standard of living;[17] a massive waste of resources accompanied by an ecological crisis which is the worst in Europe. The difficulties are increased by the inconvertibility of currencies, in other words, by the sad spectacle that the degree of economic integration in Eastern Europe is inferior to that of capitalist Europe.

The example of Yugoslavia is particularly distressing. As a result of galloping inflation, nourished by a rigorous servicing of the foreign debt imposed by the IMF and the international banks, Yugoslavia has seen its living standards reduced in a draconian manner. Average monthly wages have fallen to £135. And this average covers immense regional variations, for instance, from £215 in Serbia to £70 in Macedonia. Some observers have said that the fall in wages is worse than that which took place at the height of the capitalist crisis of 1938. The rate of unemployment is 18 per cent. There are 1.2 million unemployed, with 480,000 workers forced to seek work abroad.

As many as 7,000 enterprises, employing a workforce of 1.6 million, have been working at a loss for a number of years and, according to the new law on bankruptcy, will have to close down (*Die Zeit*, 11 December 1987). This creates an almost unbearable tension within the Yugoslav economy and society. But all this chaos is not the result of the existence of a 'command economy'. It is rather the result of the recourse to those famous 'market mechanisms', which have led to the dismantling of workers' self-management and have aggravated social inequality and mass poverty.

Under such conditions, Gorbachevism has little chance of finding positive echoes in Yugoslavia. The combination of radical perestroika and advanced glasnost has already been achieved in Yugoslavia. It has provided no solution to the endemic crisis brought about by an unnatural combination of workers' self-management, market economy, opening up to the West, and the maintenance of the monopoly of power in the hands of the bureaucracy.

The general hostility to Communism in the population of Eastern Europe is another factor which will limit Gorbachev's effect. In this matter, however, we should be cautious. The facts at our disposal do not allow us to identify this hostility towards the mechanisms of power with a hostility towards the non-capitalist socio-economic structures. Even in Poland, where the influence of the Church and Catholic doctrine is so powerful, this identification cannot be demonstrated. According to 150 surveys carried out by Polish sociologists between 1956 and 1981, 66 per cent of the people questioned expressed a wish for the world to evolve towards Socialism, whereas only 9 per cent were opposed to this. This percentage hardly changed over twenty-five years.[18] Only 12 per cent supported private ownership in medium-sized trade and industry; more than 70 per cent were opposed. More than 90 per cent opposed private ownership in large-scale industry and trade.

A study carried out by the Catholic University of Lublin six years later showed that, in spite of the decline in the mass movement, almost 80 per cent remained hostile to private ownership of the banks and the large enterprises (*Neue Zürcher Zeitung*, 6 August 1987).

The case of Hungary is the most significant because, apart from Yugoslavia, this was the country that went the farthest in the direction of 'market socialism'. Here, the balance sheet is more than disappointing.

Not only has there been a decline in economic growth similar to if not worse than the Soviet Union, but living standards have declined and a large section of the working class cannot survive without a second job.

Those conflicting developments and centrifugal tendencies in the 'socialist camp' confront Gorbachev with insoluble dilemmas. He cannot consolidate or even maintain his position within the Soviet apparatus if he remains passive in the face of the disintegration of the camp. Military intervention, however, on the model of Czechoslovakia in 1968, is ruled out because such a move would be a mortal blow to glasnost. Neither can he accept, in the long run, the presence of East European leaders who ally themselves, openly or otherwise, with his conservative opponents in the Soviet apparatus. He can have no illusions about the so-called 'reforms' of the Jaruzelski regime, a regime detested by the Polish workers. He knows, at the same time, that a process of genuine democratization in Eastern Europe, once begun, could turn very quickly into an uncontrollable torrent. The ideal solution would be to have leaderships in those countries similar to the Dubček leadership at the time of the Prague Spring, enjoying a real legitimacy in the eyes of the masses. But the crisis in the countries of Eastern Europe is already too advanced and the economic constraints on Gorbachev are too real for such a solution to be even envisaged. Underlying this problem of the reaction between the Soviet Union and the countries of Eastern Europe is the problem of their relation with the imperialist bourgeoisie of Western Europe. For the moment, Gorbachev's priority is a global accord with Washington but he is well aware that a significant section of the American political leadership, in both parties, favours demanding greater concessions from the Soviet Union in return for the desired credits. He is also well aware of the conflicts within the Atlantic alliance and of the relative decline of American hegemony in the capitalist world. Any delay in economic assistance from Washington could tempt Gorbachev to play the 'Europe versus America' card. This would entail a fundamental revision of the Soviet attitude towards the EEC and would have tremendous consequences on the political–ideological level, especially for the East German SED, but also for a number of Western European Communist Parties and for the left in the social democracy (for instance, the Benn/Scargill wing of the British Labour Party).

The economic and practical political consequences of such a turn towards Europe would be even more important. The big prize which the Soviets could hold out in any negotiations with the Western European bourgeoisie, especially with the West Germans, would be the prospect of an economic integration of East and West Germany qualitatively far in advance of what de facto exists today. Such a deal, along with increased trade possibilities for West Germany and the whole of the EEC, could win major economic credits for the Soviets from West Germany and indeed from the EEC as a whole. Such a prospect would be even more attractive for the West Germans in the face of a threatened recession in the West which would seriously undermine not only the economic prosperity of that country but also the relative stability of bourgeois political power in the Federal Republic. Washington is already very worried by the fact that the West German foreign minister, Genscher, adopted a different attitude towards Soviet proposals for conventional disarmament from that of Reagan, Thatcher and Mitterand. A deal with the Soviet Union would be even more attractive for West Germany in the long run in that it would hold out the prospect of some form of eventual reunification of Germany.

Such a shift on the part of the Soviets would have disastrous consequences for the SED in East Germany.[19] The East German bureaucracy, just like the bureaucracies in all the other East European countries, has an interest in a greater openness to the economies of Western Europe. The Hungarians are celebrating the fact that they have just done a deal with the EEC which gives them special privileges in the export of Hungarian goods. The East Germans have had such privileges for a long time, in reality if not in law. The commercial and economic advantages for the East European countries from such deals is one thing; the loss of political power, however, is another. Reunification of Germany could only mean loss of power for the SED, even if this were to take the form of a prolonged period of economic integration which maintained the existing political structures of both Germanies. These are the agonizing choices which could confront the East German if Soviet policy were to go in this direction. What is at stake here is not just the question of the relation between the Soviet Union and the countries of Eastern Europe but the changes in the whole relationship between East and West in the context of 'advanced peaceful co-existence'. What is at stake is the whole system established in Europe at the end of the second world war.

The reunification of Germany is one of the two major cards which Gorbachev holds in reserve in his negotiations with imperialism. The other is the renewal of the Sino-Soviet alliance, not necessarily as a military but as a diplomatic, political and economic alliance.[20]

There are three main obstacles to a Sino-Soviet reconciliation. The first of those, the withdrawal of the nuclear missiles directed against China, is the easiest to resolve. This problem is also linked to an accord on the Sino-Soviet border dispute and the practical, though not theoretical, abandonment of Chinese claims on territories taken from China during the time of the Russian tzars.[21] It seems that progress is being made in resolving this complex of problems.

The second problem, the withdrawal of troops from Afghanistan, is also being resolved. The third obstacle, the presence of Vietnamese troops in Kampuchea, seems a more difficult problem to resolve. Negotiations involving Prince Norodom Sihanouk may help to unblock this situation. The possibility of a summit meeting between Gorbachev and Deng Zhiao Ping has been talked about.

What has brought about a change in the strategy of the Chinese leaders is not, however, the personality, motivations, or orientations of Gorbachev, but rather what the Chinese quite correctly have seen as the rebirth of Japanese militarism. This is an almost inevitable consequence of the spectacular strengthening of Japanese imperialism in the techno-logical, industrial, and financial fields in recent years. The Chinese leaders have historical reasons for apprehension about this revival, although the relation of forces is not quite the same as in 1931 or 1937, and they know that American imperialism, regardless of the competition with Tokyo, will never take the part of People's China against Japan.

The objective basis for China's policy of equidistance from both superpowers is beginning to disappear. The international context in which Mao and his successors determined their attitude towards the USA and the USSR has changed considerably. We are still a long way from a Sino-Soviet alliance, even from a genuine reconciliation. But the pressure to elaborate a new strategy has been evident for quite some time in the ideology and in the language of Beijing.

After the visit of Prime Minister Zhao Ziyang to Eastern Europe, relations with the Communist Parties there, including the party in Yugoslavia, have been normalized. The parties in power in those countries are now referred to as 'fraternal parties' and the countries over which they govern are now described as 'Socialist countries'. It is only a matter of time before the Soviet Union and the Soviet Communist Party will be described in the same manner. The whole language of 'two superpowers', like the fifty million copies of Mao's Little Red Book, has gone up in smoke.

Is this attempt at reconciliation with the Chinese Communist Party part of a larger project of Gorbachev's, namely, to reconstitute the unity of the 'world Communist movement', embracing the Communist Parties in power, the pro-Moscow Communist Parties as well as the Eurocom-munists? It is claimed that Gorbachev intends to organize a major inter-national Communist conference to which all these parties will be invited, as well as some Social Democratic parties.

The Kremlin appears to have made a major concession to the Euro-communists: it has ceased to encourage pro-Moscow dissidents who have created splits in Spain, Britain, Sweden, and Finland, and who are a well-organized faction inside the Italian Communist Party itself.

Moscow's line is now one of reunification. There are today, however, insurmountable obstacles in the way of reconstituting the unity of the 'world Communist movement', especially one centred on Moscow. These obstacles are social–material as well as political–ideological.

The social base of hegemonic Stalinism in the old Communist International was the material dependence of the Communist Parties on the Soviet bureaucracy, the material force of which derived from its possession of power in the Soviet Union. Its ideological basis was its vision of the USSR, principal if not only bastion of the world proletariat, as well as the abandonment of any perspective of world revolution. The successive victories of the Yugoslav, Chinese, Cuban, Vietnamese, and Nicaraguan revolutions have created states which constitute an independent material base for the parties in power in those countries. This material base is more important than ideology or any other link with the Soviet Communist Party.

The Sino-Soviet split has made it possible for a number of Asian Communist Parties to follow their own independent trajectory, to develop their own praxis and to form their own cadres independently of the strategies advocated by Moscow or Beijing. Any attempt by some 'international Communist movement' to re-establish control over those parties, any attempt to make them submit to the interests of the bureaucracy in Moscow or Beijing, will run up against major material and human obstacles.

The emergence of Eurocommunism is a reflection, in the final analysis, of a *social* process of the Social Democratization of the parties concerned, their integration, to an extent qualitatively greater than at any time in the past, into the bourgeois–democratic state and into bourgeois society. This integration expresses itself in a particular practice, formation of cadres, and recruitment similar to those of the classical Social Democratic parties. This is certainly the case with the Italian and British parties, similarly with the Finnish, Swedish, and Belgian parties. The fact that the Spanish Communist Party hasn't gone so far, and that the French Communist Party developed in the opposite direction, doesn't detract from the reality of this process. In view of their social nature and their social function, the Eurocommunist parties will certainly not submit themselves to any kind of international discipline.

Now that the image of the Soviet Union has become less repulsive for the vanguard of the workers and for the left-wing intellectuals than it was during the Brezhnev epoch, future events will provide a test of the validity of this explanation of Eurocommunism. In our view, even with the greatest of efforts on the part of the Gorbachev team, the Eurocommunist parties will not return to the fold. In the case of the Italian Communist Party, the most important of the Eurocommunist parties, the entrance of the Young Communists, the party's youth section, into the youth organization of the Socialist International is a symbol of this whole development.

It is not at all certain that the Gorbachev team will put any great effort into this reunification. Real unity would have to be based on some common strategy. But such a common strategic does not exist. The whole orientation of peaceful coexistence, based on the 'progressive globalization' of problems which are to be resolved by means of co-operation with imperialism, makes the elaboration of any such common project impossible.

'The worldwide decline of the communist movement is a fact of life which requires cognizance. For Soviet foreign policy, and even more for Soviet ideology, the situation has long been an embarrassing encumbrance', writes Dev Murarka, someone close to Gorbachev's advisers.[22]

In fact, from the point of view of the Gorbachev team, this project would be counterproductive. The logic of the strategy of globalization implies a priority of collaboration with non-Communist forces: the peace movement and the Social Democracy in capitalist Europe;[23] the 'moderate' bourgeoisie in Central America; the 'moderate' possessing classes in the Arab world; the Indian bourgeoisie, etc. Any priority accorded the search for a common denominator with the other Communist Parties, including the Eurocommunist parties, which are largely minority groups inside the labour movements of their respective countries, would enter into collision with the medium-term objectives of the Kremlin.

The rapprochement between Gorbachev and the West European social democratic parties is motivated by diplomatic as well as commercial factors; closer agreement on disarmament policy, a growth in East-West exchanges, improvements in detente, and so on. A majority of social-democratic parties from Western Europe were in attendnce at the Moscow conference of Communist Parties held in November 1987. The British Labour Party and the West German SPD were the two main exceptions. Although the SPD didn't attend the conference, it is this party which has made the most pronounced turn in its relations with Eastern Europe. For a long time the SPD was the main pillar of anti-communism and anti-Sovietism in the West European labour movement, as well as the main supporter of NATO. But now the SPD has begun a permanent and institutionalized dialogue with the East German SED which has led to the elaboration of a common statement of principles.[24] Does this mean that the social democratic leaders of Europe have been taken in by the charm of Mikhail Gorbachev? Not at all. In reality, they believe that history is about to confirm the correctness of their rejection of the October revolution, of Bolshevism and of the formation of the Communist International. They believe that the realism which is today apparent in both Moscow and Beijing, a realism which has already triumphed in Belgrade and in the Italian Communist Party, will historically justify the attitude of the Social Democracy at the time of the world crisis of 1917–18: that the socialist revolution and the attempt to construct a society on the 'Marxist model' were both impossible and reprehensible. They see a growing convergence between social-democratic gradualism and Gorbachev's 'globalism'.

The effect of Gorbachev on the international workers' movement and on the anti-imperialist movement is, however, just like his foreign policy, profoundly contradictory. There is no denying the negative effect which the Gorbachevite ideology of class conciliation will have on the international workers' movement. It will strengthen the ideological offensive of the right. But the objective results of Gorbachevism will not be limited to such negative effects. The re-evaluation of the October revolution within the Soviet Union; the weakening of anti-communist attitudes in the West; the increased scope for autonomous workers' initiatives in Western Europe as well as in Japan and Canada; the increased autonomy of the South African COSATU and the Brazilian PT which would result from their refusal to follow the advice of the Kremlin – all of these are positive gains in the interests of the international workers' movement. The contradictory results of Gorbachev's new policy will be most apparent, however, in Eastern Europe. The pressure of progressive public opinion in the Soviet Union, as well as Gorbachev's orientation, will make military intervention by the Soviet Union in Eastern Europe impossible for a whole period. This will open up the possibility for large-scale independent socialist initiatives in that part of Europe. A whole new class dynamic could be opened up for the whole European continent.[25] All conservative forces, above all the imperialists, are afraid of such a perspective. They would consider the presence of Soviet troops in Eastern Europe as a lesser evil in relation to the kind of 'destabilization' that could result from uncontrollable actions by the working class. Gradualists and reformists of all kinds are trapped in the most absurd arguments. Thus a new Prague Spring would be 'dangerous' and a new explosion of Solidarity in Poland would be 'destabilizing' in spite of the impossibility of Soviet intervention. West European Social Democrats have openly expressed concern that things might 'go too far' in Eastern Europe.[26]

But the future of the revolution – the political revolution in Eastern Europe, the social revolution in Western Europe – will not depend on clever calculations, strategic projects or existential fears of groups of politicians or ideologues, whatever power they seem to possess at the moment. It will depend essentially on the depths of the contradictions which are tearing apart those societies. It will depend on whether the masses refuse to support the burden imposed on them by this crisis and on the scale of the mobilization which will result from this refusal. That is why, in spite of the gradualist convergence, in spite of the intentions of Gorbachev, the effects of glasnost on the masses of the Soviet Union, of Eastern Europe and, later, of Western Europe, far from discouraging revolution, objectively promote it.

# 11

# The Dilemmas of Gorbachev

As it becomes clearer what is involved in the Gorbachev reforms, they are running into a series of obstacles which raise serious doubts about their successful implementation. There are no less serious doubts about the nature of the fundamental objective which Gorbachev is pursuing. Is he hiding his real objective from his colleagues, from Soviet and world opinion? Or is it the case that he has no fundamental objective, that he advances pragmatically, modifying his stance in keeping with circumstances?

This is certainly true in the economic sphere. In our opinion, it would be wrong to attribute the difficulties encountered in implementing perestroika, this restructuring of the totality of economic life and management, to simple institutional obstacles – in other words, to the obstruction by intermediate layers of the more conservative bureaucracy, those most caught up in routine and inertia. There is also an intrinsic logic of the Soviet economic system – this system which is a hybrid combination of bureaucratic planning, largely socialized economy, with a survival of market mechanisms in particular areas, all of this under the control of a dominant layer that energetically defends its own privileges. It is this intrinsic logic which has to be replaced by an alternative logic.

What is striking, however, about the mass of reforms introduced by Gorbachev is that they do not appear to change the actual logic of the system as it currently functions, or, more precisely, dysfunctions. To confirm this, it is enough to examine one of the key elements of the reform: the financial autonomy of enterprises.

The directors (or, if one wishes, the 'worker collectives' – from an economic point of view there is no essential difference, although from a social point of view, there obviously is) have escaped the tutelage of the ministries: they can determine their own production; they have the right to keep a portion of the profit which can be invested further or distributed in bonuses; they can enter into contracts with other enterprises, particularly suppliers of raw materials, etc. But as long as they are not autonomous in the fields of price fixing, wages, and the major part of investments, these autonomous rights are very limited or indeed fictitious.

But a real and complete autonomy in the fields of prices, wages, and investment, would mean the end of command planning. So command planning is replaced by 'indicative' planning, something which already exists under late capitalism and which, in the light of everything that has happened in the capitalist economy in the past fifteen years, has shown itself to be ineffective, in the long term, in avoiding periodic fluctuations and crises of overproduction.[1] Attempting to reconcile the rule of the law of value with the maintenance of economic planning is like trying to mix fire and water. The enterprise is condemned to failure.

It would be useful to look at the fundamental reason for this. The ownership of the means of production, in an economic and not in a juridical sense, is, in the final analysis, the power to dispose effectively of these means of production and, at the same time, to dispose of the social surplus which enables them to increase. Where this right belongs to the state, or to some organ representing the collective *as a whole* in a manner more democratic and effective than the state – for instance, a congress of democratically elected workers' councils – then what we have is socialized ownership of the means of production and of that part of the social surplus which is destined for productive investment. In such a case, what we have is a *post*-capitalist economy. The market, the law of value, no longer determine the structure of investment or production. Market mechanisms may be used to test the economic coherence of certain decisions. Or market mechanisms may be used instead of central planning in areas where planning would be ineffective because of the low degree of socialization of labour: in services and in a whole series of areas of petty production.

Where the power to dispose of the means of production and of the social surplus destined for investment belongs essentially to enterprises that have become *independent firms*, then we have group ownership, which is only a variant of private ownership. Where this replaces collective ownership of the means of production, the market, the law of value cease merely to *influence* economic life and begin to *dominate* it and to *rule* it. In such a case we are dealing no longer with a planned or a socialized economy, post-capitalist, but with a restoration of capitalism.

Mikhail Aganbegyan, the principal economic adviser to Gorbachev, attempts to get out of this difficulty by speaking of 'a progressive restoration of the market in goods, capital and labour *in the framework of* a more flexible plan.' This is just playing with words. *Within the framework of* planning, the market cannot *rule*, just as the plan cannot rule within the framework of a market economy. This conclusion was one of the fundamental theoretical contributions of the Preobrazhensky–Bukharin debate of the twenties, a conclusion which has been confirmed by sixty years of experience, both East and West.[2]

A real market in the means of production can only exist if the enterprises are free to determine their investment choices and priorities. The incentive to do this is the right to keep their net revenue, from whence comes profit. But this implies a *model of development determined by profit*, more exactly, by the difference between the profit of the branch or firm and the average profit. Socio-economic priorities are therefore determined by the inequality of incomes and resources which structures demand. Luxury apartments will be built before low-cost housing. Colour televisions have priority over school textbooks. Clinics for the rich come before institutions for preventative medicine. The result is obvious and is plainly visible not only in Sao Paulo, Hong Kong, or Lagos, but also in New York, Naples, and Liverpool. In was also plainly visible in Petrograd in 1913 and in Shanghai in 1924.

A genuine market in labour cannot function without permanent structural unemployment, in other words, without the reserve army of the unemployed, without transforming the proletariat from an *economically* emancipated class (we don't say 'exercising political power') into an exploited class of wage-earners. Once again: this would be the restoration of capitalism, pure and simple, even if, in large-scale industry, juridical private ownership did not replace nationalized ownership of the means of production.

The economic logic which links the rule of profit to the transformation of labour power into a commodity, also means the bankruptcy of firms that operate at a loss. We are speaking here of firms that are really autonomous, that really dispose independently of the totality of their economic resources. They are engaged in *private labour*, the social nature of which is recognized only *post festum*, through the sale of their commodities. If this sale does not take place, or if the price is insufficient, they operate at a loss and go bankrupt. If they go bankrupt the workers are redundant.

The logic of profit is the logic of competition. It ensures bankruptcies, periodically on quite a large scale. Structural unemployment becomes institutionalized. The scale of bankruptcies and of the creation of new enterprises determines the inevitable fluctuations in production and employment.

It is true that the financial autonomy of enterprises can lead to bankruptcies within the framework of perestroika at the present moment. The Soviet press reported that a construction enterprise in Leningrad, employing around two thousand workers, went bankrupt in March 1987. But the workers were immediately transferred to another job in the same city. They didn't lose their wages. There is no labour market in the true sense of the term.

'Are you against the NEP, against Lenin's turn in 1921, are you a supporter of forced collectivization and rapid industrialization ('at a gallop'), without counting the real social and economic costs?' ask the leading Gorbachevites. But we are not guilty of these mortal sins.[3] We think that the solution to the specific systemic crisis which exists in the Soviet Union and Eastern Europe depends on a *combination* of central planning, democratized and rationalized by workers' and general popular control, unrestricted pluralist soviet democracy, and a larger recourse to market mechanisms in the domain of agriculture, small-scale production, and certain services.

The reference to NEP demonstrates the historical difficulty of perestroika. The NEP was essentially a return to private initiative and private property in agriculture, in certain services and in small industry. In other words, it was a greater recourse to the market in small-scale production. This recourse is perfectly compatible with socialized property and planned organization of large-scale production – with planning of the economy as a whole. Of course, this recourse to the market is full of contradictions and dangers.[4] Lenin never tried to hide this danger, especially after the introduction of NEP. The experience of the NEP which Deng Zhiao-Ping has introduced in China confirms this diagnosis and prognosis 100 per cent.[5]

But there is an obvious difference between the Soviet Union under Gorbachev and China under Deng Zhiao-Ping. Unlike China, the Soviet Union is an industrialized country. The problems of management, of co-ordination and rationalization concern large industrial enterprises, telecommunications, transport, and banks, and not agriculture and trade.

The whole experience of China, but especially of Hungary, Yugoslavia, and Poland confirms the impossibility of using the NEP model to resolve the important problems of these economies. That is why all the reforms of the financing of industrial enterprises in these countries have remained hybrid, contradictory, and incoherent.[6]

Gorbachev's real economic dilemma in the economic domain is not 'forced collectivization or NEP'. It is rather: maintenance of a socialized and planned economy or restoration of capitalism in large-scale industry. It is more than probable that Gorbachev and the other principal leaders of the *nomenklatura* will work for the former. For that reason, Gorbachev's policy of massive recourse to market mechanisms in the domain of large-scale industry is economically incoherent – if this is indeed his 'grand plan'.

The American economist, Joseph S. Berliner, of Harvard University, one of the best experts on the Soviet economy in the West, makes an assessment of what he calls the 'radical reform' of Gorbachev which is very similar to the one defended here:

> The radical extreme must entail the decentralization of planning and management. The characteristics of the model may be taken from the Hungarian experience. One may think of it simply as central planning without directive targets to enterprises. But that innocent-sounding formulation involves more than a modification of the centrally planned economy. For without the power to assign directive targets to enterprises, much of the fabric of central planning unravels. If enterprises cannot be required to produce according to directives, they cannot be held responsible for the delivery of specified intermediate materials and supplies, and the time-honoured system of material–technical supply must be largely abandoned. In the absence of directive targets, the criteria for evaluating enterprise performance must be modified, and it is then difficult to imagine any criterion other than some suitably modified form of profit. But if profit is to serve as the dominant criterion of performance it will become the effective objective function of management, and it is then necessary to assure that the prices and costs in terms of what decisions are made are reasonably reflective of marginal social benefits and costs. That must entail the abandonment of forty years of centralized administration of average cost-plus-normal profit-pricing. Similar changes would have to be introduced in the management of the labour market, the financial system, and other parts of the economy.[7]

It isn't difficult to demonstrate that this type of 'radical reform' will be effective and coherent only if the 'material interests of managers', linked to profit, goes beyond the realm of current income (and access to consumer goods), and is linked also to the long-term performance of the enterprise as a whole in financial terms. His fate, as well as that of his children, is tied to the enterprise; he is no longer simply a manager, but an owner. However, Gorbachev and his supporters in the bureaucracy won't allow this to happen. The reform will therefore be ineffective and incoherent.

In addition to the economic, there is also an institutional dilemma. Gorbachev wants to extend considerably the power of industrial managers and take away power from officials at intermediate levels, especially from the ministries. It is said that the number of officials has been reduced by 'several million' and that, in Moscow alone, sixty thousand officials have lost their jobs. We cannot speculate about those figures but it is clear, in any case, that the reduction in the number of

officials has been significant. It is obvious that the reform must meet
with considerable hostility from all those whose positions are threatened.
This fear and hostility are undoubtedly present among large layers of the
bureaucracy. These layers fear that in attacking certain pillars of the
Soviet establishment, Gorbachev risks bringing down the whole edifice.

What's more, the passivity and the proverbial irresponsibility of the
bureaucracy represent a formidable brake on perestroika.[8] Passive
resistance is more effective than active opposition. The Soviet press has
been filled with references to this obstruction, especially during the
summer and autumn of 1987. In December 1986, *Izvestia* published a
series of articles on the ministry for the construction industry where an
extensive reform was supposed to have been implemented. In fact, very
little had changed: 'Up to now, the reform has been applied only half-
heartedly in the ministry and has not produced any notable results. In
the ministry of heavy industry, as before, it is the methods of direct
control which prevail' (*Izvestia*, 20 December 1986).

Gorbachev himself is quite aware of this. In his speech in Leningrad
on 13 October 1987 (reported in *Pravda*, 14 October 1987), he said:

> To overcome the 'braking mechanism' and the forces of inertia which have
> accumulated during the course of many years in all spheres of social life; to
> conquer the social apathy which affects a large section of our workers; to
> create solid guarantees for the irreversible character of this reorganization: all
> of this today demands of the party, as it did seventy years ago, a firm political
> will, iron discipline and actions which are practical, daring, creative and full of
> initiative ...
>
> Communists have to set an example, by working according to new prin-
> ciples; they should be the first to fight the forces of inertia. At this stage these
> forces are particularly resistant. Don't believe that these forces are external to
> us; they are among us.

We know that this spirit of inertia and obstruction is to be found in
both the Central Committee and the Politburo, where Gorbachev's
power is limited. Many of his proposals have had to be revised before
being accepted. Others have been delayed or rejected.

The Secretary General is assured of the enthusiastic support of the
liberal *intelligentsia*, which is only a fraction of the intelligentsia as a
whole. He is also supported by the young modernizing managers in all
spheres of administration. But this is very much a minority group in
relation to the middle layers and the upper layers of older and more
conservative bureaucrats. This support is not enough to overcome
obstacles. Gorbachev needs broader support among the popular masses.
This support could only come from the workers, at least from that layer
which is more dynamic, more qualified, younger, and more prepared to

be active in social and political matters.

But to win support from the workers for perestroika, there has to be some material benefit for the workers themselves. Fred Halliday, writing in the British Eurocommunist magazine *Marxism Today* (November 1987), said that from the point of view of the Soviet workers: 'What matters is the kolbasa' (the sausage, as in the famous German saying: '*Es geht um die Wurst*').

In this respect, there is quite a difference between the Soviet Union and China. By eliminating the excesses and aberrations of the rural commune system, Deng was able, in a single move, to improve the material situation of hundreds of millions of peasants. Gorbachev, up to now, has only called on the workers to work harder and has reintroduced some of the practices of Stakhanovism which the workers categorically reject, while at the same time increasing prices and reducing bonuses. Under those circumstances, it is to be expected that the workers will adopt a wait-and-see attitude and, in many cases, remain sceptical of perestroika.

The Soviet press has published numerous confirmations of this. At the end of April 1987, *Komsomolskaia Pravda* published some of the thousands of replies they had received to the question: 'What changes have you seen around you during recent years?' The journal summed up the replies in this manner: 'There are no reports of victories and very few concrete results.' One reply from the city of Kirov said: 'According to the radio, the newspapers and the television, lots of things have changed. But around me, at work, everything is the same. Nothing has been implemented' (reported in the *Observer*, 3 May 1987).[9]

Here we see once again the dilemma confronting Gorbachev. If he pushes ahead with the tendency inherent in perestroika, namely, greater rights for managers, including the right to fire workers, then the wait-and-see attitude of the workers will turn into overt hostility and may even lead to explosions. In that case, the passive resistance of the majority of the apparatus will be enough to defeat perestroika.

The risks of massive unemployment are becoming clearer. According to *The Independent* (16 September 1987), *Izvestia* published an interview with Leonid Kostin, first vice-president of the State Committee for Labour and Prices, who said that 3 million workers had been made redundant in the manufacturing industry as a result of increases in productivity, 280,000 on the railways and 70,000 in the oil industry. According to Kostin, those workers temporarily 'without work' would be found other jobs quite rapidly in those regions of the country where there was a severe shortage of labour, for example in Siberia or in the Far East, or in the service industry.

According to *Sotsialisticheskaia Industria* of 29 March 1987, there are 250,000 unemployed in Azerbaidzhan and around a million in Uzbekistan. The publication of those figures was accompanied by appeals for internal migration (colonization). Around 35–40,000 unemployed Azerbaidzhanis were immediately given work in Siberia. The deputy director of the Research Institute of Gosplan, Professor V. Kostakov, has said that around 2 million workers have been 'temporarily without work' during the course of the past five years, but that the majority of them were very quickly given a new job. He estimates that this kind of 'frictional unemployment' will affect between 13 and 19 million people in the years ahead. His article appeared in *Sovietskaia Kultura* and was reported in *The Economist* of 26 December 1987.

It is a sign of the times that, for the first time since 1930, unemployment pay has been officially reintroduced in the Soviet Union. Those unemployed receive 100 per cent of their salary for three months if their 'loss of job is a result of a government decree in relation to the improvement of management in industry or in other sectors of the economy.'

It is one thing to find a job for 270,000 workers, but is quite another thing to find new jobs for 13 million. It is one thing to find another job regardless of salary or place of work, it is quite another thing to find a new job without a drop in wages and without having to move to some other place. As these problems emerge and become more apparent, there will be resistance from the workers.

According to an opinion poll published by *Moscow News* (no. 17, 1988), 85 per cent of the workers are opposed to the introduction of cuts in labour force in the enterprises. Of those questioned, 87 per cent thought that there should be reductions in 'managerial personnel of economic bodies'. Likewise, 62 per cent favoured cuts in 'the staffs of district and city executive committees, etc.' while 60 per cent thought that 'unemployment is unacceptable in the USSR in principle'. 32 per cent 'believe that some unemployment could and should be permitted'. In the same issue of *Moscow News*, Professor Boris Rakitsky made the following comments on the poll:

About unemployment. Nearly a third of those asked could accept it as a normal occurrence. That's a high percentage. I think it reflects our increasing 'socio-political immune deficiency' to other people's misfortune. What does this readiness to accept unemployment (even small-scale) mean? It means the same thing as accepting poverty, homelessness and inequality. Society and the state have a constitutional obligation to guarantee the right to work. It must stay that way. To accept 'small-scale unemployment' is to disavow one's responsibility to one's fellow citizens. I was surprised that it was educated people, scientists, teachers and young people (who do not work and do not live at their own expense) who are most socio-politically immune to injustice. Yet engineers, managers, teachers, scientists bear the most responsibility for stagnation and for bad organization in all spheres of life ... The way to efficiency lies not through staff reduction but through changing the nature of economic management.

It should come as no surprise that a section of the bureaucracy is in favour of the introduction of unemployment. Behind those different attitudes to unemployment lies a conflict of material interests between two major social groups: the mass of the workers and the privileged bureaucracy.

We find the same type of conflict over the question of the power of the recently created 'work collective councils'. According to Yevgeny Torkanovsky, writing in *Moscow News* (no. 21, 1988), there is a danger that 'enterprise self-management could be turned into a "democracy for the director"....'. The issue at stake was whether, as had been proposed, enterprise directors should be elected as chairmen of work collective councils.

> Two different approaches to the issue of industrial management have collided. One approach in question is that of the 'professionalization' of management, the other, its democratization. A stereotyped way of thinking has become deeply rooted in our society. Its propagators say that no cook could ever run an industrial enterprise [this alludes to a famous phrase of Lenin in *State and Revolution*] since certain professional knowledge is needed ... And democracy? Their answer is that democracy is merely a managerial facade, and not its backbone. Let members of the work collective give advice, but decision-making must be in the hands of the real 'master' – a competetent and responsible person. Indeed, such was the former pattern of relations between the collective and its director ... This kind of logic underlies the justification for the director's being made chairman of the work collective council. However, I'm convinced that a strong-willed director as chairman is capable of turning any council from an organ of the work collective into a body under his control and obedient to his will.

Boris Kagarlitsky is right when he points to an opposition between the market proposals of the technocrats and the democratic dynamic of glasnost. The technocrats are

> more and more defending the interests of the industrial management apparatus ...: The technocrats no longer concealed the anti-democratic character of their proposals ... The task of perestroika [for them] was to overthrow the 'tyranny' of the majority and assert the superiority of the elite.[10]

A real democracy of the producers, a genuine socialist democracy would indeed be incompatible with market mechanisms that created unemployment. In Yugoslavia, for instance, the large-scale reappearance of bankruptcies among enterprises implies an inevitable modification if not suppression of the laws on workers' self-management. It is the least profitable enterprises in each branch that are closed down. But labour productivity in these enterprises depends primarily not on the physical efforts of the workers but on the technology of the enterprise, the provision and costs of raw materials, factors which are outside the control of the workers in the enterprise. Why is it the workers who should be punished when the decisions are made by others? The workers are quite right to oppose reductions in their buying power when they see the privileges enjoyed by the bureaucracy – the dachas, the special shops, the trips abroad and so on. As long as those problems are not resolved the workers are not going to make an extra effort.

To escape from this dilemma, the Gorbachev team, undoubtedly with the support of all the upper echelons of the bureaucracy, is attempting a classic manoeuvre: to divide the workers, to set one group of workers against another group, by painting in glowing colours the considerable material advantages they can have from this experiment.

In a remarkable study which we have already referred to, David Seppo quite correctly points out that the thirty years in which Stalinist terror, with its repressive labour code, has been absent, thirty years in which there has been full employment, have created in the enterprises a relation of forces very favourable to the workers and in which their solidarity and cohesion have undoubtedly grown. Rudolf Bahro made a similar point in his major work, *The Alternative*. What we are witnessing is the rebirth of an elementary form of class consciousness, at least at the level of the enterprise, a rebirth which will make it more difficult for Gorbachev to create divisions among the workers.

If Gorbachev can't give any material benefits to the workers, at least in the short term, then he has to give them something on the political level. Hence the link, established by Gorbachev himself and by his supporters and the more clear-minded of his advisers, between perestroika and glasnost. 'The question presents itself in the following manner,' said Gorbachev to the Trade Union Congress in February 1987, 'democratization or social inertia and conservatism. There is no third way' (*Izvestia*, 26 February 1987).

But the Soviet workers won't be satisfied with vague declarations or with Gorbachev's using glasnost and democratization as a mere device to direct their attention away from the deterioration in their material conditions and away from their defence of those material conditions. On the contrary: the only point of glasnost from the point of view of the workers is that it allows them to articulate their complaints and demands. The point of democratization from their point of view is that it should lead to an increase in their trade union and political rights and in their effective power, especially within the enterprises. The question, therefore, is immediately posed: who, in the final instance, decides in the matter of lay-offs? The 'authorities'? the 'management'? The workers' collectives? Should the state have the right of veto, or the workers? If it is the workers, then 'managerial' (monetarized) perestroika loses coherence.

It is here that Gorbachev finds himself in another dilemma, more serious than those we have enumerated so far. On the one hand, he can allow the logic of glasnost to unfold more or less without doing any damage to the workers. The workers will then not only seize the opportunity to democratize their trade union structures, elect and recall factory directors, and re-establish workers' and popular control in a growing number of social areas. They will also establish independent workers' and Socialist newspapers, and engage in strikes and demonstrations. They will take part in a process of self-organization and self-activity, slowly at first, but this process will speed up and become cumulative. The trajectory is obvious: we saw it in the Prague Spring and in solidarity in Poland, with the difference that in the Soviet Union today the ideological–political conditions are far more favourable to the workers than they were in Czechoslovakia or Poland. This is a mortal threat to the privileges and monopoly of power of the bureaucracy.

On the other hand, the apparatus can try to channel all the activities of the workers and make sure that none of it escapes party control. In this case there will be recourse, sooner or later, to repression, however mild or limited. But any kind of repression directed against the workers will destroy the credibility of glasnost in the eyes of the whole of the working class and Gorbachev will lose their support.

Gorbachev is aware of this dilemma. In his speech in Leningrad (reported in *Pravda*, 14 October 1987) he stated:

Certain cadres are perplexed by the scope and intensity of the criticism that has been directed against negative social phenomena, against delays and inadequacies in our national economy, against mistakes made by certain organizations and administrations. ... We must see this criticism and self-criticism as evidence of a growing awareness, political responsibility, and social activity among our workers.

We have fought and will continue to fight against demagogy, exaggerations and one-sided criticism. But we do not allow ourselves to be intimidated by these phenomena. We will not deviate from our course and we will not succumb to the temptation to forbid this criticism. Cadres at every level must learn to take popular opinion into account and know how to influence it. We must learn once and for all to talk to the masses, *using only the methods of persuasion and dialogue among equals.*

Gorbachev is quite aware of this dilemma and challenges, in hardly veiled terms, the whole practice of Stalin. But should he then not also challenge the invasion of Hungary and Czechoslovakia, as well as the Jaruzelski coup in Poland? It would be difficult to deny that these were not examples of 'the methods of persuasion'.

But having got under way, he falls into inextricable contradictions. He doesn't hesitate to refer to Lenin's *State and Revolution*, the most libertarian of Lenin's works, the central axis of which is self-organization and workers' power. He proclaims that 'history is made by the masses'. He adds, in the same speech quoted from above:

> We talk and write a lot these days about the pressing need to inculcate into every Soviet worker *the feeling of being master of his own country.* ... It is indispensable that we create the real conditions which allow every worker and every workers' collective to exercise their rights as co-owners of the means of production.... *Only the maximum development of democracy*, as Lenin insisted, and not partial improvements and half-measures, can guarantee in a concrete manner the multiform progress of socialism. (My emphasis)

But how can one guarantee 'popular self-management' while maintaining the dogma of the single party and all the institutions which accompany this? How can the 'maximum development of democracy' be made compatible with strict party control (in fact, party apparatus control) of trade unions? Doesn't this in fact imply that the workers should enjoy all democratic freedoms: freedom of association, freedom to demonstrate, freedom of the press, the right to strike, etc.?

And how can he maintain that this exercise of the right of co-ownership of the means of production corresponds to 'the interests of *all* classes and social layers of Soviet society', when all the evidence suggests that where management is concerned, the interests of producers and the interests of administrators (bureaucrats) are opposed to each other?[11] V. Ivanov, director of the Institute of Sociological Research at the Academy of Sciences, summarized the results of an inquiry carried out in 120 enterprises throughout the country, in the following way: 'One cannot close one's eyes to the contradictions between workers and managers. This problem is becoming clearer with each study we make. The rigid division between 'them' and 'us' has had serious consequences' (*Izvestia*, 5 May 1978).

A Soviet emigré, having returned recently from a visit to the Soviet Union, described the same phenomenon in somewhat harsher terms: 'Another thing which didn't exist before, as least as it appeared to me, was the clear and total division betwen 'them' and 'us'. I suppose it existed before, but not in such an absolute form, with so much impotent hatred' (*Russkaia Mysl*, October 1986).

Among the upper echelons of the bureaucracy, among the police, and, to a large extent, among the managers there is a mortal fear of this dynamic. On no account do they want the self-organization and independent activity of the working class. Hence the warnings from Ligachev and the other leading moderate backers of perestroika as well as from the authentic representatives of the conservatives. Hence also the growing difficulties for Gorbachev in both the Central Committee and the Politburo. All of this points in the direction of 'partial improvements and half-measures' rather than 'the maximum development of democracy'.

It is in the light of this last dilemma, the most serious of all, that we can see why Gorbachev has refused to carry destalinization through to its conclusion by rehabilitating Trotsky and authorizing the publication of all his works.

The real danger for the bureaucracy is the concrete socioeconomic and political content of Trotsky's writings, those of 1905–6 and 1917–18, but especially his writings after 1921. For any unprejudiced reader Trotsky's message is clear: against the exercise of power by the bureaucratic apparatus; against the privileges of the bureaucracy and growing inequality; for the most extensive socialist democracy; for the rights of women, youth, and minority nationalities; for generalized workers' and popular control; for the real exercise of power by democratically elected soviets, which implies political pluralism, the end of the one-party system, 'the right of workers and peasants to elect whomsoever they chose to the soviets', and the legalization of all parties regardless of ideology; for the freedom of trade union organization; for scientific, literary, cultural, artistic, and ideological pluralism (which obviously implies the right of any Communist party or parties to defend their convictions).

This is a message which cannot but find a resonance among the working masses, the youth, and among the more spirited of the intelligentsia. It is a message which may well sound the tocsin of bureaucratic power. The bureaucracy will do all in its power to stop this message from being widely heard in the Soviet Union. Whether or not they succeed depends not so much on the intentions or successes of Gorbachev as on the evolution of the relation of forces among the principal social actors of Soviet society. In the final analysis, in other words, it depends on the evolution of autonomous activity within the working class.

But in limiting political glasnost, Gorbachev and his co-thinkers are confronted with a new and final dilemma: how to prevent the penetration of 'subversive' political ideas into literature, the theatre, the cinema, all of which, apparently, they want to 'liberalize'? The relation between perestroika and glasnost, between glasnost and the potential for self-organization and self-activity within the working class, leads to a contradiction within glasnost itself.

We learn from Roy Medvedev that an anti-bureaucratic play entitled *Silver Wedding* was being shown at the *Khudozhestvennyi* Theatre in Moscow at the time of the 27th Congress. In view of its radical nature, with many allusions to Stalin and Stalinism, the play was allowed to continue only after it had been viewed and approved by Ligachev.[12]

A little later the Komsomol Theatre showed a play entitled *The Dictatorship of Conscience.* In this play, the partisans and adversaries of Leninism engage in a lively dialogue (in which, of course, the Leninists win). One particular character in this play, a foreigner, played by O. Yankovsky, encouraged audience participation in the debate. One of the audience said: 'My grandfather was a Menshevik Socialist. He was shot in the thirties. Today there is a lot of talk about democratic spirit. But experience shows that there will be no true democracy as long as there is no opposition party.' After this incident, there was no more audience participation. Roy Medvedev concludes: 'Thus an interesting but carefully rehearsed debate took place on the stage. But in the life of society there is no authentic democracy.'

The case of the theatre is not an isolated one. The film *Assa*, dealing with rock music, was not allowed to be shown in Moscow cinemas. In a debate on history organized on 7 January 1988 in the Writers' Union in Moscow, the playwright Mikhail Shatrov said that an article about the procurator general at the Moscow trials, Vyshinsky, due to be published in *Literaturnaia Gazeta*, was forbidden by the censor. It has since been printed. Gorbachev himself, in an interview in the French Communist paper, *L'Humanité*, defended censorship with arguments that would support all those in the capitalist countries, such as Mrs Thatcher, who want to limit democratic freedoms, especially the freedom of the press and media.

It is hardly surprising, under such circumstances, that the question of censorship is polarizing intellectuals more and more in the Soviet Union. At the 10th Congress of the East German Writers Union, Christoph Hein made an impressive indictment of censorship, calling on the tradition of Marx and exposing it as contrary to the interests of Socialism:[13]

Censorship is hostile to the interests of the people. It is a crime against the well-known and frequently invoked wisdom of the people. The readers of our books are sufficiently independent to be able to judge for themselves. The idea that officials should decide what people can or cannot cope with is an expression of the pretensions and insolence of office. . . .

The absence or inadequacy of information and debates in the press and media concerning public affairs does injury to the political culture of our country and destroys it. Anyone who is concerned about the development of our society should be profoundly worried about this loss. The press and media shouldn't merely transmit information. They should be a transmission belt between the summit and the base, between the base and the summit, between the society and the state, between the masses and the elected leaders. When this mediation is in only one direction, there is no longer any mediation.

Behind the maintenance of a limited censorship by the Gorbachev team, there is obviously the fear that the bureaucracy will lose its monopoly in the exercise of power. That's why Gorbachev continues to use the same ambiguous formalae:

Once more, let us recall Lenin: literature is the business of the whole party. This thesis is basic and it is one which inspires us still today. . . . We should not forget that a review, a publisher, a journal are not the personal business of any individual, no matter who; they are the business of the party, of the whole people. . . . I want to emphasize once more: we are in favour of openness, without reservation, without restriction. But for openness in the interests of socialism.[14]

If the press is not the personal business of any one individual, then why tolerate that it becomes the personal business of the censors who decide what may or may not be published? If the press and literature are the business of the whole party, then how can this party, with its millions of members, delegate control to a few censors? Is there so little confidence in the ability of Communists to decide for themselves? If the press and literature are the business of the whole people, then what of the great majority of workers who are not members of the party? Can they also not judge for themselves what they want to read? Who has the right to decide for them? Is this practice not another confirmation of the view defended by revolutionary Marxists that the Soviet regime has *politically expropriated the working class.* How can this alienation of a fundamental democratic freedom be justified in the name of 'the interests of Socialism'? Is there some form of openness which is not in the interests of Socialism? Gorbachev is wrong to say: openness without limitation as long as it is in the interests of the defence of Socialism. What has to be said is: *openness without any limitation is in the interests of Socialism.*

Under Andropov there was a byzantine debate about 'antagonistic and non-antagonistic contradictions under socialism'.[15] For a Marxist, the existence of 'antagonistic contradictions' is explained by the existence of classes or sections of classes with antagonistic interests. But how can these antagonistic interests be articulated under a single-party regime, in particular one ruled by bureaucratic centralism? Limited democracy for the workers, limited glasnost, is a consequence of the existence of this single-party regime. The deputy editor of the journal *Kommunist* admitted that:

> The October revolution initially opted for party pluralism. It rejected the parliamentary system and replaced it by the soviet system, but at the beginning party pluralism was maintained in the soviets.

But then he immediately adds:

> We know better than anyone the defects of the single-party system during any period. But we are dealing here with a historical reality, with a historical choice of the people. For the moment the party is the only force really capable of organizing the battle against bureaucratism.[16]

But is it not this same party – or rather, its apparatus – which has created the conditions of stagnation, brought about the crisis of the system against which it is now necessary, in the words of Gorbachev, to organize a 'new revolution'? Wouldn't it be better to have more confidence in the workers than in the apparatus of the party, made up, as it is, of people who have material privileges to defend? Is this not an adequate reason for going beyond the single-party system?

# 12

# The Dialectic of Reform and Social Movement

Born out of the social conflict that has emerged directly from the objective contradictions of Soviet Society, the Gorbachev reforms intensify this conflict and stimulate, at the same time, the politicization and the political differentiation (polarization) of growing layers of Soviet society. This has been the fundamental socio-political dynamic of Soviet society over the past three years.

Differentiation and conflict are evident at every level of the social pyramid in the Soviet Union: within the Politburo of the Communist Party; among the nationalities; within the ecology movement; among the ideologues, the journalists, the writers, and artists; within the working class. What has been most remarkable is the appearance of independent political groups and independent journals and newspapers, evidence of a revival of independent action in certain sectors of society, although still modest in scope.

The circumstances surrounding Chernobyl and the events that followed this disaster are symbolic of this dialectic.[1] Chernobyl revealed the irresponsibility of the bureaucratic apparatus, including a section of the military apparatus. But what the catastrophe also revealed was the capacity of other sections of the bureaucracy and of important sectors of the population to react rapidly and in a manner which demonstrated their solidarity. But, above all, it revealed the limits of glasnost; the criminal delay in informing the public which undoubtedly aggravated the consequences of the catastrophe and increased the number of victims. It also revealed the existence of an independent public opinion which reacted in a manner highly critical of the authorities.

There were popular protests against the construction of nuclear power plants. Ecological groups multiplied and some of them were spectacularly successful. According to *Komsomolskaia Pravda*, the authorities were eventually forced to give in to some of the local popular pressure, and they called a halt to the construction of a nuclear power station in Krasnodar.[2] A play by Vladimir Gurarev, *The Coffin*, was enormously popular. The question was also being asked: how did it happen that, in spite of the thirty-six-hour delay in announcing the catastrophe at Chernobyl and in evacuating the population, the families of local officials were evacuated immediately?[3]

The limits of glasnost were clearly visible in this whole tragedy of Chernobyl: the delay in informing the Soviet people, with disastrous consequences for the local population; the fact that the Soviet Union's report to the International Atomic Energy Committee in Vienna wasn't published in the Soviet Union itself. Zhores Medvedev concludes that Gorbachev's honeymoon with the Soviet people came to an end with the catastrophe at Chernobyl.[4]

Another test-case is the protest movement of the Crimean Tartars. The background is well known. Because a minority of them collaborated with the Nazis, the entire nation was deported to distant territories in the Urals, in Kazakhstan and Uzbekistan. Khrushchev admitted, in his secret speech to the 20th Congress that this deportation, during the course of which 100,000 of the 400,000 deportees perished, was an arbitrary act which flagrantly violated the Soviet Constitution.

During the period of 'thaw' under Khrushchev, the survivors and descendants of the deported Tartars began a protest movement demanding their right to return to their homeland. Some courageous Communists at the time defended the rights of the Crimean Tartars. Among them were Kosterin, an old Bolshevik who miraculously survived the Stalinist purges, and General Piotr Grigorenko who, at this time, still considered himself a Communist and Marxist.[5] The most important demonstration of opposition in Moscow since the funeral of Joffe in 1928 took place when Kosterin was buried.[6]

Under Khrushchev the repression of the Tartars began to abate. The Tartar protest movement organized regular mass petitions which were sent regularly to the authorities. With the death of Brezhnev the movement acquired a new momentum and, with Gorbachev's glasnost, has been given a new lease of life. On 27 June 1987, a delegation of Crimean Tartars was received by Piotr Demichev, vice-president of the Supreme Soviet. They demanded the right to return to their homeland. According to the head of the delegation, Richat Dzhemilev, the discussion did not lead to any satisfactory conclusion (*The Independent* 7 July 1987).

As a result, the Tartars decided to move to direct action. A public protest demonstration took place in Moscow on 23 July 1987, in which three hundred took part. The hard core of the demonstration staged a sit-down strike on Red Square, holding portraits of Lenin and Gorbachev. They didn't end their protest until they had received a guarantee that they would meet with Gromyko, head of state in the Soviet Union.

The meeting took place on 27 July 1987. The Tartars were dissatisfied with the outcome of this meeting. All they had been promised was a state commission of inquiry, headed by Gromyko, which would look into their request. On 16 October 1987, *Pravda* published an official communiqué of this commission of inquiry, which stated:

> The commission has recommended to the federal, republican and local organs that they take additional measures to satisfy more fully the cultural needs of the Crimean Tartars: increased publication of literature in the Tartar language, including works by contemporary Tartar authors; the creation, where necessary, of new journals; an increase in the number of radio and television programmes in the Tartar language.
>
> The commission has analysed and recognized as unacceptable certain violations of the rights of citizens of the Tartar nationality with respect to their right to reside, work and study in the region of the Crimea. At the same time it has underlined the need, as far as legislation is concerned, to be more precise about the rules determining residence and the registration of citizens of all nationalities in the Crimea and in all the other seaside resort areas in the Soviet Union, taking into account the fact that these areas are of great importance to the whole of the Soviet Union as areas of rest and convalescence for millions of workers.
>
> The commission received almost ten thousand letters from people who requested that resolute measures be taken to put an end to the agitation of extremist tendencies that pretend to speak in the name of the Crimean Tartars but whose goal is to increase tension, provoke anti-social demonstrations and sow discord among the nations. Those who took part in the commission have noted the inconsistency of these groups in their attempts to refute the facts in the TASS communiqué of 23 July 1987, and to exonerate the traitors to their people, the Crimean Tartar nationalists, and to put them on the same level as the patriotic and honest Soviet Tartars who fought against fascism. These attempts have nothing in common with the aspirations of the Crimean Tartars; they create obstacles to the normal functioning of the organs of the state and are in conflict with the requirements of the Soviet constitution which prohibits any form of propaganda for exclusivity and any form of hostility to or defiance of the national order.

We have quoted extensively from this communiqué because it demonstrates the contradictions and tensions brought to the surface within society and within the apparatus by the dialectic which we described earlier.

The authorities recognize that the aspirations of the Crimean Tartars are just. The Tartars were victims of injustice and arbitrary prohibitions, especially the prohibition which prevented them from returning to their homeland. This was a flagrant violation of the rights guaranteed by the Soviet Constitution.

The commission's report recognizes that the deportation was not only illegal but it was also illegitimate, since, as the communiqué admits, numerous Crimean Tartars fought against the Nazi invasion. Only a minority of 'nationalist Tartars' collaborated with the enemy.

As a result of all these admissions and in view of the legitimate aspirations of the Crimean Tartars, substantial concessions were made to them. But, at the same time, their peaceful demonstrations, during which there was no evidence of 'anti-patriotic' and 'anti-Soviet' gestures or of 'hostility to or defiance of the national order', were denounced as 'anti-social', aiming to 'sow discord among the nations'.

But doesn't the Soviet Constitution guarantee the freedom to demonstrate? And does the simple request that the Crimean Tartars be permitted to return to their homeland constitute 'hostility to or defiance of the national order'? Is the freedom to demonstrate denied to any groups of citizens whose aspirations are inconvenient for the authorities? This is certainly not the spirit we find in Karl Marx's *Civil War in France*, or in Lenin's *State and Revolution*, not to mention in the Soviet Constitution of 1918 as well as in the present Constitution. All of these works describe the political liberties which Socialism guarantees to its citizens.

The inconsistency in the attitudes of the Communist Party becomes most apparent whenever the problem deals explicitly with those articles of the Soviet constitution which prohibit any propaganda which sows national or racial discord, or exalts the chauvinism of one nation to the detriment of the peaceful co-habitation of all the peoples of the Soviet Union. As we have already pointed out in chapters 2 and 7, there has existed in the Soviet Union for some years, both publicly and legally, propaganda of a Great Russian chauvinist character, both anti-semitic and reactionary. The famous *Moral Code*, published by a Komsomol official, demonstrates the same tendency. Even the sinister *Protocols of Zion*, a fabrication of the tzarist secret police, which directly inspired the anti-semitic racism of Adolf Hitler, appears to have been published once again in the Soviet Union.

On 6 May 1987, some weeks before the demonstration of Crimean Tartars, a demonstration of four hundred people took place in Moscow. It was organized by *Pamyat'* an ultra-reactionary association created allegedly for the protection of historical monuments (*Pamyat'* means 'memory'), but in fact diffusing a violently anti-semitic and xenophobic propaganda, warning about a conspiracy of 'Jews, Free Masons, and Westernizers' who want to 'undermine the Russian way of life'. (A report on this demonstration, and on a meeting of a delegation from *Pamyat'* with Boris Yeltsin, before the latter was dismissed from his post, appeared in *Moscow News* on 17 May 1987. It was also reported in some detail in the *International Herald Tribune* on 25 May 1987.)

*Pamyat'* has local organizations in Leningrad, Sverdlovsk, and Novosibirsk. The reports in *Komsomolskaia Pravda* and in *Ogonyok* underline the anti-semitic character of the propaganda put out by *Pamyat'*. A very detailed report by the Moscow correspondent of *Le Monde* (24 June 1987) gives a clear account of the overtly anti-semitic positions of the leader of *Pamyat'*, Dmitri Vasiliev: 'The Jews represent 0.69 per cent of Soviet society but they occupy more than 20 per cent of all important positions.' The editor-in-chief of the liberal weekly, *Ogonyok* does not hesitate to state the significance of Vasiliev and his followers: 'He is our Le Pen.'

The relationship between this ideology of *Pamyat'* and pure fascism is obvious to anyone who is aware of the history of fascism and neo-fascism. An article in *Leningradskaia Pravda* on 11 July 1987 reports the existence in that city of a group of young people who have formed the 'National Socialist Workers Party of Russia'. They painted swastikas on walls, stopped solitary pedestrians in the streets and forced them to shout 'Heil Hitler', and tortured a man in an abandoned house. The writer of the article explains the existence of Nazi groupuscules in the Soviet Union as a result of the routine, boring, and unconvincing character of education and official propaganda which encourages youth to look for an alternative ideology. One of the leaders of Komsomol, Viktor Mironenko, emphasizes the 'need for authority' and the quest for the 'strong man' as an explanation for the admiration for Adolf Hitler which is to be found among certain sections of Soviet youth (*Sovietskaia Kultura*, 10 May 1987).[7]

What is most striking about this whole affair is the fact that a demonstration by *Pamyat'*, in spite of its chauvinist ideology, is tolerated, while a demonstration by Crimean Tartars is considered illegal because it is alleged (incorrectly) to be chauvinistic. As we saw earlier with respect to the crisis in Kazakhstan, the nationalism of the ethnic minorities is treated very differently from the chauvinism of the Russians.[8]

The extent of mass activity in Armenia is on a scale unequalled since the October revolution. General strikes have been organized over a period of months, beginning in Stepanakert, spreading to Yerevan and then throughout the whole republic of Armenia. Councils of action were established as well as self-defence pickets. Locally co-ordinated leadership bodies were established which negotiate with local, regional and national bodies. There have been numerous demonstrations involving hundreds of thousands of people. Local authorities and the party in Armenia have capitulated completely in the face of mass demands. The conflict is no longer between the masses and the central authorities since the masses are now supported by the republican authorities.

The demands of the masses are not limited to national demands. According to *Pravda* (21 March 1988), 'the demand was raised for dismissing and re-electing leaders of enterprises and party bodies, for recalling people's deputies and expelling them all from the party if they obstructed the formation of Karabakh base committees'. The crisis cannot be reduced entirely to the decades-old conflict between Armenians and Azerbaidjanies and certainly not to a conflict between Catholics and Muslims. The detonator of the crisis seems to have been the anger of the Armenians over the degree of pollution in Yerevan caused by chemical industrial plants which had been irresponsibly situated. Totally inadequate social infrastructures in the autonomous region of Nagorno Karabakh as well as unsatisfied cultural demands contributed to the explosion. These gave real material content to the demands for greater autonomy and for the return to Armenia of the region of Nagorno Karabakh. It is only the combination of all these different factors which can explain the explosive character of the crisis.[9] Having said this, one should by no means underestimate the importance of the national question. The Soviet Union is now having to pay the price for its policies in the past: first, the policy of socialism in one country and the lack of credibility of its propaganda in favour of genuine internationalism; second, the ultra-bureaucratic, repressive and brutal policy of Stalin with regard to the non-Russian nationalities; third, the policy of Brezhnev which sought to defuse the national time-bomb by supporting bureaucratic regional mafias in the different republics. All of those policies have now been put in question by the degree of democratization under glasnost. The general strikes in Armenia marked a high point in the autonomous mass movement in the Soviet Union under Gorbachev. In the Baltic Republics there have also been large mobilizations against the local representatives of the bureaucracy.

The dialectical relationship between popular discontent, Gorbachev's reforms, and the birth of autonomous movements and actions is manifest also in the working class, the numerical majority of the Soviet Union. The Soviet press has reported a number of strikes: at the lorry plant, Kamaz, in Brezhnev; the bus conductors in Chehkov, a small town about 70 kilometres south of Moscow; at a factory which makes agricultural machinery in Tchumen in Siberia; at an electronics factory in Lithuania. Soviet television even showed a strike at a factory in Moscow where the workers were protesting against security conditions in the factory.

According to information published in the West – we don't know how accurate this is – the most important strike to have taken place up to now took place at the 'Avtodiesel' complex in Yaroslav, involving 40,000 workers. It was called by a general assembly of workers attended by 700 delegates. This dispute was over an extension of working time decreed by the management – from 7 hours 30 minutes to 7 hours 50 minutes with 15 working Saturdays. The workers proposed 8 hours and 8 working Saturdays. According to *Moscow News* (27 December 1987), from which we have taken this information, the source of the discontent was 'the fact that the administration, supported by the trade union committee, had seen its proposal as definitive, needing only to be formally approved by the works collective.' One of the most significant aspects of this strike is the fact that there emerged 'natural leaders' among the strikers who agitated on behalf of and acted as spokespersons for their fellow workers.

In general, the strikes which have broken out up to now have had to do with the consequences of the introduction of state control over quality of products. This control extends over roughly 50 per cent of industrial production. The products which do not correspond to the quality norms established by the state are not officially recognized when it comes to calculating the bonus. According to an article in *Sovietskaia Rossiia* in January 1987, many workers have lost as much as 50 roubles a month as a result of quality control, and this in a society where the monthly average wage is 200 roubles. This led to large-scale discontent among the workers and to quite a few strikes.

Other inquiries have described the situation following the introduction of quality controls as much more serious. In industrial plants in Alma Ata, it is estimated that the workers lose as much as 60 to 70 roubles a month. In Leningrad, where a pilot experiment with the 'new economic mechanism' was introduced in 1984 in 200 enterprises, an inquiry in 1987 indicated that, in the view of the workers, there had been no improvement in the situation. In December 1986, Boris Yeltsin spoke to young workers in the car factory SIL in Moscow. He summarized their responses in the formula: 'no change, no movement'. A number of inquiries confirm this impression. *Moscow News* (3 January 1988) published the results of a series of interviews carried out on the *Rossiia*, the Trans-Siberian express train that also links Moscow and Leningrad. Only 16 per cent of the passengers were enthusiastic about perestroika; 13 per cent were opposed to it and 71 per cent were 'watchful'. To the question, 'Do you see any tangible results of perestroika in your everyday life?', 36 per cent said 'yes' and 64 per cent said 'no'. An informal group involved in the defence of human rights carried out a survey among 400 inhabitants of Moscow. 90 per cent of those questioned thought that their freedom of expression was not fully guaranteed (*International Herald Tribune*, 23 December 1987).

This discontent among the workers is recognized by many of Gorbachev's supporters. A report on the big car plant in Togliattigrad, published in *Moscow News* on 4 October 1987, admitted that: 'Discontent among the workers is growing.' Gorbachev is also well aware of this. In a speech in Komsomolsk in April (reported in *Die Zeit*, 10 April 1987), he said:

> If the economic managers put social issues in the very last place, then I can say without hesitation that all our plans, our new means of production, our use of robots in production, increased use of automation and programming – all of this will come to nothing.

Gorbachev supporters insinuate quite often that the strikes and the workers' resistance are approved and supported in an underhand way by the conservative opponents of perestroika. But the weakness of this argument is apparent when we observe the way in which these same conservatives resist any extension of workers' rights within the enterprises. Jean-Marie Chauvier wrote the following comment (*Le Monde diplomatique*, May 1987), after the election of some department heads and some factory directors in accordance with the new law published in *Pravda* on 8 February 1987:

> What will become of the principle of the unity of direction of factories? Will the ballot be secret or not? Are the workers prepared for this and do they really want to share in the responsibility? Before talking about self-management, wouldn't it be better for the workers to be able to defend themselves with trade unions that are independent of management?

But surely there is no contradiction between demanding trade unions independent of the state and demanding workers' control over production, a transitory stage towards full workers' self-management. At the time of the transport strike in Chekhov, the bureaucrats clearly expressed their hostility not only to glasnost but also to democracy and to the workers (*Le Monde*, 17 December 1987):

> The city vice-chair in charge of transport, Viktor Voronin, said: 'Three years ago such a thing could be regarded as sabotage. There was talk in the streets; people have been demoralized by this democracy.' 'It is outrageous', said the head of city transport.

The more class-conscious workers, who are still probably a minority, advance cautiously. At the time of the strike in Chekhov, according to the article in *Le Monde* from which we have just quoted, the workers established a 'council of work collectives' to 'resolve the burning problems of rest periods and housing provision'. At the time of the strike in Kamaz, the workers explained their reasons for being opposed to quality control. 'Our wages are cut because of mistakes made by others. If we were in charge, then we would accept the consequences.'

This is the root of the problem. There can be no democracy or glasnost in the enterprises without workers' control over management. But such workers' control would mean a considerable reduction in the rights and powers of management. Perestroika increases the power of the managers. But *workers' self-management and control by managers are mutually exclusive.*

The French edition of *Moscow News* (*Les Nouvelles de Moscou*), in its first edition of 1988, carried two contributions on the problems of industry and how these problems are to be overcome. The first contributor was a party secretary and deputy head of a department. The other was an ordinary worker. The positions defended by both were diametrically opposed. The party secretary was a Stalinist and opposed to the election of factory directors; the worker was an authentic Communist and argued in favour of workers' self-management.

The bureaucratic Stalinist position from Anatoli Konogov was:

In this situation, which is a difficult one for enterprises, instead of the iron discipline capable of establishing order and enabling one to reach correct decisions, we are playing at democracy. But who gains from all this? The lazy ones, those who skive off from work. They're the ones that are happy now and they are rubbing their hands with glee. Disturb their idleness now and what will happen? They'll vociferously invoke democracy. They act as if they had total freedom. . . .

But when it comes to the election of the foremen, the heads of departments and the director. . . . These are like positions in the army where there are commanders and subordinates. The word of the commander is law. What would happen if every soldier could elect commanders? Some department heads, aware of the spirit among the workers, are beginning to adapt to this mentality. They wear masks and create the pretence of an accommodating bonhomie. Election of the director is ridiculous. The collective is not the proper place for resolving this problem. We don't need vague discussions. What we need is firmness on the part of one single individual who is in charge. There can be only one boss in the house. All this talk about everyone being manager is pure demagogy.

One sole director, at sector, department and enterprise level, should be in charge of everything. Under such conditions we can insist that the director carries out his duties. This will guarantee order and discipline. . . .

I am not a partisan of Stalin. I know that he did lots of things that were bad for the people. But he established order, and what order! Why was there such order then? Because everyone was afraid of the courts. Today also, we should punish without pity. This impresses people and acts as a deterrent. It's better to shoot one, if this means that the whole regiment will fight better.

The worker–Communist position from Anatoli Ptitsin was:

The workers don't find these conditions very attractive. The managers were always a problem. I remember one time that the factory functioned without either director, chief engineer or economist. How? Thanks to the enthusiasm of the workers.

Strangely enough, it was just at the time that our collective, after quite an interval, succeeded in exceeding the plan for deliveries. That was a great victory. Five or six years previously, it would not have been possible. I am certain of this because I am a worker and in constant contact with my comrades and what I saw was a new outlook that came to life among them, the view that they were the boss.

I say 'coming to life' because undoubtedly this is a long and complex process. If anyone tried to convince me that in his factory there is full democracy and all his rights are guaranteed, I wouldn't believe it....

I have heard it said that this is just another campaign, and that it will come to an end with time, just like all the others. I have heard it said that democracy is just a way of hoodwinking the people. According to this view, we should go on working in the same old way as we always did: if the boss pays me well, I'll carry out all his orders and I won't interfere in his affairs.

But this is the philosophy of a servant: the director is the boss, and I just carry out orders. It is because of attitudes like this that we have lost the habit of creative work, the habit of obeying our own conscience, of fighting against disorder in the enterprise, of seeing the state's money as our own money. We have accepted the state of affairs where someone else thinks and decides for us.

Only a small number of us question whether the decisions of this one man are right, and whether this one man, or a number of them, are capable of determining our policy. Let us remind ourselves of what the cult of personality led to. Let us remind ourselves of all the boasting and tranquillizing phrases that came from the top and from all the higher tribunals....

Today, there is no going back to the past. Only authentic (and not a fictitious) democracy in society, a rebirth among all the people of the feeling that they are their own masters, can lead to a change in the situation. This will not come about from obsequiousness but from confidence, from a free discussion of all problems, from a raised level of awareness.

The rebellious spirit which is beginning to manifest itself in the working-class milieu is even more widely spread and better articulated among youth. One has the impression that Soviet youth, especially in the big cities, is going through its pre-May 1968 phase. Pop concerts become semi-political demonstrations. When, for instance, a young guitarist in a Moscow suburb begins to improvise with a song against the war in Afghanistan, there is enthusiastic applause from his audience. In Tomsk, thousands of young people gathered on a square in the city where they protested against the education system and against the lack of democracy in the schools.[10]

The discovery of the possibility of autonomous activity leads to phenomena of political differentiation among youth. There are, for instance, opposing youth groups in Moscow, very much in the style of the (reactionary) skin-heads and the (more leftist) punks in the West. The Lyubers (so called because they come from the Lyubertsy suburb of Moscow) are against the punks, the hippies, and the supporters of pop music and rock. They want to 'clean Moscow of this vermin'. According to Boris Kagarlitsky

the psychological basis for the Lyubers' activity is nostalgia for Stalinism.... After a demonstration in Moscow on 22 February 1987 by two thousand supporters of the youth movement, to demand that the activity of the Lyubers be stopped, some newspapers declared that the Lyubers did not exist, any more than the Abominable Snowman. *Literturnaia Gazeta* informed its readers of the demonstration, while stressing that there were no grounds for it since rumours about the Lyubers had been exaggerated by irresponsible journalists.... Quite obviously, certain forces were not at all interested in mobilizing public opinion against this threat. Something else was obvious, too – that the anonymous influential protectors of the Lyubers were one and the same with those opponents of Gorbachev's liberalization who were keeping quiet for the time being.[11]

The high point of the process of politicization so far has been the appearance of independent journals and clubs during the summer of 1987. The first independent journal to appear was *Glasnost*, published by the one-time political prisoner and left-wing oppositionist, Sergei Grigoriants. *Glasnost* attacks corruption, bureaucratic privilege, and the cause of human rights. Grigoriants' flat was searched by the KGB on 2 October 1987. The Soviet news agency, TASS, accused the editor of having fraudulently used state material in printing the journal.[12] Two other collaborators on the journal were also arrested and questioned for three hours before being released.

In the meantime, other independent publications have appeared in Moscow, Leningrad, and elsewhere. Alongside the independent journals, independent clubs have also made their appearance. About fifty of these clubs held their first public conference in August 1987. One of the most interesting of these clubs is the Club for Social Initiatives (KSI), which is led by the sociologists B. Kagarlitsky and F. Pelman, the journalist G. Pavlovsky, and the philosopher M. Malzhutin.

This club is one of a number of left-wing clubs and includes in its ranks supporters of the Socialist group *Poiski* of the seventies, as well as members of the clandestine 'young Socialists'.[13] Members of the KSI consider themselves to be socialists and Marxists of various tendencies. Some of them are members of the Soviet Communist Party.

The positions of the *Perestroika* clubs in Leningrad are not as clear as those of the KSI. These include both liberals and Socialists with quite different ideas. There are also ecological clubs, as well as more radical left-wing groups who call for 'mass revolutionary self-management' and are opposed to any form of collaboration with the authorities. These clubs are to be found in Rig, Vilnius, and Kiev.

The conference of 20 August 1987 began with forty delegates from more than forty clubs. The final declaration, entitled 'Declaration of the Federation of Socialist Clubs', was signed by 16 groups, including KSI, *Perestroika*, and the *Obshchina* group.[14] During the days that followed, other groups joined the conference, among them a group of young radicals known as the 'Ernesto Che Guevara Brigade'. The final declaration was supported by 600 delegates representing 50 clubs.

A radical Socialist platform was adopted which called for the abolition of censorship, the suppression of 'special sections' in libraries and archives, the creation of independent co-operative publishing houses, freedom to demonstrate, and the erection of a monument to the victims of the Stalinist purges. Although there were quite a few Soviet journalists at the conference, the Soviet press remained silent, waiting for some sign from the top. Finally a friendly account of the conference was published in *Ogonyok* on 5 September 1987.

This fundamental dynamic of accelerated politicization is also evident in the cultural and scientific spheres and among journalists. In April 1987 the director of the Institute of Oceanology at the Academy of Sciences was dismissed for incompetence and corruption. At an open meeting of the Scientific Council of the Institute, eight candidates were nominated for the post of director, four of whom immediately withdrew from the contest. There then followed a genuine election. The person elected received 862 votes for a platform entitled 'Plan for Democratization of Relations within the Collective and within the Administration of the Institute'. Two other candidates received 679 and 566 votes respectively. The outgoing director received 2 votes.[15]

Speaking to a Komsomol meeting at the University of Moscow, the journalist Anatoli Streliani of the review *Novy Mir*, defended the idea of a completely free press (*L'Événement du Jeudi*, 5 November 1987):

We need a press that is independent of the party bureaucracy and of the state apparatus. An independent press is one that would give information on the number of dead and wounded in Afghanistan, give a daily account of the radioactivity around Chernobyl, tell us what was said at meetings of the Politburo....

If we had had an independent press ten years ago, then the engineer Medvedev who wrote that we shouldn't have a nuclear plant near Kiev and who described the catastrophe to come, would have been listened to.... Marx said that freedom of the press was not just a benefit, it was also sometimes inconvenient. Everything should be printed. If the press publishes something and there's someone who doesn't agree, then let them go to some tribunal were this can be decided. We can then defend our point of view in front of the law. There will be plenty of rubbish written. But there will also be a groundswell of change. And we need such a groundswell, even if it brings some rubbish with it. Freedom has a price that cannot be avoided. But the real question is: who profits from silence?

Confronted with this escalating pressure for democratization, the apparatus, including the supporters of Gorbachev, begin to panic. Ligachev and the head of the KGB, Chebrikov, have produced violent diatribes against the 'demagogues' and against the 'one-sided view of history' (i.e. of Stalin) which are systematically found in *Ogonyok* and in *Moscow News*. Their attacks are directed, in other words, against leading Gorbachevites like Yakovlev. Gorbachev's speech on the anniversary of the October revolution (2 November 1987) partially reflects this point of view. It represented a retreat from the policy of radical democratization. But the liberated social forces are becoming less and less controllable from the top. The exiled Social Democratic dissident, Yuri Orlov, is right when he says that the politicization of the working class is now the most likely development, and it won't be a politicization towards the right.

The panic of the apparatus increases as attacks are directed more and more at the holy of holies – the arbitrariness and prerogatives of the police and security organs. From *Moscow News* of 13 December 1987 we learn that at Kiev 'offences against work discipline' are combatted by means of inspections carried out by the militia. This type of control is manifestly illegal: stopping of cars, non-authorized checking of identities, etc. People are refusing to accept any more these flagrant violations of their rights and of legality. They protested, and the paper supported them: 'It is essential that journals and reviews like our own should point out more frequently and analyse more deeply such violations of legality and their causes.'

The fears of the bureaucracy are also evident in the return to repressive measures against freedom of the press and publication. According to the *New York Times* of 3 February 1988, which reproduced an article from *Glasnost*, new directives of 23 October 1987, kept secret until then, prohibit the editing, publication, or distribution of writings by groups that 'interfere in the ideological sphere'.

These fears reached their high point with the elimination of Boris Yeltsin in November 1987. This affair erupted at the meeting of the Central Committee on 21 October 1987. There was a confrontation at this plenum between the Ligachev group and Yeltsin, with Gorbachev playing a Bonapartist role between the two. Since the contributions to this meeting have not been published, we can only speculate as to what was the real content of the debate. According to Alexandre Adler, writing in the French newspaper *Libération* (1 November 1987), Yeltsin accused Ligachev of a 'lack of humanity' and accused Gorbachev of 'organizing a cult of his own personality'. He complained about delays in the implementation of perestroika. He demanded that the conditions of life for the masses improved immediately or as quickly as possible, since without this perestroika could not succeed. Ligachev responded by pointing out that the achievements of perestroika were somewhat meagre in Moscow, where Yeltsin was party chief.

Whatever the precise sequence of events that led up to it, the politically minded public in the USSR and abroad had quite a shock when they opened *Pravda* on 13 November 1987. There they were able to read a detailed account of the plenary session of the Moscow party committee which decided to relieve Yeltsin of his post as secretary of that committee. The elimination of Yeltsin and the manner in which this was done were a serious setback for the democratization process in the Soviet Union. It indicated once again, the limits within which the apparatus is prepared to tolerate glasnost.

But what hit the Soviet public hardest was not simply the elimination of Yeltsin, but the content and conclusions of the 'debate' in the Moscow party committee. The account of the debate in *Pravda* was reminiscent of Stalinism in the period before the purges of 1934–39.

First of all, there was no debate. Everything was decided unanimously. Yeltsin capitulated in a most abject manner. 'I agree with the critical remarks formulated with respect to myself.' But there was no mention of the substance of Yeltsin's intervention in the Central Committee which started off this whole episode. What were the real differences of opinion that underlay this whole affair? The question wasn't even asked.

The content and tone of the interventions against Yeltsin were reprehensible. All the participants in this 'debate' were highly placed and highly paid party bureaucrats. Not a single worker took part, not a single authentic representative of the party rank and file. Everything was reduced to Yeltsin's 'personal ambitions'. This was the formula used by Gorbachev himself. All the formulae used were reminiscent of

Stalinism: 'His style of work was demagogic'; 'He criticized the Central Committee for lack of democracy'; 'He was detached from us, he wasn't one of us'; 'He kept a distance from the officials of the party'; 'The whole world loves Moscow. But you, Boris Yeltsin, love neither Moscow nor Muscovites'; and so on.

And as if to make absolutely clear that this was an exemplary case, *Pravda*, on 16 November 1987, warned quite clearly against abuses of democracy which could lead to 'anarchy and chaos'. In case the workers should get carried away by their new right to elect factory directors, *Pravda* reminded them that 'the leading role of the party is inscribed in the Constitution.... That is why the committees of the party have the right to openly express their opinion on the persons recommended for this or that post' (reported in *Le Monde*, 18 November 1987).

The coup against glasnost by the direct intervention of the party apparatus was, however, not the only important aspect of the Yeltsin affair. This affair also confirmed, in a spectacular manner, the existence in the Soviet Union of a genuine dialectic between reform and social movement. The politicized elements of the population did not remain passive in the face of this setback. The independent clubs in Moscow and elsewhere reacted immediately. There was a protest by students in Moscow. There was a spontaneous demonstration in Sverdlovsk and there were reports (not confirmed at the time of writing) of a demonstration in Leningrad. There was great agitation among the workers in Moscow.

Jef Turf, head of the Flemish Communist Party, was an eye-witness to events in the biggest car plant in Moscow. The agitation, the discussions, and the work stoppages were at such a pitch on the morning of 13 November that the director of the plant gave the workers the day off, fearing that there might be a strike by thousands of workers.

This had nothing to do with the personality of Yeltsin, although his populist interventions against bureaucratic privileges and corruption, as well as his attempts to improve living conditions for the masses, made him a popular figure. What was at work here was the will of a politically conscious layer of workers and others to preserve and extend the democratic freedoms which they had won in the period 1986–87 and to prevent any abrupt going back. The Ligachev group will have to take this into account from now on. So too will Gorbachev.

# 13

# The Future of Gorbachev's Reforms

The nineteenth Conference of the CPSU held in June 1988 provided a real insight into the political situation in the Soviet Union. Gorbachev's proposals, bold as they seemed, compromised on all decisive points with the interests of the bureaucracy. The decisions of the Central Committee of 30 September 1988, as well as Gorbachev's appointment as head of state, do not basically change the unstable equilibrium within the Soviet power elite. Contrary to appearances, these decisions were the result of a new compromise, and the representatives of the party apparatus continue to hold the majority of seats on the Central Committee.

While the September moves were carried through with the bare minimum of discussion, the conference occasioned a real debate, an indication of how much things have really changed in the Soviet Union. The arguments were genuine and were very important from the point of view of the politicization of the mass of the people. The way in which the debate was contained, however, leads one to the conclusion that the democratization which has begun is still very tentative and very partial.

An important element in the preparation of the nineteenth Conference was the intervention of worker militants into the debate. Nothing like this has been seen since the beginning of the Stalinist dictatorship, which shows once again how absurd it is to maintain that nothing has changed in the Soviet Union. A typical intervention was that of the workers at the Volzhsky Motor Works (VAZ) in Togliattigrad. The workers at this plant had been told to bring their work schedules into line with other plants in the industry. But the workers rebelled. According to Anatoly Melnikov, one of the workers at the plant, writing in *Moscow News* (no. 27, 1988):

You can see from the mandates [given to the delegates to the nineteenth Conference] that the workers feel they do have an organ, the work collective council, which is really struggling on their behalf. The workers began believing it after the situation with the schedules which happened six months ago. Moscow ordered us to bring the length of our working day at the plant into line with other plants in the industry. We were working 12 minutes more. The administration obeyed. Everything seemed quite legal. But it so happened that due to a shorter working day, we'd have to work an extra six to eight 'black' Saturdays a year in order to fulfill the plan. The workers were indignant. The work collective council disagreed too. And we managed to do what we wanted to do – our old schedule remained intact.

The mandate given to delegates to the Conference from party members in VAZ had proposed an all-Union congress of work collective councils to work out a single strategy for action and had called on the CPSU to recognize the independence of work collectives, including in the choosing and appointment of administrators.

In June 1988 there was a bus strike in the Lithuanian city of Klapeda which almost paralysed this city of 20,000 people. One of the workers, Leonid Kapelyushny, reported on the strike in *Moscow News* (no. 27, 1988):

When the discontent started to gain force and cross the bounds of sensible demands, it was the Communists who assumed the right to speak in the name of the entire work collective, which took guts. One detail sticks in our minds: at the height of the developments, when the negotiations reached a deadlock, the administration and the representatives of the higher authorities decided to move the council to a quieter place. They invited some of the bus drivers to join them, so as not to be accused of scheming behind the workers' backs. At that moment one of the authorities said in a fit of temper: 'Is this really the way to strike? No clear programme, no well-founded demands, and no representatives for negotiations!' 'But it's our first strike! We're inexperienced', shouted one of the drivers. Everyone suddenly burst into laughter and just as suddenly fell silent.

It is in the light of those beginnings of working-class activity that we can appreciate the tactical choices facing the Soviet 'new left'. On the one hand they recognize quite correctly that the scepticism of the workers with regard to perestroika will only be overcome if the threat to their full employment, buying power and class solidarity at enterprise level is removed and there is a real improvement in their living standards. On the other hand they share the real fear of the Gorbachevites concerning the failure or reversal of glasnost with all that this would imply. The overthrow of Gorbachev at the present moment, before the working class has really moved into action, would mean a return to power of the most conservative and repressive elements of the bureaucracy. The workers would gain nothing from such a reversal. The majority of the 'new left' in the Soviet Union have therefore opted for an alliance with the more militant elements of the Gorbachev wing.[1] Its first major demonstration in Moscow carried banners which said: Long live Glasnost! Down with Bureaucracy! Power to the Soviets!

If it is correct to characterize Gorbachev's policy as one of more or less radical reform, should revolutionary Marxists be opposed to such a policy? Such a position would be simplistic, ultra-left and counter-productive. Revolutionaries cannot oppose reforms, regardless of where they come from, so long as they improve the living and working conditions of the working masses and thereby also their ability to struggle. To oppose such reforms would mean losing political effectiveness and all links with the masses, as well as credibility and historical justification. Revolution is not an end in itself, but is an instrument in the struggle for emancipation. If, under pretext of promoting the revolutionary struggle, we remain superbly indifferent to the real conditions of life and struggle of the masses, to the increase of their rights, powers, and freedoms, not to mention the improvements in their living conditions, or if, indeed, we would like to actually see things get worse, then the masses will conclude that these so-called revolutionaries are sacrificing the interests of the oppressed and exploited to the interests of their own political project. And the masses will be absolutely right. For workers who are terribly exploited, degraded, poor, brutalized, and divided, as well as confused about the emancipatory objectives of their struggle, will never be capable of constructing a classless egalitarian society, a society of *freely associated producers* who manage their own affairs, which is what, by definition, Socialism is.

Revolutionary Marxists fully support every struggle for reforms which promote the emancipation of the workers – reforms, in other words, which improve the conditions of life, of work, and of struggle for the broad masses. Even more, they are the best fighters for such reforms. The fundamental difference between revolutionaries and reformists is not in the acceptance or rejection of the struggle for reforms. What revolutionaries reject is any form of self-limitation of this mass struggle. They reject, in other words, any political orientation which consists in trying to prevent the mass struggle from 'excessively' disrupting social and political stability, from disrupting the power of the ruling class or ruling layer, any political orientation which tries to prevent the masses from 'going too far'. As distinct from the reformists, revolutionaries give priority to the *autonomous movement of the masses* in the struggle for reforms, which implies a constant battle for the *class political independence* of the workers in relation to other social forces. As distinct from reformists, revolutionaries prepare and systematically encourage the creation and development of all forms of self-organization of the masses – from the most embryonic forms such as strike committees to the more developed forms such as workers' councils organized on a national basis.

Such a movement could only begin as a movement for immediate demands, a movement for what are seen as reforms. It is only when the masses learn through their practical experience that these demands for reform cannot be achieved within the existing institutional framework that a real mass revolution can come into being, at least in an industrialized country where the urban proletariat are a majority of the population. For revolutionaries, therefore, the struggle for radical reforms *can*, in this way, lead to and produce revolution. For reformists, on the other hand, the fear and the rejection of revolution blocks and renders impossible any real struggle for reforms whenever the 'established order' is against reform.

But there are reforms and reforms. We have emphasized the duty of revolutionaries to support the struggle for reforms which assist the emancipation of the oppressed and exploited, which improve their conditions of life and work and increase their capacity to struggle. This obviously implies that revolutionary Marxists reject any reforms which, under the pretext of improving economic efficiency, lead to a deterioration in the conditions of life, work, and struggle for the workers. This means that a concrete analysis of the concrete situation is essential before deciding whether or not to support any concrete reform. Reforms have to be judged according to the criterion of how they affect the conditions of life and work and how they affect the ability of the masses to struggle for their own emancipation.

We must judge the nature of reforms that are proposed, put into effect, or demanded by some section of the masses according to a *class criterion*, which is the only guide in a world where so many initiatives in the larger political arena are confused, complex, and contradictory. It is with the aid of such criteria that we must judge the reforms begun by Gorbachev in the Soviet Union. *There can be no question of accepting or rejecting these reforms en bloc. What is at stake is critical support for or rejection of each reform taken separately.*

The argument is made that this process is unrealistic, that the choice is really between Gorbachev (and the possibility of some radical reforms) and the overthrow of Gorbachev. It is argued that, in the first case, progress towards some form of Socialist democracy and the achievement of a number of Socialist socio-economic objectives is at least possible. In the second case, there would be a regression towards stagnation and inertia in the internal life of the Soviet Union. The leaden weight of bureaucracy would descend on all spheres of Soviet life. To refuse to support Gorbachev *en bloc* would be tantamount today to supporting a policy of 'the worse it is the better'.

This political argument, and the analysis which underlies it, far from being concrete and realistic, is abstract and short-sighted, like every example of so-called *realpolitik*. It is based on premisses which are in themselves contradictory.

The first premiss: Gorbachev remains very vulnerable. But what is the source of this vulnerability? Obviously these are powerful social forces – the so-called conservative wing of the bureaucracy which is opposed to radical reforms and which fears their scope and intrinsic logic. But if these social forces, which are very much a minority in Soviet society, can really threaten or even overthrow Gorbachev, then it will be because the majority of Soviet society, the workers, are not mobilized in support of these reforms. So the first premiss is immediately undermined. The outcome of this process will not be decided simply by this new man, Gorbachev. The outcome will depend on the relation of forces between the different political tendencies engaged in the struggle and this depends, in the final analysis, on the social forces that support the one tendency or the other.

Under those circumstances, any action against the interests of the workers would make it more difficult to mobilize their support for Gorbachev. Some sections of the workers would become passive, while other sections would give their support to the conservatives. So, to support any of the reforms of perestroika which are anti-worker would be tantamount to facilitating the removal of Gorbachev. *Realpolitik*, paradoxically, leads to precisely the opposite result of what was intended.

Those who argue for total support for Gorbachev also rely on another hypothesis: the only choice is between Gorbachev and a return to inertia. But there is another possibility, indeed a probability, that if Gorbachev were overthrown he would be replaced by another Gorbachev, in other words, by someone a little less radical, less liberal, but still committed to the implementation of important reforms. Would such a replacement end forever the possibility of the development of autonomous mass activity? This hasn't in the least been demonstrated.

This whole analysis leads to the conclusion that the only alternative to the enlightened absolutism of Gorbachev is an obscurantist dictatorship. This is a thesis which is defended by many observers, sociologists and historians both in the West and in the Soviet Union. What is happening in the Soviet Union, according to those commentators, is a 'revolution from above'. Everything depends on what happens at the top.

The phrase, 'revolution from above', in inverted commas, generally refers to radical measures taken by governments as a way of getting out of some historical impasse in which their power is threatened. The point of the exercise is to prevent a revolutionary explosion, in other words, to prevent a 'revolution from below'. But, for this very reason, these measures are radical reforms and not a revolution in the proper sense of the term. Sometimes, such reforms are effective and achieve their goal. The revolution from below doesn't happen, or is put off for some decades.[2]

Precisely because 'revolutions from above' are reforms and not real revolutions, their results differ substantially. The radical elimination of the 'ancien régime' does not occur. It is sufficient to compare Japan after the 'Meiji' revolution to the United States, Bismarck's Germany to France, Alexander II's Russia to Italy, to see the difference.

But it is clear that the changes which are taking place in the Soviet Union do not involve, in any fashion, the transfer of power from one social force to another. What we are dealing with here are actually radical reforms, the purpose of which is to head off a genuine revolution. It is in this sense, and in this sense only, that one can use the phrase 'revolution from above' as a way of defining the Gorbachev era.[3] The analogy with enlightened absolutism is immediately obvious.[4]

We should remember that enlightened absolutism, as an instrument of conservative social forces to check and contain forces for change, is actually much older than the absolute monarchies of the eighteenth century. The writer Italo Calvino, in a novel interpretation of the rise of the Jesuits during the Catholic counter-reformation, remarks that: 'the Jesuits sought to oversee the emergence of modernity and the new through a difficult strategy of allowing openings to fresh ideas and contriving ways to close off the approaches to them. And, what is more, they could use their proverbial powers of persuasion, deceit and diplomacy.'[5]

The analogy with Gorbachev is clear. As in the period of enlightened absolutism, the initiative comes from the summit of the state. The detonator is the recognition that there are risks of social explosion which must be avoided at all costs, explosions which have been prepared over decades of accumulated and unsolved contradictions. Now, as previously, the mass of the people appear as passive spectators, sometimes showing their approval, sometimes showing their hostility or scepticism. The initiatives appear to be restricted to the governing and the privileged. The autocrat and his principal advisers appear to be the determining factors in the whole process.

Many writers on the left share this vision of the Soviet Union under Gorbachev. Rudolf Bahro sees Gorbachev as a 'revolutionary despot', a neo-Platonist, who wants to bring together 'the best, the most inspired elements from all the republics, from all walks of life, to create a new

Communist League.'[6] But this analogy with enlightened absolutism is not useful in understanding the Soviet Union. Austria in 1780 was a country of dispersed and illiterate peasants, not to mention Prussia in 1765 or Spain in 1795. But Russia has a highly educated working class, highly qualified and concentrated in large urban fortresses. Russia's proletariat is numerically the strongest in the world, bigger than that of the United States.[7] It is a country which has been refashioned, changed and educated by a century which saw the development of capitalist industry and technology and then the revolution of October, with all its consequences. The revolutionary and emancipatory potential which exists in this society was demonstrated in the Prague Spring and in the self-management movement in Poland during 1980 to 1981.

Since the Soviet proletariat is much more powerful than the proletariat of Poland, Czechoslovakia, or the French proletariat in May 1968, any similar dynamic in the Soviet Union would exist on a much greater scale. Any assessment of the possible implications of the Gorbachev reforms must take as its starting point the following general problematic: what will be the effects of these reforms on the capacities of the mass of the people for social, economic and political self-defence and self-activity? It is axiomatic for a Marxist, or, to express it more scientifically: it is a fundamental hypothesis of Marxism that the emancipation of the workers can only be the task of the workers themselves, that no variety of socialism is possible or conceivable unless it is constructed through the self-activity of the workers themselves.

The better studies of the Soviet Union today do not engage in this 'cult of the personality' of Gorbachev. They situate the Gorbachev phenomenon in the context of the new social reality of the Soviet Union. A good example of this correct approach is Martin Walker, who writes:

And the question is not simply whether Gorbachev's government can produce an efficient and modernized Soviet economy, in spite of the constraints on political reform that the party will doubtless impose. To put it that way is to fall into the Communist Party's own trap, to assume that the politics and decisions adopted by an authoritarian central government will in and of themselves determine the future course of Soviet society. If the long social revolution which produced the Gorbachev generation and the complex social system of today tell us anything, it is that a command economy cannot always deliver what was demanded, and that a totalitarian society cannot always produce the social structure that was intended. This is the wild card in the Soviet pack. Social change has its own momentum and its own logic, quite apart from the decisions taken in the Kremlin, and is steadily transforming Soviet society in its own unpredictable way.[8]

Gorbachev himself, as we indicated earlier, insists on the revolutionary nature of perestroika. It is, he says, a revolution of a special type. He explicitly refers to the precedent of the revolutions in France in the nineteenth century. This was precisely the reference point for Trotsky in distinguishing the political revolution necessary in the Soviet Union from social revolutions of the type of 1789 in France. Gorbachev writes: 'Historical analogy may be helpful in answering this question. Lenin once noted that in the country of the classical bourgeois revolution, France, after its great revolution of 1789–93, it took another three revolutions (1830, 1848 and 1871) to carry through its aims.'[9]

But the snag here is that the revolutions of 1830, 1848 and 1871 were not 'revolutions from above' of the type pursued by Gorbachev, but were genuine popular revolutions with mass mobilizations, with governments overthrown 'in the streets' and involving armed insurrections. None of this is compatible with a 'revolution from above' controlled and directed by the ruling power.

Given what we know at present, only one conclusion seems possible: the task of revolutionary Marxists, and of all Socialist and Communist forces both inside and outside the Soviet Union, as far as Gorbachev is concerned, is critically to support or reject each concrete reform measure according to whether it serves or damages the interests of the working class. This means:

1. Critical support for glasnost and for liberalization in the media, culture, and the arts; full support for a return to the freedom of expression, for ideological–political pluralism, for an increase in the political rights of citizens.

2. Critical support for measures that loosen bureaucratically centralized planning, for every measure that increases the possibility for workers and consumers to participate in the process of economic decison-making at every level.

3. Critical support for all measures that improve living conditions for the people, especially in the areas of food distribution, housing, health, public transport, education, crèches, holidays, etc.

4. Critical support for all disarmament initiatives, especially nuclear disarmament and the banning of chemical and biological weapons.

5. The rejection of all measures which reduce the rights won by the workers, rejection especially of any increase in the rights of managers and directors of enterprises, rejection of any attack on full employment.

6. The rejection of every measure which increases inequality in Soviet society.

7. The rejection of an excessive extension of the influence of the market and of market mechanisms, except in the area of small-scale production, because this undermines full employment and increases social inequality.

8. The rejection of every initiative towards peaceful coexistence with the bourgeoisie in the area of the present international class struggle; the rejection, in other words, of every manoeuvre with this bourgeoisie against the revolutions and the class struggles that are actually taking place. This obviously does not imply that we favour military adventures outside the boundaries of the Soviet Union, something which the workers and the oppressed have no need of and do not desire.

This list does not cover all the reform measures of the Gorbachev era which have been proposed or already introduced in the Soviet Union. But it is sufficiently large to establish a framework for a political attitude.

Political discussion and criticism, and a rise in political consciousness for broader masses can only come from a spontaneous political practice and apprenticeship at the base. Marx made fun of those who, under the enlightened absolutism of the Prussian kingdom, thought they could teach people to swim without actually going into the water. He made fun of those 'jumping masters' who tried to prepare jumping over a precipice with the aid of a measuring tape.

The enlightened paternalism of Gorbachev comes up against a similar obstacle. In the same way that science cannot advance without free discussion, the political apprenticeship of the masses needs freedom of action to blossom. It is essential to demand more radical political reforms and more radical social and economic measures:

1. The full elimination of censorship; the right for any specific group of citizens freely to publish books, pamphlets, periodicals, leaflets, etc.

2. The repeal of the articles in the penal code that restrict freedom of expression, in particular those that prohibit 'anti-Soviet agitation' and 'slandering Soviet power', articles that clearly concern neither spying nor criminal activities (terrorism, etc.) but institutionalize crimes of opinion and prevent or obstruct the exercise of democratic rights by the masses.

3. The release of all political prisoners, that is, of all those who are in prison or in the camps for crimes of opinion.

4. The establishment of habeas corpus. Any person arrested must be

presented with a precise charge within twenty-four hours of the arrest, and have the right to a lawyer of their choice for the defence. The lawyer must have the right to see all the evidence on which the charge is based.

5. As a protection against police arbitrariness, anyone arrested must have the right to appeal to the local soviets. The local soviets must have the right themselves to question any person arrested, without police presence. The soviets must have the right to investigate police operations.

6. The right for any group of citizens above a certain minimum number, not only to propose candidates for election to the soviets (including the Supreme Soviet) in nominating assemblies, but to run candidates, who have received a certain minimum number of votes in these assemblies, in the elections themselves.

7. The free election of trade union delegates, members of the workers' councils, and the women's councils in the enterprises, with the right to put forward several candidates, without any restriction. For a transitional period, for reasons indicated by Gorbachev himself, the freedom of such elections would have to be assured by secret ballot.

8. The right for freely elected trade union members of the workers' councils to contact each other, to consult and organize vertically within an industry and, above all, horizontally in the localities in the big urban centres, in towns, districts, regions, and republics. The elimination of the principle of 'democratic centralism' within the unions, enterprise groups, workers' councils, and all mass organizations. This principle, even in its original Leninist form, makes sense only when applied to persons freely associated on the basis of shared convictions and not to state or class bodies. At this level, to ensure that the masses will genuinely exercise the real power, the guiding principle must be that of delegated authority based on a mandate that can be taken back by the electors that gave it.

9. The re-establishment and guarantee of the workers' right to strike or carry out any other form of action in pursuance of their demands.

10. Generalized workers' control over all economic activities, at all levels of the plan and management, such as over stocks and the transport of raw materials; the use of and demands for equipment; the calculation of current production costs; the establishment of production and wage norms; the targets of the plan within the enterprise and in other enterprises; the general priorities in plans governing employment; the right of veto over layoffs and other forms of

reducing employment; etc. These are key measures for increasing real and not merely formal participation by the workers in management. These are decisive steps towards the economic democracy that the Gorbachevites talk so much about, and which is supposed to be the updated version of the 'democracy of the producers' that was talked about in the wake of the October revolution.

11. The opening of the account books in all enterprise and inter-enterprise institutions; full and complete information about industrial, commercial, and agricultural operations; publication of all the real costs of these operations.

12. The index-linking of all wages and social provisions; the establishment of a monthly index of the cost of living drawn up by independent agencies and implemented in each area by committees elected by the workers and by households.

13. An increase in the number of crèches and nurseries; the extension of maternity leave with guarantee of reemployment.

14. The elaboration of a plan for rapid transition to the 35-hour week, then to the 32-hour week, and even to the 20-hour week.

15. Strengthening the system of work inspection, under workers' control, to ensure the strictest respect for the law with respect to security and hygiene at work.

16. The construction of holiday homes adequate to allow a rapid expansion of the number of workers who can enjoy their paid holidays away from home.

17. Building more hospitals and expanding the pharmaceuticals industry so that medical care and life expectancy may improve.

18. The elimination of special shops and reserved sections in hospitals, vacation homes, special restaurants, educational establishments, etc. Workers' control and citizens' committees to ensure that these measures are implemented.

19. The introduction of the principle that no state functionary, even at the highest levels, can get greater remuneration (including non-monetary benefits) than a skilled worker.

20. The right for councils of women in the enterprises to make all decisions concerning the special needs of women workers.

21. The full implementation, within the framework of the Union, of the rights of nationalities to self-administration and self-determination.

Given the tight interlocking of the state and the Communist Party in the Soviet Union, the extension of a series of measures about glasnost to the structures of the Communist Party does not reflect illusions about the nature of this party but rather elementary democratic demands. Since at present the only real political discussions take place within the Central Committee of the Communist Party, it is logical for critical citizens to demand that these debates be published. As Gorbachev proposes that the members of party committees be elected by secret ballot, it is obvious that citizens should demand that these elections are not a mere pretence but that there are different candidates with different platforms.

Obviously this does not in any way detract from the importance of the demand for a multi-party system, that is, for the right of the Soviet workers and peasants to form freely the political parties of their choice.

Is advocating such demands asking for 'too much too soon'? Does it strengthen the position of the conservatives against Gorbachev? This is one of the most worn-out arguments. Already on the eve of the 1848 elections, the liberals accused the Communists of the time of 'playing the reactionary game' by putting forward their 'excessive demands'. The real problem lies elsewhere. It lies in the class nature of the political activity, in the different social interests that are to be expressed and articulated.

*There can be no Socialist democracy without mass mobilization, without political revolution.* To think that you can really make revolutionary changes in the Soviet Union as it is today, without the working class moving, is an illusion. To think that the working class can be made to move without appealing to its interests is to fall into the most sterile sort of voluntarist and idealist utopianism. The main thrust or both moral and material incentives for the workers in post-capitalist societies is along the lines that they have concretely manifested themselves for the last thirty years: solidarity, justice, equality, real decision-making power. Marxists would add to this the struggle for a return to real international workers' solidarity.

Speaking to a group of workers on 19 June 1986, Gorbachev stated: 'The enemy is not afraid of Soviet nuclear missiles. But it is afraid of the extension of democracy in the Soviet Union.' A Soviet Union in which real Socialist democracy prevailed would have a power of attraction for the masses of the whole world. It would, at one stroke, change the international situation. But this would mean a real Socialist democracy, one which did not merely give the workers more economic rights and powers, but gave still more rights and powers than in the most advanced capitalist countries. Gorbachev's initiatives will not produce such a democracy. It will come from the action of the masses. But Gorbachev's reforms open a breach through which this action could come, when the hopes he has raised have been disappointed.

Many Western commentators question the ability of the Soviet masses to intervene in political life in an autonomous fashion, not only in the short or medium term, but even in the long term. They emphasize the Asiatic (Mongol) antecedents of Russian power, the continuity between tzarist autocracy and bureaucratic dictatorship, the absence of mass democratic traditions – except for the tradition of village self-government which, however, disappeared with the old peasantry – and the depoliticization of the working class which resulted from the Stalinist terror and the loss of faith in Socialism.

Bureaucratic resistance to Gorbachev's reforms is put down to the 'eternal power' of the Russian bureaucracy. Marshall Goldman inscribed in his book the famous quotation from John Stuart Mill (1859):

> The Tzar himself is powerless against the bureaucratic body; he can send any of them to Siberia, but he cannot govern without them, or against their will. On every decree of his they have a tacit veto, by merely refraining from carrying it out.[10]

Lenin, towards the end of his life, also criticized the power and weight of bureaucracy in the Soviet Union:

> If we take Moscow with its 4,700 communists in responsible positions, and if we take that huge bureaucratic machine, that gigantic heap, we must ask: who is directing whom? I doubt very much that it can truthfully be said that the communists are directing that heap. To tell the truth, they are not directing, they are being directed.[11]

There is an excessive simplification in this view of Russian history, an underestimation of the insurrectionary traditions of the peasantry and, above all, an attempt to rewrite the history of the revolutions of 1905 and 1917. The colossal character of the spontaneous activity of the masses during both those revolutions is, to say the least, systematically undervalued.[12] But this view especially underestimates and wrongly evaluates the fundamental transformations that have taken place in Soviet society since the revolution of 1917. The existence now in Soviet society of a proletarian majority which is educated and qualified and irresistibly drawn towards self-activity, at least at enterprise level, creates for the first time a potential force capable of ridding the Soviet Union of its bureaucratic heap.

The chief obstacle to the achievement of Gorbachev's project is not that the obstructive force of the bureaucratic apparatus is too big. It is that Gorbachev is caught between two fires: the resistance of conservative sections of the bureaucratic apparatus on the one hand, and, on the other, the pressure of the masses for a much more profound democratization. That is why an increasingly large section of the Communist Party leadership are saying: perestroika, yes; more glasnost, no.

In the light of what is happening today in the Soviet Union, the analysis and the prediction made by Leon Trotsky half a century ago has turned out to be more realistic and more probable:

> All indications agree that the further course of development must inevitably lead to a clash between the culturally developed forces of the people and the bureaucratic oligarchy. There is no peaceful outcome for this crisis. The Soviet bureaucracy will not give up its positions without a fight. The development leads obviously to the road of revolution.
>
> With energetic pressure from the popular mass, and the disintegration inevitable in such circumstances of the government apparatus, the resistance of those in power may prove much weaker than now appears. . . .
>
> The revolution which the bureaucracy is preparing against itself will not be social, like the October revolution of 1917. It is not a question this time of changing the economic foundations of society, or replacing certain forms of property with other forms. . . .
>
> It is not a question of substituting one ruling clique for another, but of changing the very methods of administering the economy and guiding the culture of the country. Bureaucratic autocracy must give place to soviet democracy. A restoration of the right of criticism, and a genuine freedom of elections, are necessary conditions for the further development of the country. This assumes a revival of the freedom of soviet parties, beginning with the party of the Bolsheviks, and a resurrection of the trade unions. The bringing of democracy into industry means a radical revision of plans in the interests of the toilers. Free discussion of economic problems will decrease the overhead expense of bureaucratic mistakes and zigzags. Expensive playthings – palaces of the soviets, new theatres, show-off subways – will be crowded out in favour of workers' dwellings. 'Bourgeois norms of distributions' will be confined within the limits of strict necessity, and, in step with the growth of social wealth, will give way to socialist equality. Ranks will be immediately abolished. The tinsel of decorations will go into the melting pot. The youth will receive the opportunity to breathe freely, criticize, make mistakes and grow up. Science and art will be freed of their chains. And, finally, foreign policy will return to the traditions of revolutionary internationalism.[13]

That is how it will be.

# Notes

## 1. The Objective Contradictions of Soviet Society

1. Alexander Zinoviev, *Homo Sovieticus*, London 1982.

2. See in particular the commentary by the leading Czech emigré Communist, Zdenek Mlynar, in the West German journal *Sozialismus*, April 1986. Zhores Medvedev, in a recent book, has expressed a more sober and pessimistic view (*Gorbachev*, London 1986).

3. For an account of the Marxist theoretical foundation which underlies this analysis of the Soviet Union, see our essay, '*Bureaucratie et production marchande*', *Quatrième Internationale*, no. 25, 1987; also 'The Laws of Motion of the Soviet Economy', *Critique*, no. 12, 1980.

4. Jean Radvyanyi, in an interesting book significantly titled *L'URSS en révolution* (Paris 1987) emphasizes the contradictory character of Soviet reality and underlines the fact that an excessively uniform view of Soviet society has been prevalent in both East and West.

5. The tables are from *Narodnoe Khoziaistvo SSSR v 1972* g and *Narodnoe Khoziaistvo SSSR v 1984* g. The data are cited in an article by Marie-Elizabeth Ruban in *Osteuropa*, August–September 1986.

6. In this context we must point also to the obvious advance of the USSR in the field of space exploration, even in relation to the United States. See the articles on this subject in *The Times*, 10 August 1987, and also in *The Economist*, 3 October 1987.

7. The growing preoccupation of the bourgeoisie and the bourgeois state with offences involving 'insider knowledge' is also a reflection of this contradiction. The relatively easy access of 'people outside the enterprise' to inside information 'distorts competition'.

8. The report on Novosibirsk emphasizes the fact, a decade too late, that the system of economic management in the Soviet Union (and, we would add, the social and political system as well) generates 'laziness, dishonesty and a low level of morality in the population'. It could have added: the example comes from the top – the fish begins to rot at the head.

9. Heidi and Alvin Toffler, after a trip to the Soviet Union, were quite right when they wrote (*Sunday Times*, 4 January 1987):

An advanced economy demands incessant technological innovation. But technological advance in the modern world is tied up more and more with culture and the social structure. To generate a wealth of new ideas – including technological ideas – the system has to allow not only scientific theories and hypotheses, but also socially odd ideas, non-conformist art, questionable economic theories and even dissident ideologies.... What will be the consequences of 'desktop publishing' for the Soviet Union? If the authorities prevent the people from having access to computers, what price will they pay in terms of reduced living standards?

10. On the general problem of poverty in the Soviet Union, see Mervyn Matthews, 'Poverty in the Soviet Union', *The Wilson Quarterly*, autumn 1985.

11. A good description of corruption in Azerbaidzhan and Georgia is provided by the socioloist, Ilya Zemtsov, in *La Corruption en Union Soviétique*, Paris 1976. Zemtsov, professor at the Lenin Institute in Baku, was head of the information department of the Central Committee of the Communist Party in Azerbaidzhan before emigrating to Israel in 1973. For other examples of corruption see Zhores Medvedev, *Andropov*, London 1982.

12. This did not prevent General Jaruzelski from affirming, in the French journal *L'Humanité*, 3 June 1985, that 'Our state guarantees to its citizens social services, the equivalent of which is not to be found in the most advanced and richest of the capitalist countries.'

13. Abel Aganbegyan, *Perestroika*, Paris 1987, pp. 26–7. An English edition of this book is in preparation. All references which follow are to the French edition.

14. The figures for the period 1975–79 have not yet been published in the Soviet Union. Western medical experts believe that during this period infant mortality in the Soviet Union reached thirty-one per thousand ( *Wall Street Journal*, 31 October 1986).

15. Abel Aganbegyan, p. 24.

16. These data, and those that follow, were provided by Dominique Legrand in an excellent article: '*La Fièvre de la paperasse*', *Inprecor*, no. 251, 1987.

17. Ibid.

## 2. The Rebirth of Public Opinion

1. When Khrushchev made his speech denouncing Stalin at the 20th Party Congress someone in the audience shouted: 'And where were you when all these crimes were committed?' Khrushchev replied in a threatening tone: 'Who said that?' There was a deathly silence. 'Now you understand why I kept quiet', he said. This sort of thing doesn't happen today when Gorbachev denounces the measures of the Stalinist period. The atmosphere has changed.

2. On the subject of experimental theatre, see the interesting interview with Yuri Liubimov, ex-director of the Taganka, in *L'Alternative*, no. 29, 1984.

3. This information is taken from the book, translated from the Russian, by Victor Zaslavsky, *The Neo-Stalinist State*, Brighton 1982.

4. V.I. Mishin, *Sotsialnyi Progress*, Gorki 1970.

5. Official Soviet sources quoted by Zaslavsky.

6. Roy Medvedev, ed., *Samizdat Register*, London 1977.

7. The economist Tatiana Zaslavskaia and the philosopher Butenko were reprimanded for their audacity and the writer Yevtushenko was attacked in the *Literaturnaia Gazeta* for his principled criticism of the censorship. But these were mild attacks in passing.

8. Zhores Medvedev, *The Rise and Fall of T.D. Lyssenko*, London 1969.

9. Sidney Bloch and Peter Reddaway, *Russia's Political Hospitals*, London 1977. On the case of Nikitin and Koryagin, see Kevin Klose, *Russia and the Russians*, New York 1984.

10. Mark Popovsky, *Science in Chains*, London 1980.

11. Concerning the Novosibirsk report see the article by Marina Bek in the French magazine *Inprecor*, no. 193, 1985.

12. For information on demographic changes in the USSR and their consequences for the nationality question in that country, see Hélène Carrére d'Encausse, *L'Empire éclaté*,

Paris 1978. But the conclusions of this work should be treated cautiously.

13. Kevin Klase, ch. 13; Marina Vlady, *Vladimir ou le vol arrêté*, Paris 1987. Marina Vlady was Vysotsky's wife.

14. Mark Popovsky, p. 256.

15. Zalygin's speech was printed in the French weekly *Rouge*, 17 February 1986.

16. Mark Popovsky, pp. 231–3.

17. See the article published in *Literaturna Ukraina*, no. 13, 1986, one month before the accident. This article is translated in *Soviet Nationalities Survey*, vol. 3, no. 4–5, 1986.

18. Tatiana Mamonova, ed. *Women in Russia*, London 1980; see also Jacqueline Heinen, 'Work like a Man and also like a Woman', *International Viewpoint*, no. 115, 1987.

19. A. Krassikov, 'Commodity Number One', in Roy Medvedev, *Samizdat Register*, pp. 93–115.

20. On the situation of the working class and workers' resistance in the Soviet Union, see Leonard Shapiro and Joseph Godson, eds., *The Soviet Worker from Lenin to Andropov*, London 1984.

21. Two significant expressions come from V.T. Kzyma, the head of the building department at Chernobyl: 'It is very difficult, and sometimes simply impossible to sack a worker even if he is lazy.... These days it is difficult to force the workers to do even an hour more, not to mention getting them to do an extra shift' (The Ukrainian review *Vitchyzna*, no. 13, 1986, quoted in *Soviet Nationalities Survey*, vol. 3, no. 4–5, 1986).

22. A lorry driver working near an airport in northern Siberia explained, in an interview with the dissident writer, Alexander Nekritch, how his fellow workers elected him president of the trade union committee, despite the fact that he was not a party member, in the hope of getting overtime paid at the same rate as the geologists. He did not get this (*L'Alternative*, no. 29, 1984).

23. *OEKO*, no. 5, 1985. These figures were assembled by Maria-Elizabeth Ruban in her article in *Osteuropa*.

24. Michèle Kahn-Wilhelm Jampel, *L'Industrie de l'habilement à l'Est*, *Le Courrier des pays de l'Est*, no, 322. 1987.

25. Ibid.

26. It is difficult to compare the standard of living of a Soviet worker with that of a worker in Western Europe or the USA, given the big difference in price structure and buying power. If one takes the same weekly basket of goods plus one quarter of the monthly rent and one two-hundred-and-fiftieth of the cost of a television (purchase price spread over five years) one gets the equivalent of forty-one hours of work in Moscow, twenty-eight in Washington, twenty-seven in Paris, and twenty-four in London, according to Keith Bush in L. Shapiro, ed. *The Soviet Worker*, pp. 292–298. But the vagueness of this comparison is obvious.

27. See Nicolas Lamert, *Whistleblowing in the Soviet Union*, London 1985. See also Christine Revaz, *Ivan Ivanovitch écrit à la Pravda*, Paris 1980.

28. Zhores Medvedev, *Gorbachev*, London 1986, pp. 166, 184.

29. See Kevin Klase, chs. 1 and 2.

30. All these data are summarizd in *L'Alternative*, no. 27–28, 1984.

# 3. Deepening Crisis of the Soviet System

1. It is a fundamental thesis of Marxism that it is social being that determines consciousness and not consciousness which determines social being. Political and theoretical (ideological) 'errors' are obviously phenomena of social consciousness. They have to be explained by the social existence of those who make them and not by essentially superstructural mechanisms such as the psychological particularities of individuals or groups.

It is for this reason that the attempt of Eurocommunists and others to explain the crisis of the system, whether Stalinism or Brezhnevism, in terms of essentially if not exclusively superstructural phenomena are inadequate and non-Marxist.

2. As we have repeatedly warned, the 'campists' in the West will receive their hardest blows from the Soviet Union itself and not from their left-wing critics at home. Every one of their apologetic statements will be contradicted by official Soviet sources. In fact, this has been happening now for the past two years. See our article in *Quatrième Internationale*, no. 19, 1985.

3. See our article in *Quatrième Internationale*, no. 25 1987, which deals with this question in greater detail.

4. It isn't possible to list here the enormous amount of literature that has been published during the last fifty years on the question of 'the nature of the Soviet Union'. The main older works are mentioned in our earlier work, *Marxist Economic Theory* (London 1962), and in my article in *Quatrième Internationale*, no. 19. 1985. The most important examples of recent works are: Mark Rakovski, *Towards an East European Marxism*, London 1977; David Lane, *State and Politics in the USSR*, London 1985; George Konrad and Ivan Szeleny, *The Intellectuals on the Road to Class Power*, Brighton 1979; Michael Golfield and Melvin Rothenberg, *The Myth of Capitalism Reborn*, San Francisco 1980; Alex Nove, *Political Economy and Soviet Socialism*, London 1979; R. Tartarin, '*Le Mode de production de l'economie soviétique*' in *Cahiers de l'INSEA*, Paris 1979; W. Andreff, '*Capitalisme d'état ou monopolisme d'état*', in Marie Lavigne, ed., *Economie politique de la planification en system socialiste*, Paris 1978.

5. This was how all Marxist theoreticians, including Stalin himself, defined Socialism up until the late twenties. See the excellent study by the revolutionary Marxist, Alexander Zimin, *Le Stalinisme et son 'Socialisme réel'*, Paris 1983.

6. It appears that Molotov, in his final years, wrote a text in which he stated that the construction of socialism had not yet been achieved in the Soviet Union. We were also pleased to read a recent statement by the Hungarian Marxist, Tamas Szentes: '"existing socialism" in the socialist countries by no means implies a completion of the long historical process of constructing a fully developed socialist society' ('World Economic Crisis', UN University project on the Emergence of New Social Thought, mimeographed paper, 1984).

7. Mikhail Gorbachev, *Perestroika*, London 1987, pp. 49–51.

8. On the social nature of the bureaucracy, see the article in *Quatrième Internationale* May 1987.

9. See Michael Vozlensky, *The Nomenclatura*, London 1984; also David Willis, *Le Privilégiès de la nomenclatura*, Paris 1983.

10. According to David Lane, in 1977 only 43.2 per cent of members of local soviets were members of the Communist Party, and only 67.1 per cent of the executive committess of these soviets (*State and Politics*, p. 185).

11. On the relations between workers and managers in Soviet enterprises, see the interesting study by Bohdan Krawchenko, '*Arbeiter und Bosse in der Sowjetunion*', *Gegenstimme*, no. 19, Vienna 1985.

12. David Willis, pp. 100–101 Michael Vozlensky, pp. 221–3; Zhores Medvedev (*Andropov*, London 1982, p. 138) gives the following example:

High party officials became entitled to a free country cottage (*dacha*) – to at least two, if they were important enough, one close to their apartment for weekends and the other in a resort area like the Crimea, Sochi, Georgia, or the north Caucasus. For each member of the Politburo there was an official residence in Moscow (dozens of houses were built on the Lenin Hills overlooking the Moscow River), although theoretically these were government property and the Politburo members retained their own private flats. The official residences were provided with salaried personnel; guards, waiters, cooks, maids, secretries, etc. In Brezhnev's time 'maids', 'cooks' and 'secretaries' were sometimes euphemisms for high-class call-girls, employed for the pleasure of the party dignitary himself or for his guests. The dachas became more and more palatial in style, with swimming-pools and tennis courts, all built at the expense of the state. In addition, Brezhnev gave every high official the right to have a specially stocked hunting forest, guarded and banned to ordinary hunters, near Moscow or elsewhere.

On the privileges of the bureaucracy in medical care see David Willis, pp. 171–6, and on the subject of special schools for children of the bureaucracy see the same work, pp. 135–8.

13. Zhores Medvedev, *Andropov*, pp. 159–60.

14. The supporters of the theory of 'state capitalism' made a great noise during the fifties and sixties about the alleged tendency of the bureaucracy to promote 'production for the sake of production'. They claimed to have discovered a tendency for the bureaucracy to 'maximize the rate of accumulation'. The longer-term developments in the Soviet Union have completely undermined these theories.

15. See Abel Aganbegyan, *Perestroika*, Paris 1987, ch. 6.

16. There is an inherent tendency in the bureaucracy to form informal groupings for mutual support and to control their various fiefdoms. This 'federal' tendency can be found at the very highest levels of the bureaucracy. Khrushchev had his old buddies from the Ukraine, Brezhnev his associates from the 'mafia of *Dnipropetrovs'ke'* and Gorbachev his friends from Stavropol. On this subject see Abel Aganbegyan, p. 102.

17. See our *Marxist Economic Theory*, ch. 15.

18. A good example of this is to be found in the experience at the chemical complex in Shchokino, where the bureaucracy tried to divide the workers in its effort to 'rationalize' employment. See Martin Walker, *The Waking Giant*, London 1986, pp. 41–2.

19. Mel Leiman, *Some Theoretical Aspects of Socialism in the East and West*, manuscript, p. 8.

20. *SSRV v Tsifrakh (v 1984 godu)*, pp. 50f. *Finantsi i Statistiki*, Moscow 1985.

21. Abel Aganbegyan, pp. 37–8.

22. See our response to Alex Nove's *Economics of Feasible Socialism*, 'In Defence of Socialist Planning', *New Left Review*, no. 159, 1986.

23. Boris Komarov, *The Destruction of Nature in the Soviet Union*, London 1980.

24. David Willis describes in details many of the operations of the 'grey market', for instance, exchanging theatre tickets for shoes or sweets, exchanging meat for a place in a holiday home for the butcher's family, etc.

25. David Willis, pp. 41, 51.

26. Abel Aganbegyan, pp. 157–8.

27. Marshall C. Goldman, *Gorbachev's Challenge*, New York, 1987, pp. 114–15.

28. Mark Popovsky, *Science in Chains*, London, 1980, pp. 202–3.

29. Marshall C. Goldman, pp. 112–13, gives details of the Paton Institute. Details concerning the space industry are in *The Economist*, 3 October 1987.

30. Harley D. Balzer has made a recent analysis of the causes of this contradiction in the American publication, *Issues in Science and Technology*. They are to be found, according to this analysis, in bureaucratic management and bureaucratic dictatorship and not in the system of collective ownership or central planning. See also the article by Karl-Ernst Lohmann in the German journal, *Argument*, special volume AS 135, Berlin 1985.

31. Abel Aganbegyan, pp. 93, 104–5. According to the State Committee for Science and Technology '40 per cent of Soviet scientific inventions which are being used abroad are not yet being applied in Soviet industry' (*Sotsialisticheskaia Industria*, 18 April 1981).

32. The formula 'state Socialism' is even more ambiguous. For Engels this term applied to nationalization measures undertaken by a bourgeois state.

33. May 1968 had interesting repercussions also in Eastern Europe, particularly in Czechoslovakia and Yugoslavia.

34. The GDR is an exception because it is partially integrated into the EEC through agreements with West Germany.

35. The constraints exercised by Western banks on Poland and Yugoslavia are very severe. These banks supported Jaruzelski's coup against Solidarity because, in their view, the elimination of the right to strike is a necessary precondition for Poland's repayment of its debts.

36. Stephen Cohen, *Rethinking the Soviet Experience*, Oxford 1985; Moshe Lewin, *The Gorbachev Phenomenon*, Berkeley 1988.

37. Cohen, ch. 5.

## 4. Gorbachev: his Background and what he Represents

1. See our article, 'The Role of the Individual in History', in *New Left Review*, no. 157 1986; also the important article by our friend, Roman Rosdolsky, ' *Über die Rolle des Zufalls und der "Grossen Männer" in der Geschichte*', *Kritik*, no. 14, Berlin 1977.

2. Zdenek Mlynar, 'My School Companion, Mikhail Gorbachev', *Unita*, 9 April 1985.

3. Emile Vandervelde, *Trois conceptions de la Révolution Russe*, Paris 1939.

4. All of these details are from Christian Schmidt-Häuer, *Gorbachev, The Path to Power*, London 1986, pp. 53ff.; Martin Walker, *The Waking Giant*, London 1986, pp. 12–14; Mark Frankland, *The Sixth Continent*, London 1987; Zhores Medvedev, *Gorbachev*, London 1986, pp. 31–5; Michel Tatu, *Gorbachev*, Paris 1987, pp. 30–40.

5. Martin Walker, p. 257, writing about the Geneva summit, says that 'days in advance of the summit's opening, and before the White House press corps reached Geneva, Soviet spokesmen were giving daily briefings at the Geneva press centre, dominating the story for those journalists who had begun to arrive.' This was the biggest and the most succesful 'public relations' exercise which the Soviet Union had ever carried out in the West. David Willis (*Les Privilégiés de la nomenclatura*, Paris 1983, pp. 21–3) and Dev Muraka (*Gorbachev*, Paris 1987, pp. 56–8) insist on the working-class origins of Gorbachev and the traumatic experience he had as a young man in the war.

6. Michel Tatu, p. 46.

7. Urel Schmiederer reduces these sub-groups to four in '*Die Logik der Gorbatschowschen Reformen*' *Sozialismus*', no. 7–8, 1987.

8. See Anton Kolendic, *Les Derniers Jours*, Paris 1982.

9. Schmidt-Häuer, pp. 63–4; Michen Tatu, pp. 10, 86–7.

10. An obvious sign of this disenchantment was the large number of Brezhnev books unsold in the shops.

11. Soviet sociologists, for this reason, are turning increasingly to the use of public opinion surveys. A party, not to mention a state, which is really and democratically representative of the working class would not need to use such indirect means to know what the workers think.

12. Its main characteristics are: poor representation of the working class in the Communist Party; few factory meetings; the presence at such meetings not only of workers but also of management, party officials, and what under the circumstances could hardly encourage sincerity, the police; constant pressure to conform; penalization of any kind of criticism; fear to draw attention to oneself or to appear as an 'oppositionist'; general absence of real political and trade-union democracy.

13. On the KGB, see Zhores Medvedev, *Andropov*, London 1982, chs. 7–10.

14. Ibid., pp. 92–98; Patrick Meney, *La Kleptocratie*, Paris 1982; see also the book mentioned in chapter 1; Ilya Zemtsov, *La Corruption en Union Soviétique*, Paris 1976.

15. For instance, Zhores Medvedev, *Gorbachev*, ch. 6.

16. The quotation from Gromyko is from Michel Tatu, p. 15. Since Gorbachev came to power the KGB is represented in the Politburos of fifteen republican parties. Previously, it had been represented in seven (Martin Walker, p. 139.)

17. Gorbachev has returned many times to the theme of the 'leading role of the party' in perestroika. Obviously the party apparatus is worried. In his speech at the end of the Central Committee meeting, at the time of the Yeltsin affair, he said: 'It is the Communist Party and its cadres that will assume the greatest responsibility for success in carrying out these new tasks.'

18. See Zhores Medvedev, *Gorbachev*, pp. 166–7.

19. *Pravda*, on 13 February 1986, published a letter from a certain N. Nikolaev from Kazan, demanding the closure of special shops, restaurants, etc. reserved for the bureaucracy. A similar letter appeared in *Sovietskaia Rossiia* on the same day.

20. The one-time Soviet official at the UN, Arkady Shevchenko, has denounced the special privileges of Soviet diplomats in his book, *Breaking with Moscow*, New York 1985. This ex-official is a newcomer without political conviction, but his descriptions have the ring of truth.

21. According to Martin Walker, Aliyev led the fight against corruption, particularly in Azerbaidzhan. In view of the evidence given by Zemtsov, this conclusion should be treated with caution.

22. Not only Ligachev, but also Gorbachev himself, have systematically rejected the demand for the suppression of bureaucratic privilege as 'demagogy'.

23. *EKO*, no. 8, 1985.

4. The only veteran to speak at the 27th Party Contress, the ex-miner K.G. Petrov, complained in the *Pravda* of 2 March 1986 that a device for reducing vibration, invented by the Siberian Institute of the Academy of Sciences, had not been manufactured and put into service. He asked why they weren't concerned with the health of the miners.

25. *Pravda*, 27 January 1986. Yeltsin added that he himself had not had the courage to speak his mind at previous congresses. The kind of courage required can be seen in the case of Lev Karpinsky, one of the national directors of Komsomol, whose career was abruptly brought to an end in 1975 when he raised the demand for democratic reforms. There have been many similar examples. See the article by Stephen Cohen in *The Nation*, 3 May 1986.

# 5. Perestroika and Gorbachev's Economic Reforms

1. Catherine Samary, *Plan, Market and Democracy*, which is no. 7/8 of *Notebooks for Study and Research*, Paris 1988.

2. O. Latsis, 'On the Transformation of the Economic Mechanism', *Kommunist*, no. 13, 1986.

3. Abel Aganbegyan, 'Why do we Make Four Times More Tractors than the USA?', in *Literaturnaia Gazeta*, reproduced in the French magazine *Les Temps modernes*, July–August 1987, pp. 232f. In his book *Perestroika*, Aganbegyan estimates that the productivity of Soviet agriculture is 20 per cent that of the USA.

4. On the Novosibirsk report, see chapter 2 above.

5. These concerned a limited number of enterprises and branches where the power of directors to determine the price and range of commodities was increased. The results, according to Aganbegyan, were mediocre (*EKO*, no. 6, 1986).

6. The 1987 harvest appears to be no better than the 1986 harvest.

7. Dev Murarka, *Gorbachev*, Paris 1987, p. 90. An English edition of this book is planned. All references are to the French edition.

8. Zhores Medvedev, *Gorbachev*, London 1986, pp. 204–7. The system of distributing kolkhoz land to small brigades is described by Karl-Eugen Wädekin, 'Agriculture', in Martin McCauley, ed., *The Soviet Union Under Gorbachev*, London 1987, pp. 129–34.

9. Abel Aganbegyan, *Perestroika*, Paris 1987, p. 145.

10. The *Sunday Times* of 12 July 1987 carries interesting details on the appearance in Moscow of private hospitals where fees are seven times that of public hospitals.

11. On the role of cars in changing the aspirations (and ideology) of the middle layer of the bureaucracy, see Martin Walker, *The Waking Giant*, London 1986, pp. 74–76 and David Willis, *Les Privilégies de la nomenclatura*, Paris 1983, ch. 7.

12. Abel Aganbegyan, *Perestroika*, p. 200.

13. Ibid., p. 201.

14. Ibid., p. 129.

15. Ibid., p. 100.

16. Marshall C. Goldman, *Gorbachev's Challenge*, New York 1987, pp. 55–6.

17. *Pravda*, 2 March 1986.

18. Tatiana Zaslavskaia, 'The Human Factor in Social Justice' in *Sovietskaia Kultura*, 23 January 1986.

19. See our 'En défence de la planification socialiste', *Quatrième Internationale*, no. 25, 1987.

20. See Alex Nove, *The Economics of Feasible Socialism*, London 1985.

# 6. Glasnost and Gorbachev's Political Reforms

1. 'We need glasnost as we need the air' (Mikhail Gorbachev, *Perestroika*, London 1987, p. 78).
2. In an interesting commentary on the Gorbachev reforms, which appeared in the West German Eurocommunist journal *Sozialismus* (no. 2, 1987), the Czechoslovak 'reform Communist', Zdenek Mlynar, who knew Gorbachev well, emphasizes the fact that the bureaucracy is not a new class and does not behave as one. We obviously agree with this point of view, which we have defended for decades. But history shows that an important *section of a class*, with specific interests, can take power in order to defend those interests, to the point where a (political) revolution is required to get rid of them. In the political and theoretical discussion which is taking place in the Soviet Union today about the nature of the bureaucracy, the term 'caste' is being used more and more. Trotsky, as is well known, made use of this term also.
3. In his speech to the 27th Party Congress, Gorbachev said:

Whenever the country faces new problems the party finds ways of resolving them, restructures and remoulds leadership methods, demonstrating its ability to measure up to its historic responsibility for the country's destiny, for the cause of socialism and communism. This is where the task of enhancing the role of the party organization rises to its full stature.

The text of Gorbachev's report to the 27th Party Congress, which took place in February–March 1986, can be found in Mikhail Gorbachev, *Towards a Better World*, London 1987, pp. 83–202; also in Mikhail Gorbchev, *Selected Speeches and Articles*, Moscow 1987, pp. 341–469. The above quotaion is from *Towards a Better World*, p. 175.
4. Dev Murarka, Paris 1987, *Gorbachev*, p. 88.
5. Zdenek Mlynar, in the article cited above, in *Sozialismus*, April 1986, insists that the long period of depoliticization of the Soviet masses has reduced the risks of an explosion from below.
6. *Writing and Speeches*, Moscow 1987, p. 452. Leon Trotsky (*Literature and Revolution*, Ann Arbor 1968, pp. 9, 137) wrote:

The development of art is the highest test of the vitality and significance of each epoch.... To reject art as a means of picturing and imaging knowledge because of one's opposition to the contemplative and impressionistic bourgeois art of the last few decades, is to strike from the hands of the class which is building a new society its most important weapon. Art, it is said, is not a mirror, but a hammer: it does not reflect, it shapes.... If one cannot get along without a mirror, even in shaving oneself, how can one reconstruct oneself for one's life, without seeing oneself in the 'mirror' of literature. Of course, no one speaks of an exact mirror. No one even thinks of asking the new literature to have a mirror-like impassivity. The deeper literature is, and the more it is imbued with the desire to shape life, the more significantly and dynamically it will be able to 'picture' life.

7. Caspar Ferenczi-Brigitte Löhr, *Aufbruch mit Gorbachev*, Frankfurt 1987, pp. 253–9.
8. Friedrich Hitzer (ed., *Zeitzeichen aus er Ferne*, Hamburg 1987) has collected together some of the most radical positions adopted by Soviet intellectuals on the great variety of issues related to perestroika and glasnost.
9. The Soviet sociologist, Aleksei Myasnikov, complained publicly about the case of a worker who was arrested because he had complained about a 'hooligan director'. Those who had spoken out in the worker's defence were also persecuted. Myasnikov submitted an article to the journal *Sovietskaia Rossiia*, but it was not published. He was sentenced in 1980 to three years deprivation of freedom under Article 190 of the Soviet Constitution for writing a 'slanderous' article attacking the Soviet state. See Aleksei Myasnikov, 'Open

Letter to Gorbachev', *Labour focus on Eastern Europe*, vol. 9, no. 2, October 1987, pp. 15–16.

10. Friedrich Hitzer, pp. 475–480.

11. Between 1963 and 1981, according to official Soviet sources, there were 4,900 cases of recall of members of soviets, practically all at local level. This makes an average of 250 per year or 650 per legislative period, which is 2.5 years in the Soviet Union. Since there are 2.3 million elected members of soviets, those recalled constituted only 0.03 per cent of the total. The reasons for recall had, in all cases, to do with 'morality'; alcoholism, sometimes corruption.

12. Selections of letters to the Soviet press have been published in the West. See, in particular: Uwe Engelbrecht, *Glasnost, neue Offenheit*, Cologne 1987.

13. *Le Monde diplomatique*, December 1987.

14. Marshall C. Goldman, *Gorbachev's Challenge*, New York 1987, pp. 230–31.

15. According to Aleksei Shkolnikov, president of the Control Committee of the Supreme Soviet, thirteen thousand economic officials have been dismissed (*Le Monde*, 21 November 1986).

16. By a strange coincidence, Rust landed in Red Square on Frontier Guard Day. Rumour in Moscow was that the frontier guards were too drunk from all the celebrations to notice Rust's incursion. The story is also an apt comment on Gorbachev's campaign against alcohol.

17. *Keesing's Archief*, September 1987.

18. The *Komsomolskaia Pravda* of 3 July 1987 condemned excessive police violence against hippies in Moscow.

19. Gérard Streiff, p. 230.

20. *Pravda*, 6 July 1987; as reported in *The Times*, 7 July 1987.

21. The Moscow correspondent of *Le Monde* reported on 20 August 1987 on an article published on this topic in the Soviet weekly, *Ogonyok*. This article argued that the deterrent effect of capital punishment was an illusion and it called for its suppression on humanitarian grounds. Two writers in *Moscow News* argued on similar grounds, recalling Lenin's opposition to capital punishment. But according to *Le Monde*, these articles found very little echo in the public. During the first quarter of 1987 the Soviet press reported sixteen cases of death sentences or executions.

22. Jean Radvanyi, *L'URSS on révolution*, Paris 1987, pp. 164–5.

23. Ibid., p. 166.

24. The following quotations are all from Gorbachev's book, *Perestroika*.

25. See the document, 'Dictatorship of the Proletariat and Socialist Democracy', adopted by the 12th World Congress of the Fourth International, in *Inprecor*, no. 10, 1977.

26. Gérard Streiff, p. 203; Jean Radvanyi, p. 170.

27. According to *Moscow News* (22 November 1987), the Academy of Sciences of the USSR has set up a commission to fight manifestations of bureaucratism within itself. It has received an avalanche of letters condemning bureaucratic abuse throughout the whole of society. The vice-president of the commission concluded:

In my view, 'bureaucratology' is an extremely interesting object of social research. The sources of bureaucracy, its social base, the layers of the population materially involved, its processes of self-preservation and self-defence are all problems unexplored by sociologists. It is essential to know what this bureaucracy is.

28. In the period leading up to the 27th Party Congress, the journalst T. Samolis emphasized the links between the immovability of *nomenklatura* officials, the material privileges inherent in their position, and the constitution of a kind of 'administrative layer of the party' (*Pravda*, 5 December 1986; 27 December 1986; 13 February 1987).

# 7.  Gorbachev and the Limits of Destalinization

1.  These figures are from Roy Medvedev, *Let History Judge*, London 1972, pp. 48ff.; and from Anton Antonov-Ovseyenko, *The Time of Stalin*, New York 1981. In view of those figures and in view of the disastrous consequences of the terror for both industry and national defence, the apologetic comment, 'The role of the purges in providing a mechanism for the integration of the society is often ignored', is scandalous (David Lane, *State and Politics in the USSR*, London 1985, pp. 80–81.

2.  The search to find information about one's father, his physical fate as well as his intellectual–moral identity, is a theme in *Starik* (*The Old Man*), a novel by Yuri Trifonov, one of the great Soviet novelists of the recent period. Trifonov himself was the son of a Red Army organizer in Leningrad who was killed in the purges of 1937.

3.  The *Moscow News* of 13 December 1987 informs us that Alexander Shliapnikov, the most important working-class leader in the Bolshevik Party, people's commissar in the first Soviet government and member of the Central Committee for many years, was rehabilitated by a decree of the Supreme Court of 31 January 1963. This rehabilitation was a result of a long and hard battle carried on by his family, especially by his daughter, Irina.

4.  Nikita Khrushchev is buried in a cemetery within the walls of the Old Novodevichy convent, on the Moscow river. His grave is always covered in flowers, put there by old political prisoners who owed their freedom to his decision to open Stalin's camps (see Martin Walker, *The Waking Giant*, London 1986), p. 221). Mikhail Shulman, creator and first director of the Red Army dance and choir ensemble, arrested in 1937 and having spent nineteen years in the camps, tells in his memoirs, published in samizdat form in Moscow in 1976, how, during the period after his liberation, when he was looking for a flat in Moscow, he was able to arrange a meeting with the head of the executive committee of the Moscow city soviet, thanks to the discreet assistance of the assistant chief of the militia, who said to him once, 'while having a quiet smoke together: "Me too, I had a brother who was sent to the camps ... he died there"' (*L'Alternative*, no. 4, 1984, p. 87).

5.  The two quotations are from Mark Frankland, *The Sixth Continent*, London 1987, pp. 236–7.

6.  Martin Walker, p. 222.

7.  Quoted in Ibid., p. 221.

8.  On the debate among Soviet historians, see Christian Schmidt-Häuer and Maria Huber, *Russlands zweite Revolution*, Munich 1987, pp. 97ff.

9.  Ibid., p. 108.

10.  Albert R. van Goudoever, *The Limits of Destalinization in the Soviet Union*, London 1986, p. 56.

11.  The third Moscow trial took place in March 1938. Krestinksy was the only one at the beginning of the trial to plead innocent and he rejected *en bloc* all the accusations. He eventually gave in under torture and confessed.

12.  See in particular the memoirs of the chief of the general staff of the Soviet army, Marshal A. Vassilievsky, *La Cause de toute une vie*, Moscow 1984. Facing page 80 in this book is a group photo titled 'The Top Marshals of the Soviet Union'. In the group are M. Tukhachevsky, C. Voroshilov, A. Yegorov, S. Budionov, and V. Bliukher, and the year is 1935. Three of those five marshals were shot by Stalin in 1937.

13.  Kontratiev is known as the creator of the economic theory of 'long waves'. During the twenties he was director of an institute devoted to the study of the contemporary international economy which he founded in Moscow.

14.  Less well known abroad than Kontratiev, Chayanov was the author of a celebrated article which was published in Germany in 1924, titled 'The Theory of Non-capitalist Economic Systems'. He was author of a 'peasant utopian' work, *The Voyage of my Brother Alexis to the Land of the Peasant Utopia*. He was a militant of the Soviet co-operative movement after the Russian revolution. At the same time, the Agrarian Academy in Moscow was closed down and its leading members were arrested. Kontratiev and Chayanov were executed in 1937.

15.  Albert van Goudoever, p. 56.

16. However, the head of ideology at the time, P.N. Pospelov, stated at a congress of historians that Bukharin had never been a spy or a terrorist (Robert Conquest, *Russia After Khrushchev*, New York 1965, p. 44).

17. Albert van Goudoever, pp. 56–8.

18. See the biography of Rakovsky in Gus Fagan, ed., *Christian Rakovsky, Selected Writings on Opposition in the USSR 1923–1930*, London 1980, pp. 7–64.

19. An international petition was circulated calling for the legal rehabilitation of all those condemned in the Moscow trials, including Trotsky. It was signed by important leaders of the international labour movement. See the list of signatures in *Inprecor*, 2 November, 16 November, and 30 November 1987.

20. Gorbachev himself, in a speech on 2 November 1987, spoke of 'thousands' of victims of Stalin's 'excesses', whereas the real number is in millions. This was a strong blow to his credibility.

21. See especially, *The Revolution Betrayed, Stalin*, as well as the numerous articles in *Writings of Leon Trotsky*, published by Pathfinder Press. A two-volume edition of his writings on Russia has been published in German, *Schriften über Russland*, Hamburg 1988.

22. The text of Gorbachev's speech is in the *New Times*, no. 45, 1987.

23. Trotsky exposed a great number of these falsifications in his book *The Stalin School of Falsification*, New York 1962. The original edition of this work was published in New York in 1937.

24. The full text of Lenin's Letter to the Congress, known as his Testament, was first published in English in the *New York Times* of 18 October 1926. It was included as a supplement to *The Real Situation in Russia* by Trotsky, published in 1928. It is also included in Leon Trotsky, *On the Suppressed Testament of Lenin*, New York 1970.

25. Leon Trotsky, *The New Course*, London 1972. His 'Letter to the Central Committee' of 8 October 1923 is contained in Leon Trotsky, *The Challenge of the Left Opposition (1923–25)*, New York 1980. *The New Course* is also contained in this collection (quotation from p. 126). *Documents of the Left Opposition*, London 1975, pp. 7–8, 48–49.

26. Leon Trotsky, 'Declaration of the Thirteen', in *The Challenge of the Left Opposition*, vol. 2, pp. 83–4; 'The Platform of the Opposition', ibid., pp. 311–12 (emphasis in original).

27. Translated from the German version of the stenographer's report of the trial, *Prozessbericht*, Moscow 1936, p. 185.

28. There is a historical dimension to this reconquest of the truth which is of particular concern for the countries of Eastern Europe: the crimes of Stalin against the Communists and the workers and peasants of Poland; the calumnies with regard to the Czechoslovak leaders in 1968; the truth about the Hungarian revolution. We will return to those questions in chapter 10.

# 8. The Ideological–Moral Crisis

1. Dev Murarka, *Gorbachev*, Paris 1987, p. 192.

2. *Vremia*, 6 September 1985, quoted by Dev Murarka, p. 212.

3. Mikhail Gorbachev, *Towards a Better World*, London 1987, p. 88.

4. See the article by Boris Mohaev in the special issue of *Les Temps modernes*: *L'URSS en transparence*, pp. 153ff. This article was originally published in *Literaturnaia Gazeta*, in 1984.

5. The film director, Roland Bykov, in conversation with the French journalist, Ignacio Ramonet, spoke about censorship (Le Monde diplomatique, July 1987):

It was a permanent scandal. As often happens in matters of censorship, there were colossal absurdities. For instance, my film, *The Telegramme*, was banned in the cinemas although it had been shown four times on television and everyone had seen it. They are a bunch of inept people, a small clique of bureaucrats who think that the truth will frighten people. Only mediocrity and vulgarity has the right to exist. Talent and, a fortiori, genius, are dangerous.

6. All of these quotations are from Gorbachev's report to the 27th Congress in *Towards a Better World*, pp. 82–200.

7. K.S. Karol in the special issue of *Les Temps modernes: L'URSS en transparence.*

I looked for some answers in Moscow in 1984, as a simple tourist, then again in 1985 in Leningrad, Tblisi and Moscow ... What I saw was very different from what I had seen at the time of my previous trip in 1970, at the beginning of the Brezhnev era. The social differences were much greater than before and they were obvious for all to see. For the first time, people spoke to me about 'bogatye liudi', rich people, even millionaires, as if their existence in the land of the soviets was normal, even necessary.

8. *Moscow News*, 22 November 1987.

9. In view of these judgements by the Soviet leaders themselves, and by the workers quoted, the statement by Smith that the conformist character of the art and literature of socialist realism corresponded to the tastes if not the needs of the majority of the people seems to be crudely apologetic (in R. W. Davies, ed., *The Soviet Union*, pp. 157–8).

10. Mikhail Gorbachev, *Perestroika*, London 1987, pp. 21–2.

11. V.I. Lenin, 'The Immediate Tasks of the Soviet Government', in *Selected Works* (in one volume), London 1969, p. 409.

12. Imitating the vocabulary of reactionary neo-conservatives in the West, certain Gorbachev supporters have begun to speak of the envy and jealousy which motivates those on low incomes when they criticize the high incomes of the affluent. See in particular the article by Nikolai Shmelev in *Novy Mir*, June 1987.

13. Gorbachev devoted a part of his report to the 27th Party Congress to the 'ideological subversion' organized by imperialism. At the time of Lenin, not to mention Marx, when Socialist ideas were credible and still on the offensive, the bourgeoisie were on the defensive. The notion of 'ideological subversion' of the labour movement by bourgeois ideology was inconceivable. The Communists not only didn't fear a confrontation with bourgeois ideas, they systematically provoked such a confrontaation. What the Soviet bureaucrats fear is the resonance that these ideas might have in the Soviet Union, not because of their value or because of their intrinsic ideological content, but because of the critique of real conditions in the Soviet Union which these ideas carry, a critique which, unfortunately, contains a large amount of truth.

14. See especially Jean Radvanyi, *L'URSS en révolution*, Paris 1987, p. 144; John B. Dunlop, *The New Russian Nationalism*, New York 1985; N. Poljanski and A. Rahr, *Gorbachev der neue Mann*, Frankfurt 1987, ch. 7; It appears that Andropov had begun to react against this current.

15. Mark Frankland, *The Sixth Continent*, London 1987, pp. 80ff.

16. W. Poljanski and A. Rahr, p. 288.

17. See Ilya Zemtsov, *La Corruption en Union Soviétique*, Paris 1976, and Patrick Meney, *La Kleptocratie*, Paris 1982.

18. At the beginning of Soviet planning, the writer Ilya Ehrenburg devoted a satirical novel to the theme of raising rabbits in Siberia: *The Adventures of Lazar Rotschwanz.*

19. This affair acquired a somewhat macabre dimension because one of the main lieutenants of Brezhnev, Sharaf Rachidov, first secretary of the Communist Party in Uzbekistan and member of the Politburo, was the real 'godfather' in all those robberies. He died of a heart attack in October 1983. Some people say he committed suicide but he was, in any case, given a solemn funeral and was buried in a tomb of honour in the central park in Tashkent. But when the scandal broke in public he was dug up, the monument and the tomb were destroyed, and the ground was ashphalted over.

20. According to an article in the daily *Trud*, reported in *Business Week* in July 1987.

21. Zhores Medvedev (*Andropov*, pp. 143–4) is right when he says:

This is why the new initiative against corruption cannot be explained entirely as emanating from the top. It was also the result of great pressure from below, expressed in the letters: the same kind of force which brought Solidarity to life in Poland so quickly in August 1980 and made the organization ten million strong.

22. The *Observer*, 12 July 1987.
23. J.V. Stalin, Letter of 28 December 1928, *Werke*, vol. 11, p. 278.
24. The programme says:

To the extent that the necessary socio-economic and ideological conditions have matured, where all citizens participate in leading, and where the corresponding international conditions also exist, the socialist state, as Lenin saw it, 'becomes more and more a transitional form between state and non-state.'

Let us remember that, for Lenin, this transition takes place before the full development of a Socialist society. In explicitly incorporating this international condition into the programme, the authors have once again departed from the Stalinist thesis of the completion of Socialism in a single country.

25. Sensing obscurely that there is something wrong with their reductionist definition of Socialism, the authors of the new programme of the CPSU use a variety of formulae, some of them totally contradictory. We learn that 'a socialist society has essentially been constructed in the Soviet Union', that 'socialism has completely and definitively triumphed in our country', that 'the working class strengthens its vanguard role in perfecting socialism' and then, to our surprise, we learn that the Communist Party is engaged in constructing the Socialist phase of Communist society. But if the 'Socialist phase' is only being constructed, how can one speak of an already completed Socialist society?

26. Friedrich Engels, *The Origins of the Family, Private Property and the State*, London 1940, pp. 194–5.

27. How can one, on the one hand, fight against 'the private property mentality' and the 'tendency towards private enrichment', while on the other hand admitting that private property is 'the principal material incentive'?

28. V.I. Lenin, *Selected Works*, pp. 328–9 (emphasis in original).

29. All references to the programme of 1919 refer to the *Programme of the All-Russian Communist Party*, adopted at the 8th Party Congress in March 1919. This programme is printed in *Communism in Action, A Documentary History*, New York 1969, pp. 16–46. Page references in the text refer to this edition.

30. Leon Trotsky, *The Revolution Betrayed*, New York 1972, p. 186:

Foreign policy is always and everywhere a continuation of domestic policy, for it is conducted by the same ruling class and pursues the same historic goals. The degeneration of the ruling stratum in the Soviet Union could not but be accompanied by a corresponding change of aims and methods in Soviet diplomacy. The 'theory' of socialism in one country, first announced in the autumn of 1924, already signalized an effort to liberate Soviet foreign policy from the programme of the international revolution.

31. The programme contains a number of references to disarmament, in particular to nuclear disarmament. But alongside formulae which speak of the need to eliminate aggression and avoid war, there is also a formula which speaks of 'wiping out' any aggressor, which leaves some doubt about the utopian belief in 'winning' a nuclear war.

32. The new programme states, in its first chapter, that 'social justice' has already been achieved. But, in chapter two, the goal of the party's 'social policy' is defined as 'striving towards a more perfect realization of social justice'. In other words, it has not yet been perfectly realized.

33. Karl Marx, in *The Civil War in France*, in Marx/Engels, *Selected Works*, London 1968 p. 291, in praising the measures of the Paris Commune, says: 'The police, which up to then had been an instrument of the central government, was immediately divested of its

political attributes and became the responsible instrument of the Commune, recallable at any time.'

34. The new programme insists, rather heavily, on the fact that:

the transition from socialism to communism is determined by the objective laws of society, which cannot be neglected. Every precipitate attempt to introduce communist principles, without taking into account the degree of material and intellectual maturity to society, is destined to fail, as experience proves, and may possibly do economic and political damage.

# 9. Gorbachev's Foreign Policy

1. The text of the treaty was published in *Neue Zürcher Zeitung*, 12–13 December 1987. Kissinger has stated quite clearly that the elimination of all nuclear weapons is not desirable (*International Herald Tribune*, 7 December 1987).

2. See the forceful and very pertinent refutation of the different elements of this myth by Vice-Admiral Antoine Sanguinetti in *Le Monde diplomtique*, October 1987. The British weekly, *The Economist*, 28 November 1987, shares this view, though expressed more prudently.

3. These armies are not for any offensive intervention against the West.

4. See in particular Marshal Gretchko, *The Armed Forces of the Soviet Union*, Moscow 1977; also W.D. Sokolovski, ed., *Militärstrategie*, Berlin 1965. In a symposium led by Major-General Milovidov, published in Paris 1973 under the title, *L'Héritage philosophique de V.I. Lenin et les problèmes de la guerre contemporaine*, it is stated in a totally irresponsible manner that: 'The statements by bourgeois ideologues, that there will be no winner in a nuclear world war, are profoundly wrong and harmful.'

5. On the development of Soviet military doctrine on this question, see Hans Jürgen Schultz, *Die sowjetische Militärmacht*, Frankurt 1985.

6. See the interesting study which appeared in the weekly *Die Zeit*, 11 December 1987.

7. See the account of statements by a leading Gorbachevite at a conference in the Aspen Institute in Berlin, in *Frankfurter Allgemeine Zeitung*, 4 June 1987. This politician recognized quite openly that no power could win a nuclear war. But a more conservative ideologue, S. Sanakoev, has written in the journal *Mezhdunarodnaia Zhizn* no. 4, 1987, that 'nuclear parity' is of truly 'historic' importance because it has created 'a relatively new situation': 'If imperialism were to launch a new war, under today's conditions, it would mean catastrophe for itself.' Only for itself? Not for the Soviet Union also, and indeed, the whole of humanity?

8. Mikhail Gorbachev, *Perestroika*, London 1987, p. 140. In the same book, and on the same page, Gorbachev writes that the dictum of Clausewitz, that 'war is the continuation of politics only by different means', does not apply to nuclear war. Lieutenant-General Serebriannikov advocated exactly the opposite view in February 1987: see the quotation from his article in Hans-Henning Schröder, '*Gorbatschow und die Generäle*', in Margareta Mommsen and Hans-Henning Schröder, *Gorbatschows Revolution von Oben*, Frankfurt 1987, pp. 111–12.

9. Dmitri Zgerski, *New Times*, no. 47, 1987.

10. We must distinguish the socio-economic conditions for the (re)production of weapons of mass destruction from the scientific-technical knowhow which makes their production theoretically possible. The former must be eliminated. The latter cannot be suppressed except at the cost of a colossal intellectual and material regression for the human race. Those who advocate such a regression share the obscurantist view that knowledge contains the germ of an inevitable moral and political degeneration. This fatalist thesis detaches historical catastrophes from their context and from their specific social causes, making 'human nature' itself responsible. In the final analysis, this is just another version of 'original sin'.

11. This idea has been attributed to Trotskyists in numerous Russophile publications in the Soviet Union.

12. In his speech of 2 November commemorating the seventieth anniversary of the October revolution, Gorbachev restated this calumny (*Moscow News*, November 1987).

13. The initiator of the theory of exterminism is the British historian E.P. Thompson. See his contribution in E.P. Thompson, ed., *Exterminism and the Cold War*, London 1982. According to this theory, the stationing and firing of nuclear weapons has reached such a level of mechanization and automatization that they are on the point of escaping from human control, making a nuclear war inevitable if nuclear weapons are not eliminated very soon.

14. Another means of 'burying' capitalism, in Khrushchev's perspective, was the 'non-capitalist road of development' which would be adopted, according to the programme of the 22nd Congress in 1961, by important third-world countries, if not the majority of them. The results in India, Egypt, and Indonesia, and especially the emergence of the dependent semi-industrialized countries such as Brazil, South Korea, Mexico, Singapore, Argentina, and Taiwan, has obliged the pragmatic Gorbachev to abandon this perspective. The overthrow of capitalism by the masses in these countries is not part of his schema of things.

15. Mikhail Gorbachev, *Towards a Better World*, London 1987, p. 105.

16. Perestroika, p. 137.

17. Mark Frankland, *The Sixth Continent*, London 1987, pp. 268, 271–3.

18. 'Global' problems made their appearance before nuclear weapons. Imperialism was a global problem, as were the two world wars. The world Socialist revolution, placed on the agenda by the Third International, was also a 'global' problem!

19. There is an additional contradiction in this simplistic view. The overlapping of the great civil and military monopolies, their interconnections with finance groups, etc.: this whole analysis of the structure of monopoly capitalism has disappeared.

20. Mikhail Gorbachev, *Perestroika*, p. 211.

21. See the article by Gregory Meiksins, 'Soviet Perceptions of War', *New Left Review*, no. 162, 1987.

# 10. The 'Socialist Camp', The Communist Parties and the Social Democracy

1. On Gorbachev's visit to Moscow, see Vaclav Havel, in Freimut Duve, ed., *Glasnost*, Hamburg 1987 and Hans Starek, 'Prestavba Rules – But What Is It?', *Labour Focus on Eastern Europe*, vol. 9, no. 2, 1987.

2. See Kevin Ball, 'Only Rock'n'Roll', *Labour Focus on Eastern Europe*, vol. 9, no. 2, 1987.

3. See Gus Fagan, 'Rumania: Misery Under the Conductor', *Labour Focus on Eastern Europe*, vol. 10, no. 1, 1988.

4. The German weekly *Die Ziet* has published a remarkable series of interviews with critical Marxist intellectuals and artists from the German Democratic Republic. See in particular the following issues from 1987: 22 May, 5 June, 12 June, 3 July, 10 July, 17 July, 24 July.

5. See the American journal *Across Frontiers*, Spring 1986, which has also published the song reproduced here.

6. See the remarkable collection of interviews with leading Stalinists in the Polish Communist Party: Teresa Toranska, *Oni, Stalin's Polish Puppets*, London 1987.

7. The British Liberal politician Brian May writes (*Le Monde diplomatique*, June 1987):

The 'Brezhnev doctrine', by means of which the Kremlin attempts to maintain communist rule in Eastern Europe, is founded on strategic rather than ideological requirements. It is not communist fervour but rather the fear of losing control of territory judged essential to the defence of the USSR which led Brezhnev to declare that the Soviets would invade Czechoslovakia even at the risk of a third world war.

8. Martin Walker, *The Waking Giant*, London 1986, pp. 254–6.
9. See Dev Murarka, *Gorbachev*, Davis 1987, pp. 122–5.
10. Christian Schmidt-Häuer, '*Neue Weltsicht aus dem Kreml?*', *Die Zeit*, 19 September 1986.
11. *Le Monde*, 13 January 1988 and 7 January 1988.
12. The West German Communist Party (DKP) has systemtically and correctly campaigned against the *Berufsverbot* in West Germany but has been obliged to defend the same *Berufsverbot* in Czechoslovakia.
13. We are quoting from the German version of this interview, which appeared in *Die Zeit*, 15 January 1988.
14. On this matter, see Teresa Toranska, *Oni.*
15. Bernard Lecomte wrote in *Le Vif–L'Express*, 27 November 1987:

For the Kremlin, however, the revolt in Brasov was a source of real concern. The events in Rumania must be added to the demonstrations in Warsaw and in East Berlin, the strikes in Skoplje and the violence in Kosovo, the revival of the opposition in Czechoslovakia, the demonstrations of the Latvians, the Estonians and Armenians. The politics of Gorbachev in the Soviet Union are giving rise to new hopes from one end of the Eastern Bloc to the other. It was a little like this in 1956, when Khrushchev's report to the Twentieth Congress led many people to believe that the Stalinist period was definitely over. This led, as we know, to the Prague Spring and the Hungarian revolution. 1988 risks being a momentous year for Gorbachev.

16. The new financial measures in Hungary – progressive tax on income and value added tax – have met with strong public opposition and some votes against in the Hungarian parliament. On the general economic problems of Hungary, see Marshall C. Goldman, *Gorbachev's Challenge*, New York 1987, pp. 148ff. On the views of the opposition and the effects of these measures on the working class, see Gus Fagan, 'Janos Kadar's Legacy', *Labour Focus on Eastern Europe*, vol. 9, no. 3, 1988.
17. *The Economist*, 28 November 1987 and 16 January 1988.
18. Stefan Nowak, 'Values and attitudes of the Polish People', *Scientific America*, no. 7, 1981.
19. For an excellent study of the East German situation see: Günther Minnerup and Peter Brandt, 'Eastern Europe and the German Question', *Labour Focus on Eastern Europe*, vol. 9, no. 2 1987.
20. There is also a commercial aspect to this improvement in relations between the Soviet Union and China. In 1986, trade between these two countries reached its highest level for twenty-five years (2.6 thousand million, imports and exports combined). In 1985 the level was 1.9 thousand million and in 1982 only 363 million. In spite of this increase, the Soviet Union comes only fifth place, after Hong Kong, Japan, the United States and East Germany.
21. For the Chinese communists it was always a matter of principle, inherited from the early bourgeois-democratic revolutionaries, not to recognize the 'unequal treaties' imposed on China in the nineteenth century by foreign powers. A large section of Siberian territory was annexed by Tzarist Russia as a result of such 'unequal treaties'. The whole question becomes obviously less simple the moment one takes into consideration the peoples who have populated those territories in the meantime and their right to determine their own fate.
22. Dev Murarka, *Gorbachev*, p. 370.
23. 'I have received the Consultative Council of the Socialist International led by Kalevi Sorsa, and have met Willy Brandt, Egon Bahr, Filipe Gonzalez and the other Social Democratic leaders, and each time we noted that our views on the crucial issues of international security and disarmament were close or identical.' Gorbachev, *Perestroika*, p. 206.

24. The document of common principles is contained in *Kultur des Streits – Die gemeinsame Erklärung von SPD und SED*, Cologne 1988.

25. One of the most astute representatives of Charter 77 in Czechoslovakia, Jiri Dienstbier, has understood this quite well and has put forward some interesting ideas in 'A Strategy for Europe', *Labour Focus on Eastern Europe*, vol. 10, no. 1, 1988.

26. Egon Bahr, the creator of the SPD's *Ostpolitik*, openly defends the thesis that any change in Eastern Europe could only be possible with the consent of the Soviet Union. See Egon Bahr, *Fwur eine neue Ostpolitik*, Berlin 1988.

## 11. The Dilemmas of Gorbachev

1. On this subject see our other works: *Late Capitalism*, London 1975; *Marxist Economic Theory*, London 1962, 1968.

2. On the Preobrazhensky–Bukharin debate, see: E. Preobrazhensky, *The New Economics*, Oxord 1965; E. Preobrazhensky, *The Crisis of Soviet Industrialization*, London 1980; N. Bukharin, *Le Socialisme dans un seul pays*, Paris 1974.

3. In *My Life*, (New York, 1960) Trotsky claimed that, far from having hesitations about NEP, or opposing it, he had proposed abolishing the requisitioning of surplus agricultural products and replacing it with a tax almost a year before the party introduced this as the foundation of NEP. In fact, the *Trotsky Papers* (The Hague, 1971) reproduces a letter from Trotsky to the Central Committee in February 1920 which confirms this statement.

4. On this matter there are numerous quotations from Lenin. We will content ourselves with just one (V.I. Lenin, 'Economics and Politics in the Era of the Dictatorship of the Proletariat', in *Selected Works*, London 1969, p. 499):

> Peasant farming continues to be petty commodity production. Here we have an extremely broad and very sound, deep-rooted basis for capitalism, a basis on which capitalism persists or arises anew in a bitter struggle against communism. The forms of this struggle are private speculation and profiteering versus state procurement of grain (and other products) and stated distribution of products in general.

5. See our 'La NEP en RP de Chine', *Inprecor*, 19 January 1987.

6. We have already pointed to the interesting work of the Hungarian economist, Janos Kornai, on the fundamental incompatibility of the political domination of the bureaucracy on the one hand, and, on the other, the combination of central planning and market mechanisms. He points out that, within the framework of the Hungarian economic reforms, the bureaucracy is becoming *polycentric* and is transforming itself into a network of bureaucracies, each group becoming more independent, but each preserving its privileges.

7. Joseph Berliner, 'Planning and Management', in Abram Bergson and Herbert S. Levine, eds., *The Soviet Economy Towards the Year 2000*, London 1983, p. 371.

8. On the passivity and idleness of the bureaucracy see the appendix to Michael Vozlensky, *The Nomenklatura*, London 1984.

9. On the scepticism of the workers, see the article by David Seppo, '*Une classe ouvrière sceptique*', *Inprecor*, 19 October 1987; also David Seppo, 'Economist Reform and Democracy in the Soviet Union', *Labour Focus on Eastern Europe*, vol. 9, no. 3, 1988.

10. Boris Kagarlitsky, 'Perestroika: The Dialetic of Change', *New Left Review*, no. 169, 1988, p. 80.

11. Numerous Soviet studies recognize this, in particular Tatiana Zaslavskaia, in *Sovietskaia Kultura*, 23 January 1985, and A. Butenko, in *Moskovskaia Pravda*, 7 May 1987.

12. Roy Medvedev, '*Panorama de la vie culturelle en URSS en 1986*' *La Nouvelle Alternative*, no. 4, 1986.

13. *Die Zeit*, 4 December 1987. An anthology of all the texts of Karl Marx against censorship and for the freedom of the press has been published by Iring Fetscher: Karl Marx, *Pressefreiheit und Zensur*, Frankfurt 1969.
14. Mikhail Gorbachev, 'Democracy is the Essence of Perestroika and Socialism', speech to the Central Committee on 8 January 1988, published in the supplement to *Moscow News*, no. 4, 1988.
15. On this debate, see in particular Dev Murarka, *Gorbachev*, Paris 1987, pp. 148–9, 173.
16. O. Latsis, 'Socialism Should Work for Man', *Moscow News*, no. 2 1988.

## 12. The Dialectic of Reform and Social Movement

1. On the Chernobyl catastrophe, see David Marples, *Chernobyl and Nuclear Power in the USSR*, London 1987
2. Zhores Medvedev, p. 269; The article in *Komsomolskaia Pravda* was reported in the *New York Times*, 28 January 1988.
3. On popular unrest, especially in Kiev, see David Marples, pp. 148–51.
4. Zhores Medvedev, p. 269.
5. Demoralized and broken by continuous persecution, Piotr Grigorenko finally lost his Communist convictions and, in exile in the United States, became a reactionary ideologue.
6. See Piotr Grigorenko, *Mémoires*, Paris 1980, pp. 485–6.
7. The neo-nazis in Leningrad are not an isolated case. According to the Soviet press, a similar group exists in Lithuania. See the Lithuanian *Komsomolskaia Pravda*, 28 October 1986.
8. In his *Testament*, Lenin solemnly warned the party against the dangers of Great Russian chauvinism, which would undermine the appeal of the Soviet Union for the oppressed peoples of Asia and undermine the cohesion of the Soviet Union itself.
9. See the interesting article by Roy Medvedev, 'The Emergence of the National Problem in Soviet Transcaucasia', *Labour Focus on Eastern Europe*, vol. 10, no. 1, 1988.
10. For an interesting and informative account of progressive movements among Soviet youth, see Boris Kagarlitsky, 'Soviet Intellectuals and Glasnost', *New Left Review*, no. 164, 1987.
11. Boris Kagarlitsky, p. 22.
12. Sergei Grigoriants spent four years in prison between 1975 and 1980. In 1983 he was sentenced once again, this time to seven years in prison and five years exile, for 'anti-Soviet agitation and propaganda'. He was released in February 1987 along with another 139 political prisoners.
13. The most complete account of the independent clubs is given in Alexander Severukhin, 'The Development of the Independent Socialist Clubs', *Labour Focus on Eastern Europe*, vol. 9, no. 3, 1988.
14. The 'Declaration of the Federation of Socialist Clubs' as well as other documents from these clubs are to be found in *Labour Focus on Eastern Europe*, vol. 9, no. 3 and vol. 10, no. 1, 1988. See in particular the 'Declaration of the Historical-Political Club *Obshchina*' in vol. 10, no. 1, 1988.
15. *Moscow News*, 25 October 1987.

## 13. The Future of Gorbachev's Reforms

1. See Boris Kagarlitsky, 'Perestroika: The Dialectic of Change', *New Left Review*, no. 169, 1988.
2. In liberating the serfs by means of an autocratic act of government, the Tzar,

Alexander II, undoubtedly postponed the first authentic Russian revolution by more than forty years.

3. The description of Gorbachev's reform programme as an authentic 'revolution from above' is quite common both East and West. Two West German writers, regular contributors to the German liberal weekly, *Die Zeit*, Christian Schmidt-Häuer and Maria Hüber, have titled their last work *Russlands Zweite Revolution* (Russia's Second Revolution).

4. Our late friend, Roman Rosdolsky, has analysed in masterful fashion the most exemplary case of enlightened absolutism, that of Emperor Joseph II of Austria: Roman Rosdolsky, *Die Groisse Stuer- unsd Agrarreform Josefs II*, Warsaw 1961.

5. *New York Review of Books*, 8 October 1987.

6. Rudolf Bahro, 'Il Principe', *Tageszeitung*, 14 February 1987.

7. There are 115 million wage-earners in the Soviet Union today, against about 110 million in the United States.

8. Martin Walker, *The Waking Giant*, pp. 270–271.

9. Mikhail Gorbachev, *Perestroika*, p. 50.

10. Marshall Goldman, *Gorbachev's Challenge*, New York 1987.

11. V.I. Lenin, 'Political Report of the Central Committee of the RCP to the 11th Party Congress', *Collected Works*, vol. 33, Moscow 1966, p. 288.

12. On the self-activity of the masses in the Russian Revolution of 1917, see: A. Rabinowitch, *The Bolsheviks Come to Power*, New York 1976; David Mandel, *The Petrograd Workers and the Fall of the Old Regime*, London 1984; David Mandel, *The Petrograde Workers and the Soviet Seizure of Power*, London 1984; Leon Trotsky, *The History of the Russian Revolution*, London 1965.

13. Leon Trotsky, *Revolution Betrayed*, New York 1972, pp. 287–290.